PERCEPTIONS
OF BATTLE

George Washington's Victory at Monmouth

J. R. DACUS

BROOKLINE
books
Pennsylvania & Yorkshire

Brookline Books is an imprint of Casemate Publishers

Published in the United States of America and Great Britain in 2024 by
BROOKLINE BOOKS
1950 Lawrence Road, Havertown, PA 19083, USA
and
47 Church Street, Barnsley, S70 2AS, UK

Hardcover Edition: ISBN 978-1-955041-27-0
Digital Edition: ISBN 978-1-955041-28-7

A CIP record for this book is available from the British Library

Printed and bound in the United Kingdom by CPI Group (UK) Ltd, Croydon, CR0 4YY
Typeset in India by DiTech Publishing Services

For a complete list of Brookline Books titles, please contact:

CASEMATE PUBLISHERS (US)
Telephone (610) 853-9131
Fax (610) 853-9146
Email: casemate@casematepublishers.com
www.casematepublishers.com

CASEMATE PUBLISHERS (UK)
Telephone (0)1226 734350
Email: casemate@casemateuk.com
www.casemateuk.com

Cover image: George Washington and his generals needed a victory to shore up the Revolutionary effort. They got it at Monmouth. *Washington Receiving a Salute on the Field of Trenton. 1776. Copy of print by William Holl after John Faed, published circa 1860s NAID: 532914 Local ID: 148-GW-566 Photographs and other Graphic Materials Covers: 1931–1932*

Contents

Prologue

On May 6, 1778, the camp at Valley Forge was buzzing with excitement. The air was as electric as one of Dr. Franklin's experiments and as emotional as one of Patrick Henry's orations. It was 9:00 am. Drums beat assembly, officers shouted orders, and excited troops began forming into their companies and regiments. Today was an important celebration for the soldiers of the Continental Army of the United States, indeed the entire rebellious population of the 13 former British colonies. Good news had recently arrived from Europe. The king of France had agreed to a treaty of friendship that would open the floodgates of support from that powerful country that up to now had been a helpful, clandestine, but incomplete, source of military supplies and money.

Once the brigades assembled, the chaplains read an article from the *Pennsylvania Gazette* detailing the French alliance, followed by a prayer of thanksgiving. The regiments marched from their ramshackle huts to converge upon the parade ground. The announcement of the new French alliance caused a frenzy of excitement. George Washington had prepared a ceremony to show the Continental Army's appreciation of their new ally as well as demonstrate their recently learned skills with the weapons and tactics taught to them by their new inspector general and drill master, Baron von Steuben.

From south of the parade ground came the men of the Pennsylvania Line, a large number of Irish descent, along with the Virginians of William Woodford and Charles Scott, and Enoch Poor's New Hampshire brigade. From the southeast part of the outer line of defenses marched the Massachusetts men of John Glover, Ebenezer Learned, and John Paterson's brigades. Alongside the Bay Colony were the Virginians of George Weedon and John Peter Muhlenberg's brigades. The Continentals marched proudly from all parts of the camp, forming into their respective divisions, as they made their way to the open area near the center of the sprawling military village.

The large area of newly grown spring grass that served as the parade ground filled up quickly as the various units took their places. There was little consistency in the soldiers' uniforms. After the long winter soldiers wore only the ragged remnants of regimental coats or civilian garments. Others had hunting shirts or frocks. Some had clothing made from torn and worn blankets. There was a myriad collection of coats made from odds and ends, but each soldier had placed a bit of green sprig in his hat.

At first glance, their arms were as varied as their apparel, but a closer look revealed that most were equipped with variations of the French Charleville or British Land Pattern "Brown Bess" muskets. The weapons were cleaned and burnished, as the men who carried them were as neat as possible under the circumstances.

The army finished forming up along the edge of the parade ground as a party of officers rode up from the Schuylkill River. Leading the group on a beautiful white horse was a tall, almost massive, figure, the commander in chief, George Washington. He had attended church services earlier in the day with the New Jersey regiments, thanking the "Almighty Ruler of the Universe"[1] for interceding for the rebellious colonists. Washington and his staff rode slowly along in front of the massive display of military might, appearing to inspect but also showing respect for the stalwarts who had stood by the Continental Congress, George Washington, and their cause, during the miserable months at Valley Forge. After a cursory inspection, the big man on the white horse placed himself in a position where he could observe the fruits of the winter's training.

At 10:30 on that beautiful morning, a single cannon fired. The various regiments and battalions formed into two ranks as they had been practicing for days. Officers passed through, inspecting each soldier, straightening them out as much as possible with the wide variation of uniforms. Then each man carefully loaded and primed his musket.

A second cannon shot sounded across the encampment and the regiments began to march. They stepped out smartly, rank upon rank of disciplined troops, across the parade ground in view of the reviewing officers, halting next to a line of 13 cannon. The platoons turned to face the commander in chief and his staff. It was a stirring sight for the civilian onlookers as well as Washington's staff to witness thousands of American soldiers marching in unison, then abruptly halting and facing their commanders. For the senior observers, it appeared as if the hard months of training were paying off. The soldiers, as well as their leaders, had rarely seen so many men acting in complete unison. Here on the flat, grassy parade ground they could see their brother soldiers, thousands of them, marching as they had never marched before. Grizzled veterans remembered watching the British soldiers perform complex maneuvers expertly on the battlefield, often under fire, and realized with pride that the Americans were approaching that level of military ability.

Another booming cannon shot, and the magnificent display went to a higher level. Touch holes were sparked and 13 field pieces crashed out in unison, echoing across the assembled army and into the neighboring hills of the Schuylkill Valley. The assembled soldiers followed with a *feu de joie* that rippled from one end of the army to the other: the soldier closest to the cannon fired first, followed by the soldier next to him, and so on down the line. The effect was electric: flashes of powder followed by clouds of smoke, that were in turn pierced by more flashes as the soldiers along the line touched off their powder. This was repeated and again until it reached the far end of the entire army. Then the second rank fired in succession, and the fire moved down the line to the artillery. As the smoke began to clear, a signal was given and thousands of voices shouted, "Long Live the King of France!"

The celebration wasn't over. After the "Huzzah" for the king of France, the artillery fired another 13-gun salute, and the soldiers fired another *feu de joie*. At the end of this round of firing, the troops shouted, "Long Live the Friendly European Powers!" The procedure was repeated a third time. Smoke swirled and the smell of powder filled the nostrils of the onlookers and participants: then 13 cannons, the ranks of firing and finally a shout of, "Prosperity to the American States!" It was a moving experience, a symbol of the army's new abilities. Such a ceremony had been attempted the previous October as a celebration of the victory at Saratoga, but it had not been carried out with the same numbers or professional execution as this one.

The Grand Review completed, the soldiers were dismissed to a feast while the officers went to their own impressive reception under a giant canopy. The officers' wives, including amiable Martha Washington, pretty and vivacious Kitty Greene, broad Lucy Knox, and dignified Lady Stirling, mingled with junior officers as well as the generals. Washington, typically taciturn and reserved, on this occasion mixed easily with his officers as they enjoyed eating and drinking in boisterous merriment. There were games and races, the lethargy of winter forgotten. One of the victors in a race was a young officer from Virginia, John Marshall.

About mid-afternoon, General Washington left his officers and the ladies to visit with the enlisted soldiers mounted on his favorite gray horse, Blueskin. His red-brown hair, cued in back, was visible under his broad tricorne hat. The commander in chief moved with an easy familiarity despite his aristocratic appearance. He was a common sight in the camp, riding daily through the hundreds of crude huts, playing at wickets with the soldiers on occasion.

His presence was accepted without undue excitement. Dismounting, he acknowledged their greetings and joined them in toasting the new treaty. Washington had an intangible quality. In his company, one felt a spirit of comradeship despite the general's unmistakable air of authority. Speaking to many of the soldiers by name, he made his way through the crowd until he reached the edge of the gathering. Remounting his magnificent charger, he snaked slowly through the men who spontaneously cheered as he passed. He doffed his hat in acknowledgement of their salute and briskly cantered off to meet his wife at the Potts' House, his personal quarters.

Officers and their wives toasted until about 5:00 pm with a final toast, "Long live George Washington!" Morale was high, as optimism swept through the assembled leaders. Perhaps the campaign of 1778 would be the last? Even their stoic commander in chief, not always an optimist himself, looked forward to what the summer might bring. He felt content enough to pardon two soldiers sentenced to death. The general on this "truly joyful day is pleased to pardon William McMarth of the Artillery and John Morrel of Col. Henry Jackson's Regiment."[2]

CHAPTER I

Background to Battle

Washington

The man who rode through the army at Valley Forge that day in 1778 was 46 years old. A tall man, over six feet in a period when such a height made one noticeable, he was a natural athlete. He was known to be an accomplished dancer and "the best horseman of his age."[1] An imposing figure, he was naturally quiet in a crowd, possessing the "gift of silence."[2] Unlike many prominent figures of his time, or any time, he often took time to think before he spoke. He also possessed a great temper; Thomas Jefferson thought that "his temper was naturally irritable and high toned; but reflection & resolution had obtained a firm and habitual ascendancy over it. If ever however it broke it's bonds he was most tremendous in his wrath."[3]

Washington's path to Valley Forge started in the French and Indian War, where he showed his personal courage and leadership ability. A loyal officer, he had lobbied for a British commission even as he fought against Virginia's, and Britain's, enemies. But the man who arrived in Philadelphia during the troubles with Great Britain to attend the First Continental Congress in 1774 was not the same man who had fought alongside the British in the French and Indian War. Years of British economic and administrative decisions had turned the successful plantation farmer into a politically aware rebel.

The situation had changed dramatically by the time Washington arrived at the Second Continental Congress in May of 1775. The battles at Lexington and Concord had taken place and an army of colonists laid siege to the British army in Boston. Now an ardent Whig who was prepared to defend his rights as a British subject through force, he arrived at the Congress. Rumors of his willingness to raise troops to relieve Boston added to the perception he might serve in an important military capacity. He was placed on every committee dealing with military affairs. John Adams acknowledged his usefulness: "Colonel Washington appears at Congress in his uniform, and by his great experience and abilities in military matters is of much service to us."[4] Even as delegates debated using military force, others pleaded for a reconciliation with their mother country with an "Olive Branch Petition."

There was no "Continental" army when the Second Continental Congress first met but that changed in June, after Congress adopted the militia forces in New England outside Boston. With the adoption of the "army," there was a need for a commander that would represent all the colonies, not just New England. Washington, the wealthy Southerner, filled the bill. Though not as experienced in war as former British officers Horatio Gates or Charles Lee, he was a wealthy, native-born American. His physical presence was imposing. He looked like a general. Another delegate said of him: "...he is Clever, & if any thing too modest. He seems discret & Virtuous, no harum Scarum ranting Swearing fellow but Sober, steady, & Calm. His modesty will Induce him I dare say to take & order every step with the best advice possible to be obtained in the Army."[5] Congress gave him the post of commander in chief of the Continental Army on June 19, 1775. Two days prior, the British had stormed and captured Breed's Hill at great cost. The colonies and Great Britain were at war.

Background to Valley Forge

From taking command of the Continental Army to that celebration on May 6, 1778, there were to be a series of highs and lows, of successes and failures for the new commander in chief. Meeting with the army at Boston on July 2, 1775, was an educational experience for George Washington. His first impressions were of a confused, dirty mass of humanity that could not be disciplined. As the new commander in chief, he was forced to bring men of many backgrounds, abilities, and interests together. With the help of Horatio Gates and Charles Lee, and a great deal of patience, he started the process of forming the diverse group of men into an army. Fortunately, the British remained quiet in Boston, giving the new army time to build some type of organization. On January 25, 1776, Henry Knox, a Boston bookseller, brought guns from recently captured Fort Ticonderoga. Washington had the guns emplaced on the dominating Dorchester Heights on March 4 and the redcoats left Boston on March 17, never to return. Washington was voted a gold medal by Congress.

The high point of driving the British from Boston was soon followed by a low point as the following battles around New York City in 1776 were not nearly as successful as the siege of Boston. Still learning the ropes of commanding an army with no permanent infrastructure and backed by a government that was also in its infancy, Washington suffered defeat after defeat. The causes were various but for the most part it was due to his or his army's ineptitude, inexperience, or some combination of the two. Defeated badly on Long Island, he earned some respect for his skillful withdrawal from Brooklyn but then nearly lost a third of his men after the British landed behind part of the army at Kip's Bay. Outflanked again at Pell's Point and New Rochelle, the army was pushed off Chatterton's Hill but managed to bloodily rebuff the British at White Plains.

The lowest point was the disastrous loss of Fort Washington on November 16, 1776, due almost entirely to Washington's own indecision. Noting its exposed position, he ordered stores to be evacuated and the troops inside to leave if threatened. Unfortunately, he issued his orders in such a discretionary manner that the fort's commander and Brigadier General Nathanael Greene thought it better to defend the fort than evacuate it. The British easily took the fort. It was the worst defeat of the early war, resulting in the British capturing almost three thousand soldiers and a vast amount of badly needed stores. Washington avoided a second humiliating setback by evacuating Fort Lee in New Jersey a few days later; despite his mistakes, George Washington was a serious student of war who appeared to be learning from his errors.

Oddly, despite the defeats around New York and his forced retreat from New Jersey into Pennsylvania, Congress felt that extreme measures were necessary and gave Washington full control of military operations:

> Resolve, That General Washington shall be, and he is hereby, vested with full, ample, and complete powers to raise and collect together, in the most speedy and effectual manner, from any or all of these United States …to take, wherever he may be, whatever he may want for the use of the army, if the inhabitants will not sell it, allowing a reasonable price for the same; to arrest and confine persons who refuse to take the continental currency, or are otherwise disaffected to the American cause; and return to the states of which they are citizens, their names, and the nature of their offences, together with the witnesses to prove them: That the foregoing powers be vested in General Washington, for and during the term of six months from the date hereof, unless sooner determined by Congress.[6]

After an ignoble retreat across New Jersey, Washington's successful raid on the Hessians at Trenton and the follow-up attack on the British near Princeton as 1776 became 1777 proved that his ability to command and maneuver his army was improving. The French/German volunteer Johan de Kalb, so-called Baron, said of Washington after his twin victories, "[Washington] does more every day than can be expected from any general in the world, in the same circumstances, and that I think him the only proper person (nobody actually being or serving in America excepted), by his natural and acquired capacity; his bravery, good sense, uprightness and honesty, to keep up the spirits of the army and people, and that I look upon him as the sole defender of his country's cause."[7]

More importantly, the battles showed that success for the Revolutionaries would not be measured by battlefield victories but by keeping the army in the field. The British were forced out of New Jersey by the presence of Washington's small army and its ability to attack or run away at will. It was another high point in Washington's military schooling.

The Continental Army camped in the rugged area around Morristown, New Jersey in the winter of 1777. The British began their campaign in the spring of 1777 with several attempts to entice Washington out of his defenses for a major battle. His army was not in shape to come out of the hills and fight the British, so the Continental Army refused battle.

Frustrated, Major General William Howe, the British commander, placed his army on ships and sailed out of New York. The ships, under the command of his brother Richard "Black Dick" Howe, were sighted sailing up Delaware Bay on July 30, 1777. But the fleet withdrew, leaving Washington to wonder if they were returning to New York. Perhaps the fleet was moving up the Hudson River to support the British invasion forces under Major General John Burgoyne? Or was the fleet coming back to attack Philadelphia? Washington's army marched to and fro to match the British movements, giving the impression of confusion. A few weeks later the British were spotted in Chesapeake Bay. They landed at the Head of Elk on August 25 and, after resting to refresh and regroup from the arduous voyage, began a march toward Philadelphia.

Confronting Howe's advance in Pennsylvania, Washington lost badly at Brandywine Creek on September 11, 1777. Washington was easily outflanked due to his poor dispositions, flawed plan, and confusion resulting from conflicting intelligence reports. Only through the fighting spirit of his officers and men, as well as his own dramatic personal intervention which he made by riding from threatened point to threatened point and directing reinforcements to those areas, was a battlefield calamity prevented.

A few days later, the British under Howe maneuvered Washington out of position and occupied Philadelphia on September 26, 1777. Washington felt that he had to do something to offset the psychological blow from the loss of the capital. On October 4, 1778, Washington tried a four-pronged attack on British forces camped near Germantown. Fog, confused officers, and an overly ambitious plan combined with Washington's poor decision to slow the attack to dislodge a small British force in his rear at the Chew House, turned a promising beginning into a near disaster. It compared with the defeats at New York City as one of the lowest points of the war.

But it was only the 1777 campaign and not the war that ended with these two defeats and the loss of Philadelphia. By keeping the army together, Washington's perception was somewhat optimistic despite the setbacks. After Brandywine he wrote John Hancock, the president of Congress: "Notwithstanding the misfortune of the day, I am happy to find the troops in good spirits; and I hope another time we shall compensate for the losses now sustained."[8] After the action at Germantown, he again wrote Hancock with cautious hope: "Upon the whole, it may be said the day was rather unfortunate, than injurious... The Enemy are nothing the better by the event, and our Troops, who are not in the least dispirited by it, have gained what All young Troops gain by being in Actions."[9] Despite the setbacks, Washington demonstrated an ability to survive defeat and keep his army together and in shape for another battle.

After the twin defeats of Brandywine and Germantown and the British occupation of Philadelphia, Washington had to find winter quarters for his army. Following a council of war, he settled on an elevated area northwest of the city at the Valley Forge. It was a position that allowed the army to stay close enough to the Quaker City to disrupt British foraging expeditions yet far enough away to prevent the British from stealing a march on the Continentals. It was a relatively formidable position, being situated on heights with the Schuylkill River on two sides. While the main camp was at Valley Forge, supplies, hospitals, and support facilities were spread out as far away as Reading. The cavalry was dispersed for easier foraging in New Jersey.

Conditions at the camp were miserable due to logistical failures. Congress was unable at times to procure the resources the army needed. There was also a question of who should provide supplies. Should the states provide certain types of supplies or should the Congress? Who should Washington go to with his requests for support? A new country and new army needed time to sort things out. Some civilian leaders and generals were impatient. For the army, the winter proved to be another low point in morale.

A Plot?

Not all the low points in Washington's command were due to defeat on the battlefield. In addition to the duties involved in commanding an army, Washington also had to deal with government and military politics as the army moved into winter quarters. Many in Congress, the army, and the people at large were growing dissatisfied with the overall course of the war, the lack of success in Washington's theater, the commander in chief's abilities, or the loss of Philadelphia. Many members of Congress were rightfully aware of their duty to criticize what they felt were unsound decisions by members of the government or military. Added to these apprehensions was the historic aversion, dating from the English Civil War, to a standing army with a strong leader, which Washington now represented. Samuel Adams wrote succinctly of this traditional thought: "A standing army, however necessary it may be at some times, is always dangerous to the liberties of the people. Soldiers are apt to consider themselves as a Body distinct from the rest of the Citizens. They have their Arms always in their hands. Their Rules and their Discipline is severe. They soon become attachd to their officers and disposd to yield implicit Obedience to their Commands. Such a Power should be watchd with a jealous Eye."[10] Fear of another Cromwell was very real to the Americans.

During the bleak wintertime, events took place that some believed were an attempt to usurp George Washington as commander in chief or at least curb his power and influence. Some honestly thought a change would be best for the rebels' efforts toward independence. Some were jealous of Washington's popularity, especially with the bulk of the army. Some were arrogant and egotistically believed they knew better than Washington. A few simply hoped to advance in rank and position if he were removed and his supporters dispersed. After Washington's twin defeats at Brandywine and Germantown, New Jersey Congressman Jonathan Sergeant wrote fellow congressman James Lovell: "Thousands of lives and millions of property are yearly sacrificed to the insufficiency of our Commander-in-Chief. Two battles he has lost for us by two such blunders such as might have disgraced a soldier of three months standing, and yet we are so attached to this man that I fear we shall rather sink with him than throw him off our shoulders."[11] One trait never criticized was Washington's courage or personal bravery, which he had demonstrated on many occasions under fire.

Some of the senior officers were critical of Washington's abilities. Once an admirer of Washington, the German adventurer Johan de Kalb wrote: "... as a General he is too slow, even indolent, much too weak is not without his portion of vanity and presumption. My opinion is that if he gains any brilliant action he will always owe it more to failure or to faults of his adversary than to his own capacity. I will even say that he does not know how to profit by the clumsiest mistakes of the enemy."[12]

After Horatio Gates' victory at Saratoga in October of 1777, many openly advocated Gates as the new commander in chief. Dr. Benjamin Rush lamented the differences between Washington's army and that of Gates:

> I have heard several officers who have served under General Gates compare his army to a well-regulated family. The same gentlemen have compared General Washington's imitation of an army to a uniformed mob. Look at the characters of both! The one on the pinnacle of military glory, exulting in schemes planned with wisdom and executed with vigor and bravery... See the other outgeneraled and twice beated obliged to witness the march of a body of men only half their number through 140 miles of thick settled country, forced to give up a city the capital of a state, and after all outwitted by the same army in retreat. If our Congress can witness these things with composure and suffer them to pass without an inquiry, I shall think we have not shook off monarchical prejudices and that like the Israelites of old we worship the work of our own hands.[13]

Of course, there were many differences in the two armies and their battles, but on balance comparing Washington's two defeats at Brandywine and Germantown to Gates' major victory at Saratoga was not good for the Virginian.

Soldiers often criticize other soldiers, or leaders, but in one case the interception of a letter proved to be an irritant for Washington. The so-called "Conway Cabal" involved the contents of a letter from Thomas Conway to Gates that was leaked to Washington. It supposedly read: "Heaven has been determined to Save your Country; Or a Weak General and bad Counsellors would have ruined it."[14]

Thomas Conway was a skilled soldier, born in Ireland but in the service of France before joining the Continental Army. Despite his excellent abilities in training and leading troops, he was exceedingly ambitious and derisive of his fellow officers, and his loyalty to the American cause went only as far as it would help his career. He told a fellow general: "I depend upon my military promotion in rank to increase my fortune and that of my family. I freely own to you it was partly with a view of obtaining sooner the rank of Brigadier in the french army I have joined this."[15]

Corpulent with a doughy looking face, Gates was also an experienced soldier who helped Washington organize the army around Boston in 1775. Unfortunately, he also was a self-promoter who had intrigued on several occasions to gain a new command. During Washington's Trenton/Princeton campaign in 1777/1778, Gates was absent from the army ostensibly due to illness, but he was busy in Philadelphia ingratiating himself with Congress. A competent administrator and organizer, he made quite a scene when advocating for the command of the Northern Department, as described by a member of

Congress: "It is impossible for me to give you an Idea of the unhappy Figure which G.G. made on this Occasion. His Manner was ungracious, and Totally void of all Dignity, his Delivery incoherent and interrupted with frequent Chasms, in which he was poring over his Scattered Notes, and the Tenor of his Discourse a Compound of Vanity, Folly, and Rudeness. I can assure you that notwithstanding his Conduct has been Such as to have eradicated from my Mind every Sentiment of Respect and Esteem for him."[16]

His success at the battles around Saratoga, made possible in large part by the efforts of his subordinates but still essentially his victory, was enough to make Gates the darling of many who were dissatisfied with Washington, the status of the army, or the course of the war. While he did not openly lobby for Washington's position, he would have gladly accepted it.

Washington deftly used the supposed contents of Conway's letter as an opportunity to confront his critics. In the ensuing scuffle, many opponents of Washington, including Gates and Conway, were intimidated into declarations of loyalty to the commander in chief. Still, there were those that continued to entertain doubts about the commander's ability, the course of the war, or Washington's popularity, or simply felt jealous of his position. It is not unusual in time of war to question such things.

Another incident prompted consternation for Washington and most of the senior officers of the army. Congress, on June 12, 1776, had provided for a Board of War to unify the Congressional responsibilities in supporting the army. The Board would coordinate efforts to meet army logistical requirements and assist Washington in administrative operations. A variety of civilians had served on the Board over the year with mixed results. In the fall of 1777 Congress created a new Board of War with new authority. The president of the Board would report directly to Congress, making him senior to Washington in important decisions and able to interfere in the day-to-day operations of the army. No longer just a body to support the army, the Board would render Washington merely a tactical commander and leave the operational and strategic decisions to its members. Two of the members of the Board were advocates of replacing Washington or limiting his power: Horatio Gates, who was to head the board, and Thomas Mifflin, former quartermaster general.

Mifflin was a proud, wealthy Pennsylvanian who served as George Washington's aide when the war with Britain began. Slightly overweight and fond of the bottle, he proved a capable field commander and efficient in mobilizing Pennsylvania's resources to assist the Revolutionary War effort. He ran into trouble when appointed as the quartermaster general. It was a difficult job in the best of circumstances and the early war years were not the best of circumstances. Officers, including Washington, criticized him for his lackluster performance at that job. He resigned just before the army marched into Valley Forge. Unimpressed by Washington's inability to defend Pennsylvania and resenting the harsh criticism he had received, Mifflin became anxious to limit, or replace, the Virginian.

As part of its increased power, the Board of War appointed Thomas Conway to the post of inspector general of the army. It was a position established by Congress and accepted by Washington. The inspector general would oversee organizing and carrying out uniform methods of training for the army. The regiments of the army often trained using different systems such as *New York's Regulations of 1757* or *Pickering's Plans for the Discipline of Militia*, a weakness that hindered deployment on the battlefield. At first glance, Conway appeared well qualified, and he was also a favorite of many Congressmen. His efforts at training his own men, his knowledge of European drill, and his deep military experience made it appear that he was the perfect officer. Unfortunately, Conway was not the man for the position. His egotism and disdain for his fellow officers made it unlikely that he would be able to work with them. Colonel Alexander Graydon recalled how upon seeing the poorly uniformed junior officers of the Continental Army, Conway snarled: "Did Congress see you before they appointed you?"[17]

In addition, he was promoted to major general despite the seniority of many others which caused nine other brigadier generals to write a letter of complaint to Congress. Washington referred to the Irishman's arrogance in a letter to Richard Henry Lee: "General Conway's merit, then, as an officer, and his importance in this army, exists more in his imagination than in reality; for it is a maxim with him to leave no service of his own untold, nor to want anything which is to be obtained by importunity."[18] Conway's recent letter to Gates demeaning Washington made him an anathema to the commander in chief. When he arrived at camp, Washington and the senior officers treated him with a cold contempt. Confronted with conditions so uncomfortable as to make it unlikely that he could perform his duties, he never officially took his post.

But the Board of War and Congress were not finished in their attempts to curtail Washington's power. In January of 1777 it was decided that a new invasion of Canada was to be attempted. It was done without consulting Washington and the expedition would be independent of him, answering directly to the Board of War, a body originally never intended to control military field operations. The Marquis de Lafayette was chosen as its commander with Conway as the second in command. Poorly planned, the excursion never got off the ground. Lafayette refused the position unless he answered to the commander in chief, and wanted fellow Frenchman Johan de Kalb to be his second in command. Few logistical resources were allocated, regiments would have to be pulled from the main army, and when Washington was asked to support it, he responded tepidly. The commander in chief believed such an invasion could occur only after the British army completely left the Thirteen States. Ultimately Conway skulked away, and the matter was dropped. Lafayette thought the actual reason for the Board's invasion plans was more sinister, and alluded to Conway's participation: "I inquired in his caracter, I found that he was an ambitious and dangerous man—he has done all [in h]is power by a cunning maneuvres to take off my confidence and affection for you."[19] He felt Gates and the others wished to separate the young man from the commander in chief with whom he was developing a strong bond of friendship.

Even while commanding the army and dealing with the daily activities of the various duties associated with that command, Washington faced opposition from the new Board of War, members of Congress, and Revolutionary leaders outside of the army. Artillery pieces were assigned to different units and regiments were transferred without Washington's knowledge or approval. Friends wrote him of machinations in Congress and by other civilians against his continued command of the army. An example of these notes was a letter from his friend Doctor James Craik: "The Morning I left Camp I was informed by a Gentleman, whom I believe to be a true Friend of yours, that a Strong Faction was forming Against you in the New board of War and in the Congress… At my Arrival in Bethlehem I was told of it there, and was told that I should hear more of it on my way down I did so, for at Lancaster I was Still assured of it. All the way down I heard it, and I believe it is pretty general over the Country. No one would pretend to affix it on particulars, yet all Seemed to believe it, it was Said Some of the Eastern & Southern Members."[20]

Using his own connections in Congress Washington set out to return the Board of War to its support mission. He requested Congress to send some of its members to see the condition of the army. Providentially, a committee from Congress, called the Committee at Camp, arrived at Valley Forge on January 28, 1778, to look at the state of the army. Consisting of Gouverneur Morris, Francis Dana, John Harvie, Nathaniel Folsom, and Joseph Reed, this group of men set out to find out how badly things were going with the army and its leadership. Washington presented them with a letter on January 29 outlining the state of the army and its needs.[21] After reading the letter and spending time with the army, the visitors realized the difficulty of the actual conditions facing its commander in chief.

Congress sent the Committee at Camp, Francis Dana, Nathaniel Folsom, Joseph Reed, John Harvie, and Gouverneur Morris, to view the situation at Valley Forge. Washington convinced them that the situation was dire and they reported the reality to their fellow members. *National Archives (Photograph 148-GW-184; General George Washington and a Committee of Congress at Valley Forge. Winter 1777–78. Copy of engraving after W. H. Powell, published 1866; 1777–1778 (artwork 1866); Records of Commissions of the Legislative Branch, Record Group 148; National Archives at College Park, College Park, MD*

Gouverneur Morris wrote Governor George Clinton of New York describing how the committee's eyes were opened: "The American army, in the heart of America, is at the point of deserting, having nothing to eat."[22] He continued his thoughts in a letter to John Jay: "An army of skeletons appears before our eyes, naked, starved, sick, discouraged… The powerful American Senate is not what we have known it to be. Continental money and Congress have both depreciated."[23] They stayed in a nearby house until March 12 and then furiously went to work trying to make the changes Washington recommended.

The Committee's reports from Valley Forge, Congress' support of Washington, the unwillingness of Conway to take his post, and Gates' lack of participation in the Board of War were factors that led to the Board losing much of its power. Washington also had several new adherents. With the

Board of War's loss of prestige and power, Gates returned to command in the Northern Department.

Had there been a plot against Washington? The Conway letter, the changes in the Board of War, Congressional backbiting, and disillusionment with Washington led the commander in chief to think so. Writing to an aide after the events, he stated his position:

> I thank you sincerely for the part you acted at York respecting C—y's Letter; & believe with you, that matters have, & will, turn out very different to what that Party expected. G—s has involved himself in his Letters to me, in the most absurd contradictions—M. has brought himself into a scrape he does not know how to get out of, with a Gentn of this state—& C—, as you know, is sent upon an expedition which all the world knew—& the event has proved, was not practicable. In a word, I have a good deal of reason to believe that the Machinations of this Junto will recoil upon their own heads, & be a means of bringing some matters to light which by getting me out of the way some of them thought to conceal.[24]

There were still some who disliked Washington, were jealous of his popularity, or thought he was not a good general. Members of Congress had their favorites in Charles Lee or Horatio Gates. Some believed the war was not going as well as it should have been and thought a change at the top level, no matter how much they respected Washington, would be beneficial. Some of the critics would be silenced if Washington could just achieve a victory.

Washington was most concerned about the conditions of the army and did what he could to improve this situation. He spent many hours writing to Congress about the state of these soldiers, as seen by himself, thus leading to the Committee at War's visit. Each day he rode throughout the camp, seeing for himself what needed to be done. In doing so, he gained a familiarity with the common soldiers that would be exemplified by his mixing easily with them at the May 6 celebration of the French alliance. For the most part the rank and file of the army, closely associated with Washington every day, respected and even admired the general.

His popularity with the soldiers was reflected by the historian Mercy Otis Warren in a letter to her husband James: "The toast among the soldiers, Washington or no Army."[25] Captain Ezra Sheldon of the First Connecticut well-represented the typical soldier's view when he wrote: "I am content should they remove almost any General Except his Excellency… even Congress are not aware of the Confidence The Army Places in him or motions would never have been made for Gates to take Command."[26] Note that Sheldon was aware of some machinations to usurp Washington. Although Washington's position and ability as commander in chief was still subject to criticism and intrigues, the soldiers of the army were with him.

New Quartermaster

The army suffered terribly that bleak winter from disease and the lack of proper supplies, though it was more from the ineptitude of the quartermaster and commissary departments than the weather or the enemy. Many soldiers deserted. Officers requested furloughs in dramatic numbers. The supply situation improved dramatically when Nathanael Greene, one of Washington's favorite field generals, took over as quartermaster general on March 24, 1778.

Greene was born in Rhode Island in 1745. A handsome man who walked with a slight limp, he was raised as a Quaker, but after church leaders saw him at a local militia event, he was asked to leave his local congregation. Growing up, he worked diligently at his mill. Elected to the colonial assembly in 1770, he helped organize the so-called Kentish Guards. Because of his limp he was not allowed to be an officer and remained a private.

Hearing of Lexington and Concord, he rushed to Cambridge to join the Revolutionary Army. After a few days, he was sent back to Rhode Island. The state formed three regiments in 1775 and, recognizing that despite his limp Greene was a natural leader, appointed him a brigadier general of militia on May 3, 1775. After serving on the lines outside Boston, he was appointed a brigadier general in the Continental Army on June 22, 1775, where he took command of the militia and marched them to the siege lines outside Boston. Recognizing his leadership abilities, George Washington immediately took a liking to the genial and intelligent Rhode Islander.

Greene served in a variety of command positions in the campaigns of 1776 and 1777. His abilities were questioned after he advocated the continued occupation of Fort Washington even as it was surrounded and threatened with destruction. When the fort surrendered with humiliating losses, many critics pointed fingers at him. The distinguished doctor Benjamin Rush called Greene "a sycophant to the general, timid, speculative, without enterprise."[27] Despite the Fort Washington debacle, the commander in chief avoided pointing a finger at his subordinate and continued to show confidence in him.

At Valley Forge, Greene was not happy with his new assignment as quartermaster, preferring field duty. He wrote after taking the post: "There is a great difference between being raisd to an Office and decending to one; which is my case. There is also a great difference betwext serving where you have a fair prospect of honor and laurels, and where you have no prospect of either let you discharge your duty ever so well. No body ever heard of a quarter Master in History as such or in relateing any brilliant Action. I engagd in this business as well out of compasion to your Excellency as from a regard to the public."[28]

Although he performed well as quartermaster general, Nathanael Greene wanted to return to a line command. He got that chance at Monmouth. *National Archives Mezzotint (full length) by V. Green from painting by C. W. Peale, The George Washington Bicentennial Commission*

Despite his misgivings, Greene plunged into his new assignment with alacrity. His ability to rectify the supply situation was one of the factors that helped encourage Washington when the Virginian anticipated the upcoming campaign.

Steuben

Living conditions for the Continental soldier at Valley Forge were dirty and disease ridden. Hunger was a constant and brutal companion. Arriving in mid-December, it took until the middle of January to get the entire army into crude huts. It was a struggle to survive. Frequent rain, mixed with snow and intense cold, made conditions miserable for soldiers clad in little but what they had brought to camp. It was unlikely that the army would be able to improve its combat efficiency if it was struggling just to survive. Washington's decision to appoint one of his more capable combat commanders, Nathanael Greene, as quartermaster made it possible for the army not only to survive but to improve itself.

Another source of improvement was the arrival in camp of Baron Friedrich Wilhelm Ludolf Gerhard Augustin von Steuben. A former Prussian officer, the stout, energetic soldier was touted to Congress as a former member of Frederick the Great's staff and a lieutenant general in that service. These were blatant lies that the baron did nothing to refute. He had been a captain in

Baron von Steuben provided the basic training the Continental Army needed to stand, counterattack, and defeat the British army at Monmouth. *The Miriam and Ira D. Wallach Division of Art, Prints and Photographs: Print Collection, The New York Public Library. "Major General, Baron Steuben"*

the Prussian service with experience in an infantry unit and on staff during the Seven Years War. He was a "baron" in one of the many small principalities that made up Germany at that time, a somewhat honorary title with no accompanying lands or wealth. He spoke little English and blustered about loudly but it was soon obvious he was both able and willing to help the rebels.

Washington saw something he liked in the man; perhaps it was Steuben's offer to serve as an unpaid volunteer: "…the Object of my greatest Ambition is to render your Country all the Services in my Power and to deserve the title of a Citizen of America by fighting for the Cause of your Liberty. If the distinguished Ranks I have Served in in Europe Should be an Obstacle, I had rather Serve under Your Excellency as a Volunteer, than to be a Subject of Discontent to Such deserving Officers as have already distinguished themselves amongst you."[29]

The office of inspector general was open after Conway's abdication and Washington saw an opportunity. Washington usually was a good judge of people, and he appointed Steuben as inspector general with the staff rank of major general, tasked with training the American army to European standards. "The Baron Steuben, a Gentleman of high Military rank, profound knowledge and great experience in his profession, is placed at the head of this department."[30]

Very quickly Steuben assured the members of Washington's staff that he knew his business. Young officers Alexander Hamilton and Benjamin Walker were fluent in French and they were assigned to help the new inspector general. Steuben gave them orders in French which they translated into English. The two officers stayed up nights to organize and write a manual. The manual was copied by hand and distributed to the officers of the army. Then Steuben began his work in earnest.

Fortunately, most of the soldiers were veterans with some type of previous experience. New recruits were often men who had served in the militia or previously in the Continental Army, although unfortunately there had been no consistent or uniform set of drill regulations. With this foundation of experience Steuben went to work. He formed a model company of one hundred soldiers, primarily drawn from Washington's Life Guards. He carefully and personally instructed them in the manual of arms and basic drill movements. It was quite a sight, the robust German clad in resplendent uniform covered in medals and ribbons, yelling out commands and gesticulating with enthusiasm, amid his less spectacularly dressed and confused American students trying to carry out his orders. But his patience and zealous attitude soon won the Americans over and they responded to his instructions. This is not to say he wasn't frequently frustrated. He wrote to a European officer, "You say to your soldier, 'Do this,' and he does it…" but it wasn't the same with the Americans. To the Continental soldier he had to say, "'This is the reason why you ought to do that,' and then he does it."[31] He became so frustrated at one point that he used every swear word he could think of in French and German. Then he turned and implored Captain Walker, his newly appointed aide, to swear in English at the independent-minded Americans to complete the tirade.

After several weeks of instruction, the model company was broken up and dispersed among the other units to train them in Steuben's drill. He formed another model company to repeat the process and forced junior officers to take part in drills; something many had avoided, believing it was beneath them. The baron held classes for all the officers to teach them how to maneuver their units en masse on the battlefield using the movements being taught their troops in daily drills. Washington watched the efforts, and the results, of Steuben's training. He believed that only an army as good as that of the British could win the war.

Drill was not the only aspect of camp life that von Steuben tried to improve. Alarmed by the poor sanitary conditions of the American encampment, he addressed the proper layout of such a camp. He organized latrines away from the kitchens, laid out proper company, regimental, and brigade streets, and instructed troops where to bury carcasses of butchered or dead animals that were decomposing in alarming numbers around the camp.

After the ceremonies celebrating the French alliance on May 6, Washington felt that Steuben's training was showing results.

> The Commander in Chief takes particular Pleasure in acquainting the Army that their Conduct yesterday afforded him the highest Satisfaction; The Exactness and order with which their Movements were performed is a pleasing Evidence of the Progress they are making in military Improvement, and an earnest of the pleasing Perfection to which they will shortly arrive, with a Continuance of that laudable Zeal and Emulation which so happily prevails; The General at the same time presents his thanks to Baron Steuben and the Gentlemen under him for the Indefatigable Exertions in the duties of their Office, the good effects of which are already so apparent.[32]

Whatever the supply difficulties the army had experienced during the awful winter, its education had not been neglected. Despite all the problems that winter, Washington wrote to his brother: "the Army is in exceeding good spirits."[33]

Some believed that Washington himself was making a difference in troop morale and training. Baron de Kalb noted that Washington "does more every day than can be expected from any general in the world, in the same circumstances, and that I think him the only proper person (nobody actually being or serving in America excepted), by his natural and acquired capacity; his bravery, good sense, uprightness and honesty, to keep up the spirits of the army and people, and that I look upon him as the sole defender of his country's cause."[34]

The setbacks of the previous fall, the poor living conditions at Valley Forge, and even the strange cabal that may have been trying to replace Washington as commander in chief, might have cast a pessimistic cloud on the upcoming campaign season for the Virginian. Instead, the arrival of new recruits and returning veterans, the French alliance, Greene's excellent work as quartermaster, the failure of the "Conway Cabal," and the efforts of von Steuben helped to restore the confidence of the army and its commander. Writing to fellow Virginian Thomas Nelson, Jr., Washington optimistically said: "Matters appear abroad to be in as favourable a train as we could wish, and if we are not free and happy, it will be owing to a want of virtue, prudence & management among ourselves."[35]

A Gift for the General

As if to underscore the optimistic mood, Washington was given a gift by a fellow Virginian. Captain Henry Fauntleroy had just returned to the army that spring from recruiting duty with a pair of matched pistols owned by his brother-in-law, Thomas Turner. A short note was attached:

> Altho' I have not the honour of being personally acquainted with your Excellency, neverthless I am far from being a Stranger to your distinguished merit, both in private and publick life; your indefatigable zeal, and unwearied attention to the true Interest of your native Country, since the commencement of these differences, must excite the warmest sense of gratitude in the breastt of every American that is not callous to the rights of humanity; That it may please the supreme Disposer of human Events, to crown you with success in this important struggle, & speedily put an end to the distressing Scenes of this unnatural War, is the fervent wish of your, Excellency's respectful & Obedient h'ble Servt
> Thos Turner.
> P.S. I have transmitted to your Excellency a pair of pistols &c. &c. your acceptance of which will confer a singular obligation on[36]

Presented to the commander in chief, the beautiful pistols with silver inlays on the butt and brass barrels seemed to augur success. Obviously happy with the gift, Washington made sure that Turner received a thank-you note through his nephew George Lewis: "Altho I am not much accustomed to accept presents, I cannot refuse one offered in such polite terms as accompanied the Pistols & furniture you were so obliging as to send me by Captn Fauntleroy. They are very elegant, & deserve my best thanks, which are offered with much sincerity.

The favourable Sentiments you are pleased to entertain of me, & the obliging and flattering manner in which they are expressed add to the obligation."[37]

Oddly enough, Washington had once romantically pursued Fauntleroy's sister. Another sister had married Turner.

After starting out at a low point with plots, jealousies, and inefficiencies, the situation for Washington had changed. The new drill instruction, a new quartermaster general, and the alliance with France boded well. The month of May brought spring to full fruition, and, like the new pistols, the army and its commander were ready for battle. Valley Forge had turned into a high point of his generalship. Now he only needed to crown his efforts with a triumphal campaign.

The Opponent: Henry Clinton

While the group of men grandly termed the "Continental Army" suffered through winter at Valley Forge, the British army was quartered in and near Philadelphia. Some of the redcoat soldiers took over public buildings, some built themselves huts, and the officers took shelter in private homes. Cavalry took over several churches as their stables. The countryside was quickly denuded of trees around the outer line of fortifications as the occupiers, and those residents who remained, needed firewood as well as construction material. Except for a short period when American Forts Mifflin and Mercer closed the river, the local people who remained in Philadelphia did not suffer under British occupation. Once Fort Mifflin was evacuated on November 15, 1777, and Fort Mercer on November 18, 1777, life in the city was comfortable for the Loyalists—those still supporting the Crown, often called Tories—as well as for William Howe and his men.[38]

Balls and dances were held and there was a gaiety about the whole occupation. Officers formed their own theater, spent nights drinking and dancing at the City Tavern and Indian Queen, or gambled at the London Coffee House. Howe exercised his troops by foraging throughout the countryside or chasing local militia. He personally kept up a vibrant social life. Loyalists eagerly feted the occupiers, joining in the parties and merrymaking. To make things even better for Howe, as the new year of 1778 dawned, he received the welcome news that he would be able to go home to England and leave the god-forsaken colonies to his successor, Sir Henry Clinton. Unable to destroy the army of rebels in the last two years of campaigning, and suffering criticism for his inability to do so, Howe had asked to be relieved several times. Now his wish was granted.

In contrast to the growing optimism of George Washington, the new commander of His Majesty's forces in America, Sir Henry Clinton, was not in the mood for rejoicing or celebration. The 40-year-old professional had longed for the post as senior British officer in America since he arrived in the colonies in 1775. Many would have thought it a great honor to be the commander in chief of the British army in the 13 colonies. But recent events had made the change in command a hollow honor. Handsome, with a slightly petulant look, his body developing the heavy looks common to many senior British officers, Clinton found himself in a difficult situation. The lack of promised personal glory, conflicting orders, and his government's contradictory positions transformed what should have been the chance of a lifetime into the prospect of a gloomy summer for the most senior redcoat in America.

A sour and contrary man, Clinton's mood was not helped by his equally contrary orders. When originally tapped for the position to lead His Majesty's Forces, he had been told that he could hold or give up Philadelphia, go after Washington, or make his own plans. But the official entry of France into the conflict, unofficially involved since the start of the war in 1775, resulted in great changes in London's plans. Clinton was now ordered to send many of his troops elsewhere and limit his own operations in North America. He was to give up Philadelphia. Unlike Washington, he had been a soldier all his life and had varied military experiences in many different locations. He could be counted on to do his duty.

Despite his many foibles, there was no doubt that Henry Clinton was a brave and intelligent man. As a young man, Clinton had grown up in New York, where his father was the governor. One of his friends was an affable young man named William Alexander, who would later claim the Scottish title "Lord Stirling" and serve as a general in the rebel army. Clinton served in the local militia and participated in combat during the attack on the French fortress of Louisburg. When the family returned to Britain, he obtained a commission in the Guards and served with distinction in Europe during the Seven Years War. Clinton finished the war in the prestigious position of aide de camp to Prince Ferdinand of Brunswick and seemed to be destined for great things. He was named colonel of the 12th Regiment of Foot in 1766 and married Harriet Carter the following year. The couple appeared to be honestly in love as Harriet's family connections and fortune were negligible. Acknowledged by many as a thoughtful, tactically competent officer, he was promoted to major general in 1772. With the help of his cousin, the Duke of Newcastle, Clinton was elected a Member of Parliament for Boroughbridge. The sky appeared to be the limit and the possibilities endless. The loving couple

S.ᴿ HENRY CLINTON.

Sir Henry Clinton was a capable professional officer plagued by events out of his control and his crusty personality. *Line engraving by H. R. Cook, from John Andrews'* History of the War with America..., *London, 1785–86. Naval History and Heritage Command*

lived in harmony at their country estate with their four children. Henry and Harriet were enormously fond of each other and thoroughly enjoyed their offspring. Then, on August 29, 1772, just before Henry was to take his seat in Parliament and place the capstone on his career, Harriet died in childbirth, although the baby lived.

Genuinely bereaved, Clinton went into a deep depression; nothing would console him, not even his loving children. His promising career seemed irrelevant. He did not take his seat in Parliament, instead deciding to travel abroad with his friend Henry Lloyd, a Russian spy. Leaving his children with relatives, he traveled for two years, primarily in the Balkans, observing the Russo-Turkish War, until his friend moved on to Russia. Clinton returned to Britain just as the troubles with the 13 American colonies came to a climax.

The future held no promise for Henry Clinton at this point; he needed distraction and sought active service. Using his influence, Clinton obtained permission to go to America to assist Lieutenant General Thomas Gage, the commander of British forces dealing with the rebellious colonists in Boston. In 1775, Clinton was one of three major generals who crowded into the HMS *Cerberus*, appropriately the name of the three-headed dog of mythology, for the trip to Massachusetts. Clinton, perhaps still depressed from his wife's death, did little to socialize with his fellow generals, William Howe and John Burgoyne, but got along amiably enough. Boston seemed crowded when the three major generals joined the lieutenant general/governor.

When the three generals arrived in Boston on May 25, 1775, the battles of Lexington and Concord had already taken place and a large, motley army of colonists besieged the seaport. Clinton noticed that the peninsulas at Charlestown and Dorchester dominated the city and, having a habit of voicing his tactical opinions, perhaps learned as an aide to a prince, he recommended that the British occupy both heights. Gage and the others ignored his advice. When the colonists fortified the heights above Charlestown northwest of Boston, on Breed's Hill, Clinton recommended an amphibious landing behind the Americans at the base of the peninsula. William Howe, the senior major general and future replacement for Gage, ignored Clinton's idea and decided on a frontal assault meant to awe as well as defeat the Americans. Clinton distinguished himself in Howe's bloody victory on June 17, known as the battle of Bunker Hill, by organizing a group of about 500 men, transporting them across from Boston, and flanking the heights in the final push that displaced the recalcitrant colonists.

Howe replaced Gage as the latter returned home in a cloud of controversy, but the new commander took no action concerning the other dominating heights near Boston, those at Dorchester. The Americans didn't wait and occupied the heights on March 4, 1776, using recently arrived guns from Fort Ticonderoga brought overland by Henry Knox and his men. This sealed the fate of British forces in Boston. Dominated by the guns overlooking their fleet from Dorchester, the British evacuated the post on March 17, 1776.

The British army reorganized in Halifax, Nova Scotia, and Clinton was given his first independent command. Ordered to meet with American Loyalists in North Carolina, he arrived in that province only to find that Loyalist forces had been recently routed at the battle of Moore's Creek Bridge and the royal governor was in flight. Nevertheless, he again demonstrated his personal courage and led raids on rebel posts in the vicinity of the coast. Clinton proceeded south to attack Charleston, South Carolina on June 28,

1776. Poor understanding of local water conditions, the inability of the army and navy to cooperate, and a strong rebel resistance turned the assault into an embarrassing fiasco with finger pointing from all sides. Clinton returned ignominiously to New York.

When the British landed on Long Island and began their campaign to capture New York City, Clinton distinguished himself by planning and leading the successful flanking movement that dislodged the American forces on August 27, 1776. He was knighted and promoted to lieutenant general. Returning to the main army, he was personally insufferable: he constantly offered unwanted and contrary advice, gradually alienating his fellow generals. He criticized Howe's decisions and lack of initiative. Socially he did himself no favors and did not interact well with the other officers, calling himself a "shy bitch."[39] He often found himself at odds with many others, including fellow general Lord Cornwallis. Unlike most of the others, he was of the "German" school, an officer whose service in the last war had primarily been in Europe. This made him popular with the German troops and those British soldiers who had campaigned in Europe but suspect among those who had fought the last war in America. Howe managed to get rid of Clinton for a short time by detaching him on an independent command which easily captured Newport, Rhode Island on December 28, 1776. Despite this minor victory, which provided an excellent base for the Royal Navy, Clinton was frustrated and asked to return to Britain. The request was granted, and he boarded ship for home in the spring of 1777.

Clinton was reassigned to America after only a few weeks of leave. Frustration set in quickly as he was assigned to a stagnant command of the forces in and around New York City. He advised William Howe against going after the Americans in Pennsylvania and recommended advancing up the Hudson to meet Major General John Burgoyne's thrust down from Canada. Instead, Howe sailed off to Pennsylvania to chase George Washington out of Philadelphia. Howe found martial glory in defeating Washington in major engagements at Brandywine and Germantown, sweeping the rebels from Philadelphia, and sending Washington flying into the country. Meanwhile, brooding Henry Clinton sat in New York with a garrison too small for offensive operations. Far to the north, flamboyant John Burgoyne was earning his share of glory by defeating the Americans there, including the capture of the massive fortress at Ticonderoga. Clinton was sidelined, out of the picture. Clinton, eager for his own glory and ever wary of any slight or criticism, bristled at the inactivity. When Burgoyne encountered trouble in the wilds of New York, Clinton eagerly pushed a small force up the Hudson, capturing several small rebel forts but ultimately finding himself unable to distract the American forces that eventually destroyed Burgoyne.

Clinton again petitioned to return to Britain. Instead of ending his career as a gentleman member of Parliament, however, he was ordered to take command of the forces in America in March of 1778 upon the relief of William Howe. At this point Clinton was hardly the same enthusiastic officer he had been when he first arrived back in 1775 but he was prepared to do his duty.

The *Mischianza*

In addition to the contradictory orders, Clinton's reception by the army upon his appointment as commander in chief was disheartening. Rather than being met by an enthusiastic staff, he was forced to endure the performance of the so-called *Mischianza*, a lavish party, in honor of the departing William Howe.

Lieutenant William Hale of the 45th Regiment's grenadier company and part of the 2nd Grenadier Battalion spoke for many when he wrote his parents: "Whether you can send a better Gen. than Sir William Howe, I know not, one more beloved will with difficulty be found."[40] There were some who spoke out about his failure to destroy Washington's army or to support Burgoyne the previous fall during the disastrous Saratoga campaign. Despite the criticisms leveled against him Howe was well respected by the army. Four or five junior officers, with the assistance of dashing young Captain John Andre, aide to General Charles Grey, decided to throw a farewell party for the outgoing commander in chief.

The event, on May 18, 1778, was given the name Mischianza or Meschianza, an Italian term implying a medley of entertainment. It was intended to be the biggest farewell ever given to a commanding officer by his subordinates. Without a doubt, they achieved their purpose.

A giant tent, about 180 feet long and 30 feet wide, was erected on the grounds of the mansion of Charles Wharton in Walnut Grove. The ground there sloped down several hundred yards to the Schuylkill River. From Knight's Wharf at the foot of Green Street, a parade of extravagantly decorated galleys, barges, and boats brought the guests, in order of rank, to the festivities. In several of the boats were musicians, playing music as the four hundred or so guests approached the landing.

After a two-hour voyage, covering only one mile, the participants landed and proceeded to take a position around an area marked off for jousting. Crowds of spectators were kept at bay by soldiers as two groups of seven women were seated opposite each other, the ladies chosen to represent the two sides, the Knights of the Blended Rose or the Knights of the Burning Mountain. Guests were treated to elaborate ceremonies of introduction and then to a series of jousts.

That was only the beginning. Throughout the rest of the night there was no lack of entertainment as the guests strolled through the gardens or took refreshment in the capacious tent. The bands provided stirring music for dancing, which was interrupted at 10:00 pm by a dazzling display of fireworks and again at midnight by a full meal. All through the night, until daylight, there was dancing and drinking as would befit the greatest military celebration of any kind.

Dashing American Captain Allan McLane and his company of light troops provided the only negative note during the glorious celebration. They daringly attacked part of the British perimeter around Philadelphia as the Mischianza was in full swing. McLane was a wealthy young man born in Pennsylvania and living in Delaware when the war began. He had been in the war since fighting at the Great Bridge in 1775 and was respected for equipping his men at his own expense. McLane was a man of action, on this night leading his men as they threw combustibles and explosives at British positions to cause panic in the British outposts. Such was the excitement of the Mischianza that his foray went nearly without notice.

Many would criticize the extravagance of the Mischianza, both in England and America, but all who participated fondly remembered it. One who could hardly have felt any need for remembrance was Henry Clinton. It would be hard to follow in the steps of so popular a commander as William Howe. One small consolation for Clinton was that Charles Grey's aide John Andre, who had planned the extravaganza for Howe, joined Clinton's staff and became as loyal a supporter to the new commander in chief as he ever was for William Howe.

Orders

The esteem and respect for Howe might have given Clinton a feeling of insecurity but he did receive a note of confidence from a former enemy, Continental Army Major General Charles Lee: "General Lee presents his most sincere and humble respects to Sir Henry Clinton. He wishes him all possible happiness and health and begs, whatever may be the event of the present unfortunate contest, that he will believe General Lee to be his most respectful and obedient humble servant."[41]

The timing of his ascent to command was another reason that Clinton showed a lack of enthusiasm for his new assignment. Looking forward to a campaign to test Washington and the rebels, he found the initiative was quickly plucked from his hands. Days after giving him command of the army, Lord Germain, Secretary of State for the Colonies, sent a new message that essentially ordered Clinton to go on the defensive. In view of the new French alliance with the American rebels, he was to send three thousand troops to Florida, five thousand more to the West Indies, and six hundred Marines to Halifax. He was also instructed to consolidate his remaining forces in New York by giving up Philadelphia and possibly Newport. If things went terribly wrong, he could evacuate the 13 colonies completely, including New York City, and go to Halifax. The possibilities of glory and honor as a successful general seemed to be torn from his fingers before he had a chance to demonstrate his abilities, placing him in a situation that he had not counted on when he first coveted the position back in 1775. Now, the new commander wrote about the dubious assignment: "For neither honor nor credit could be expected from it, but on the contrary a considerable portion of blame, howsoever unmerited, seemed to be almost inevitable."[42] He would have to evacuate Philadelphia immediately. He had no choice when given such orders. "I cannot misunderstand them, nor dare I disobey them. I am directed to evacuate Philadelphia. My fate is hard; forced to an apparent retreat with such an army is mortifying."[43]

Clinton did have one difficult choice. In following his instruction, he was forced to decide whether to evacuate by sea or overland. The sheer size of his army and the number of Loyalists that would need to be moved precluded any single movement entirely by sea. There simply were not enough ships. He could leave the loyal residents of Philadelphia to their fate and evacuate his army by ship, or he could take his army overland to New York and place many of the Loyalists on ships with much of his non-essential baggage. Even after deciding on the latter course, he found that hundreds of Loyalists and their belongings would still have to go overland with him. The choice to cross through New Jersey to New York City would also open him up to attack from George Washington and the Continental Army. On the other hand, getting out of Philadelphia might be an opportunity for Clinton to meet Washington in a general engagement that could result in martial glory. "And I was, moreover, not altogether without hopes that Mr. Washington might be tempted by his superior numbers and many other advantages to measure his strength with me in the field."[44]

His decision on when to evacuate was spurred on by news of the Americans' new allies. Intelligence that a French fleet was coming to America that could blockade the Delaware, attack the fleet en route to New York, or even blockade New York to prevent his entry gave Clinton an impetus to move sooner than later. But Clinton's timing was complicated by political events taking place across the Atlantic.

The Carlisle Commission

An additional headache for Clinton was political posturing in London. During the winter Parliament and the king made known through various bills that Great Britain would be willing to compromise with the colonies. Parliament declared another offer of peace would be made and it was decided to send three envoys to talk to Congress. Clinton would have to put his planned evacuation on hold until these commissioners had a chance to do their work. On June 6, 1778, the so-called Carlisle Commission arrived in Philadelphia aboard the HMS *Trident*. It consisted of young Frederick Howard, the fifth Earl of Carlisle, the former governor of West Florida George Johnstone, and William Eden, Lord of Trade. Technically, this commission also included Lord Howe, and to his embarrassment, Henry Clinton. Washington left any negotiations to Congress.

Essentially the commission was there to treat for peace, but peace was improbable. Parliament was willing to offer some self-government and possible representation in the House of Commons. Parliament had given the commission the authority to grant pardons, appoint new governors, discuss the suspension of offensive Parliamentary policies, make treaties, and generally give the Americans much of what may have satisfied many colonists back in 1775. Parliament had suspended the Intolerable Acts, punishing laws passed in response to the Boston Tea Party, and the Tea Act. These were some of the most offensive actions that had helped turn the Americans into rebels but the time when their revocation would have proved effective had long since passed. The flowing words of the Declaration of Independence, the destruction of towns like Falmouth, Massachusetts, and the shedding of the blood of thousands of colonists had thrown many Americans into the arms of the rebels. The Commission would use any method to persuade the colonists to renounce their rebellion, including attempts to bribe American officials.

It was not only rebellious Americans but some British and American Loyalists as well who felt the time for reconciliation had passed. A Hessian officer noted the reaction to Parliament's actions prior to the commission's arrival: "The common English soldiers are so angry about the Act of Parliament on non-taxation, etc., which is posted here that they tear down these proclamations at night."[45] The peace commissioners were facing a tough audience from both Whigs and Tories.

Whatever its avowed purpose, the Carlisle Commission and the impending retreat of the king's army from Philadelphia made it look as if the British were dealing from a position of weakness. How could they hope to make the Americans come to the peace table if the British army was leaving Philadelphia and Parliament was meekly changing laws to placate Congress? When the commission managed to get word to Congress of their mission and willingness to meet, Congress took over a week to reply and said they would only negotiate if two items were agreed to: American independence and British forces' withdrawal from the 13 states. The members of the commission could not give their agreement to either of these points of negotiation and eventually realized the complete futility of their mission. There were rumors of failed attempts to bribe some prominent American rebels that only served to prove how desperately the British wanted a reconciliation of the two combatants.

Valley Forge

On May 7 the Continental Army began to implement an important directive given to them by Congress back on February 7. Each commissioned officer of the army was to take an oath:

> I, do acknowledge the United States of America to be free, independent and sovereign states, and declare that the people thereof owe no allegiance or obedience, to George the third, king of Great Britain; and I renounce, refuse and abjure any allegiance or obedience to him: and I do swear (or affirm) that I will, to the utmost of my power, support, maintain and defend the said United States, against the said king George the third and his heirs and successors, and his and their abettors, assistants and adherents, and will serve the said United States in the office of which I now hold, with fidelity, according to the best of my skill and understanding. So help me God.[46]

General Orders on May 7 gave detailed instructions on how the entire army would take the oath.

Just as Clinton had to formulate plans for his evacuation, Washington needed intelligence to make his own plans. Reports from townspeople that the British were evacuating Philadelphia reached George Washington in early May. On May 7 he sent French and Indian War veteran William Maxwell's New Jersey brigade into New Jersey to cooperate with the local militia under hawk-nosed Brigadier General Philemon Dickinson, brother of John Dickinson of the Continental Congress. Their orders were to harass the British army and gain intelligence of their movements: "The detachment under your comd is designed to answer the following purposes—become a security to this Camp, & the Country between the Schuylkill & Delaware.

Militia played a significant role in the Monmouth campaign. Philemon Dickinson was an important commander of the New Jersey irregulars. *The Miriam and Ira D. Wallach Division of Art, Prints and Photographs: Print Collection, The New York Public Library. "Gen. Phil. Dickenson"*

interrupt the communication with Philadelphia—obtain intelligence of the motion, and designs of the enemy—and, aided by the Militia, prevent small parties of the Enemy from patrolling, to cover the market people; whilst large Parties, especially if any attempt should be made on this side the Delaware to destroy the Vessels above Bristol, are to be harrassed as much as possible, till notice there of can be communicated to me."[47]

A gruff Scots-Irishman, Maxwell was the perfect man for the job. After militia service in the field against the French and Indians, he had served for years as a commissary in the British army. A tough man to get to know, he had a wealth of experience in this new war. Maxwell was part of the ill-fated Canadian campaign in 1776. He commanded the first corps of light infantry in the Continental Army and had participated in the battles of Brandywine and Germantown. What made him perfect for this present work was his previous cooperation with the New Jersey militia and his knowledge of his native Jersey countryside. Maxwell had worked with Dickinson before and his New Jersey Brigade would be on home ground. Many of Maxwell's men were new recruits and it was hoped that skirmishing with small bodies of the British would provide them with needed experience. Washington wrote Dickinson to harass the British in such a way as they "…may be greatly injured by concealed and well directed fire of Men in Ambush. This kind of Annoyance ought to be incessant day and Night, and I would think, be very effectual."[48]

Congress pushed Washington to make plans for the spring campaign season, resolving that: "General Washington be authorized and directed forthwith to convene a council, to consist of the major generals in the State of Pennsylvania, and the general officer commanding the corps of engineers, and with the advice of the said council to form such a plan for the general operations of the campaign as he shall deem consistent with the general welfare of these states: That Major Generals Gates and Mifflin, members of the Board of War, have leave to attend the said council." On May 8 he held the first of these councils of war. Both Gates and Mifflin chose to attend the conference, but they did so in a subordinate capacity. After briefly reviewing the situation throughout the 13 states, Washington asked the generals "that after full and candid discussion of the matter in council, each member would furnish him with his sentiments in writing on some general plan, which, considering all circumstance(s,) ought to be adapted for the operations of the next campaign."[49] The next day he received a lengthy reply from the council with the basic recommendation to "remain on the defensive and wait events; without attempting any offensive operations of consequence, unless the future circumstances of the enemy, should afford a fairer opportunity, than at present exists, for striking some successful blow."[50]

British intentions were hard to discern. The redcoats became aggressive: on May 9, an expedition set out from Philadelphia and burned Continental supplies, boats, and two frigates. British troops roamed the countryside foraging and skirmishing with local militia. Washington could only wonder—if the British were going to evacuate Philadelphia, why would they be so active? He sent notes requesting Maxwell with the militia from Pennsylvania and New Jersey to try to obtain information on this new enemy movement.[51] The British raiders returned to Philadelphia without a major engagement.

The British reaction to the alliance between the colonies and the French was a topic of many reports that Washington received. His cavalry commander Stephen Moylan wrote on May 13 of this problem, "there has been no positive account of war having been declar'd but to have been two days after the last packet left England, there being but one dissenting Lord against the motion."[52]

In addition to sifting through intelligence about Clinton's plans, Washington also went through these reports to see what the effect of a war between France and Britain on the fledgling United States might be.

Washington's anticipation of the spring campaign was laid out in the General Orders for May 16: "It is not improbable that the army may soon find it necessary to make a sudden & rapid movement–The Commander in Chief reminds the Officers of the order of the 27th of last March respecting Baggage–if there should be any who have been inattentive to it, they must abide the consequences of it, as it is determined that no hindrance to the Motions of the Army will be suffered to happen on Account of an Incumbrance which out to have been removed."[53] He referred to a notice he sent out about officers accumulating possessions while in camp and how the excess baggage might prove a problem if the British did leave Philadelphia with little notice.

Washington also instructed his quartermaster Nathanael Greene to begin preparations for the upcoming operations: "From many concurrent circumstances it appears that the enemy are preparing to evacuate Philadelphia, whether their design is to withdraw altogether from the Continent or to concenter their forces at new york cannot be ascertained—in case the latter shd be the case it will be proper to have provision of forage made on the road to the No. River for such body of Troops as may be ordered to march from hence in consequence."[54]

He wrote the commissary general, Ephraim Blaine, on May 17: "Very frequent and recent intelligence from the City of Philadelphia induces me to think that the Enemy mean to evacuate the place."[55] Despite the preparations to move when he had concrete knowledge of British plans, Washington felt he needed still more information. He decided to send out a detachment to ascertain British intentions.

Barren Hill

The orders to send troops to other areas and assume a concentration in New York or Halifax did not stop the British from the tactical offensive. In another blow to a man with an easily bruised ego, Clinton was forced to step aside as Sir William Howe conducted one last offensive operation before leaving the colonies. Technically, Clinton took over as commander on May 11, 1778, but Howe could not pass up one last chance for a major blow at the Americans and a chance to capture the Marquis de Lafayette, the young French officer recently moved from staff to field command in the Continental Army.

On May 18, a full week after the British change of command and the same day as Howe's magnificent farewell Mischianza celebration, Washington sent a detachment under the Marquis de Lafayette "to interrupt the communication with Philadelphia—obstruct the incursions of the enemy parties and obtain intelligence of their motions and designs." He also included a warning: "In general I would observe that a stationary post is inadviseable, as it gives the enemy an opportunity of knowing your situation and concerting successfully against you."[56] Lafayette took a detachment of a little over 2,000 men with five cannon and moved toward Philadelphia. He took up a position on Barren Hill across the Schuylkill River about 14 miles northwest of Philadelphia. Unfortunately, he ignored Washington's warning and failed to move from his position, remaining fixed in place for several days.

British patrols reported the position and strength of Lafayette to Howe and the outgoing commander in chief could not resist one last opportunity. Shunting aside Clinton, Howe took personal command of an expedition to capture the over-eager and imprudent Frenchman and a substantial part of Washington's army. On the night of May 19 and morning of May 20, Howe led three columns totaling some 10,000 men out of Philadelphia to surround Lafayette's position and cut him off from the main American position across the Schuylkill 10 miles away. It appeared as if Lafayette, and Washington, had both made great mistakes. Lafayette had stayed too long at a position too far from support and backed by the river. Washington had sent out too large a party for just a reconnaissance, attracting the full attention of the British.

At first, Howe's plan worked perfectly, helped by the fact that many of the militia who were supposed to be screening the American position disappeared. Luckily for Lafayette, Captain Allan McLane's scouts captured British messengers who gave up the whole British plan and Lafayette was able, though not without some drama, to draw off his force and place the Schuylkill between himself and the British. "Howe's last and likewise unsuccessful expedition,"[57] as one British officer termed it, referencing Howe's previous inability to destroy Washington's army, proved to be a failure. Howe's command of the attempt to capture Lafayette was another insult for Clinton but Sir William finally sailed back to England on May 24 aboard the HMS *Andromeda*.

Washington was still concerned that the British would try some attack on his army either as a distraction to support an evacuation or as a major attempt to destroy the Continental Army, thereby enabling them to hold Philadelphia. He wrote militia commander Philemon Dickinson: "Some reports say they mean to make a push against us here and that this is the most common opinion."[58] Howe's attack at Barren Hill only reinforced that perception.

The Marquis De Lafayette proved to be one of the few foreign officers who provided sterling service to the Continental Army. Unfortunately, glory in battle evaded him at Monmouth. *"Portrait of General Lafayette and a view of his landing in New York in 1824" The Miriam and Ira D. Wallach Division of Art, Prints and Photographs: Print Collection, The New York Public Library*

In addition to watching the British activities in Philadelphia and preparing for the upcoming campaign, Washington had a variety of other concerns. Court martials, a new commander for Fort Pitt, Loyalist disruptions in Maryland, Congress and the various state governments, and operations in Massachusetts and Rhode Island all consumed the commander in chief's time. He also had to interact with the British commander on prisoner of war matters as well as respond to a letter from the Carlisle Commission. Washington chose to let the Congress deal with the commission.

On May 29 Washington was still evaluating the activities of the British in Philadelphia, writing William Maxwell: "It is yet a matter of uncertainty whether the Enemy intend to embark or to march across New Jersey."[59] Washington further encouraged Maxwell to be prepared to interdict a British withdrawal across New Jersey. "If the Enemy attempt to cross the Country, you are, as before directed, in conjunction with the Militia, to break up and obstruct the Roads, and make their march as difficult as possible."[60] Despite this lack of certainty, he ordered the army to prepare to march and organized the route and composition of the units that would move out first. He consolidated three of the Continental Dragoon regiments under Colonel Stephen Moylan in readiness for the beginning of the campaign. Patrols watched for British activities that might indicate when the enemy was moving and whether they would be going by land or sea. Where would they go? Would it be New York or Charleston? No matter which rumor proved true, Washington wanted to be prepared. If it was that the British were leaving by land, Washington would take the army to Coryell's Ferry and cross the Delaware River.

CHAPTER 2

Valley Forge and Philadelphia

Evacuation

With his decision to take the bulk of his forces across New Jersey to New York, Henry Clinton conducted his evacuation of Philadelphia with an attention to detail that showed why he was one of the better commanders in the British army. Even though it would be almost impossible to hide the actual evacuation, he did everything he could to confuse the Americans about the details. He continued sending expeditions out into the countryside for forage and to acquire information. He ordered continued construction of new fortifications around the city, although a sharp eye would notice larger cannons were being replaced with light field pieces that would be easier to remove. Washington and his officers had to guess how big the evacuation would be. Would it be total, would the British really give up Philadelphia without a fight? Would they send out the army to destroy Washington before they left? Were they going to leave by ship or go overland across New Jersey? If they went overland, what route would they take?

The British soldiery was not happy with the talk of peace commissioners and an evacuation. Elias Boudinot, commissary of prisoners, was in Germantown arranging prisoner exchanges when he felt the anger of the soldiers: "The commissioners had like to have been mobbed by the british Light Infantry two nights ago—They hung Lord North in Effigy with the two acts of Parliament in his Hands. They cannot bear the thought of Peace."[1] Frustrated by the proximity and reputed weakness of the rebels, many of Clinton's officers wanted one last shot at Washington. Couldn't they move out and attack him at Valley Forge? Clinton understood their frustration. He also wanted to defeat Washington in battle and end the war but in the meantime, he tried to distract his officers and men with a schedule of hard work and training. Washington would have to wait, as Clinton had his orders.

The rebels outside Philadelphia were not the only confused Americans. The departure of Howe and Clinton's preparations combined as the basis of rumors that swirled throughout the close-knit Loyalist community in town. They could not help remembering the fate of the Loyalist population of Boston when it was evacuated after that siege ended in 1776. In 1778 the Loyalists who left Boston remained spread out in Halifax, New York, and England, unable to return home. Prospects for their return depended on a total British victory, which remained uncertain at this point. The Loyalists of Philadelphia, who had eagerly greeted the arrival of the king's troops the previous fall and supported their occupation of the city, now faced a fate like their Boston relations. A military evacuation of Philadelphia would be a terrible event for those who had counted on the continued rule of the king's law. During the British occupation of the city, they had conducted themselves in such a way that the return of the Continental Congress and the Pennsylvania legislature boded no good for them.

Joseph Galloway, an often sickly, refined, Loyalist Philadelphia politician and former member of the First Continental Congress, was typical of many. Galloway was a leading lawyer in Philadelphia when the war broke out. A member of the American Philosophical Society, he was also a friend of Benjamin Franklin. He was a delegate to the First Continental Congress in 1774 but alienated many of the more radical members with his conservative views. He wrote his own plan for reconciliation with the mother country that was rejected by the other members of the Congress. He did not serve in the Second Continental Congress, leaving Philadelphia to live on his country estate in fear of radical mobs. He joined the British forces in New York late in 1775, thinking they were going to liberate Philadelphia immediately, and also was part of a plan to capture Congress.[2] When Howe took the city in 1777, he returned to become the leader of the civil government there during the British occupation.

On May 22 Brigadier General Sir William Erskine informed Galloway about the evacuation. Galloway then met with Clinton on May 25, asking him to keep the army in Philadelphia. When Clinton said he would comply with his orders and evacuate, Galloway conducted a campaign attempting to get Clinton to change his mind, ignore the orders, and remain. In an effort to get the orders changed, he wrote letters to members of Parliament and other influential men in England, including Lord Dartmouth, the former secretary of state for America.[3] It was all for naught, and in the end Galloway had to come to terms with the evacuation. Troops were being sent to the Caribbean and other places, forcing the consolidation of His Majesty's forces in North America. Loyalists were soon in a panic; they were told to try and make peace

JOSEPH GALLOWAY.
Member of the Congress of 1774

Joseph Galloway was an ardent Loyalist and former friend of Benjamin Franklin. He was shocked and dismayed when the British decided to abandon Philadelphia. The Miriam and Ira D. Wallach Division of Art, Prints and Photographs: Print Collection, The New York Public Library. "Joseph Galloway, member of the Congress of 1774," New York Public Library Digital Collections

with the rebel Congress if the British had to evacuate. Unwilling to rely on the mercy of those same rebels they had previously humiliated or abused, many Loyalists flocked to the British military leaders to try to find a place on one of the dozens of transport vessels anchored along the river. Galloway assisted them, organizing them into groups of those Loyalists who wished to leave by water with Lord Richard Howe's transports, and those who wished to travel overland with Clinton.

The Delaware

While Washington sifted through his intelligence reports and sent out patrols, Clinton's operation to secure the Delaware River crossings was conducted with the professionalism that would be expected from the experienced and skilled officers of the British army. In the middle of May, the 55th and 63rd Regiments established redoubts near Cooper's Ferry to protect the rest of the army's crossing. Slowly, a few regiments at a time, the first elements of the army moved to the river, protected by light infantry under the command of Brigadier General Alexander Leslie. A British warship, HMS *Vigilant*, took position just north of the crossing to protect the vulnerable troops from American surprise. Wagons loaded with the army's baggage, and the possessions of hundreds of Tories, crossed the river on June 8. There was not enough room on the ships for the Loyalists, now refugees, and their belongings. The bulk of the luggage would go overland.

The last preparations for sailing took place during the second week in June. Seasick Loyalists who had come aboard the week before watched as munitions and supplies were loaded. The two Anspach Regiments of German Mercenaries, who had only arrived in Philadelphia that spring, boarded ships on June 9.[4] The soldiers too sick or infirm to walk across New Jersey were loaded on board on June 11. A massive show of canvas sail indicated the fleet of transports leaving Philadelphia on June 17, followed by the ominous warships of Admiral "Black Dick" Howe, the brother of Sir William Howe. They carried about three thousand Philadelphia Tories, any extra members of the soldiers' families (Clinton's orders allowed only two women per company to march with the army overland), and the two regiments of German troops. Among the evacuees were the disgraced members of the Carlisle Commission.

Once the crossing area was secured, the British army began the long march to New York, accompanied by a wagon train that would eventually stretch out 12 miles due to the excess baggage and plunder the Tories brought out of Philadelphia. From June 15 to 18 the massive, clumsy column of soldiers, horses, guns, wagons, and other vehicles crossed the river for the overland journey to New York City across New Jersey. The 15th Regiment left its fortifications at Billingsport, New Jersey, and joined Clinton's main force on June 18. Last to leave Philadelphia were the elite of the army: the Ranger Corps, light infantry, the Jaegers, and the British and German grenadiers. These troops were the most versatile and would serve in various important assignments throughout the upcoming days as flank guards, the advance guard, and the rear guard.

Among the last troops leaving town were recently recruited regiments of Loyalists. Since the beginning of the war, the British Ministry had believed that there were large pools of loyal manpower just waiting to join the cause against the rebels. The belief among the bureaucrats in London, fostered by Loyalists like Galloway, was that if they were provided the safety of protection for their families, large numbers of these American Loyalists would flock to the king's banner. Regiments were formed and local Loyalists were recruited, but their numbers never lived up to the expectations of the British generals or their masters back in Britain.

As soon as the British began their march, local militia began harassing them. Although few of the Imperial force were killed or wounded in the haphazard attacks, these skirmishes reminded the redcoats that the soft days of garrison duty in Philadelphia were over. The climate also took its toll on the troops as the extreme heat and humidity of the New Jersey summer led to the soldiers being easily fatigued. Troops who had been relatively inactive for the last seven months were not used to rough marching and suffered accordingly. It was an ominous warning of what a march through New Jersey would entail, as noted by Jaeger Captain Johann Ewald:

> The 18th. The army set out one hour before daylight. The jagers formed the advanced guard, followed by the Hessian grenadiers, the provision wagons containing supplies for the entire retreat, and then the army. The light infantry, rangers, and provincials brought up the rear. As soon as day broke the militia received us with sharp rifle fire, and a part of the light troops of Washington's army hung on our rear guard. The skirmishing continued without letup. Many men fell and lost their lives miserably because of the intense heat, and due to the sandy ground which we crossed through a pathless brushwood where no water was to be found on the entire march.[5]

After the entire army crossed the river, Clinton could choose one of several paths to New York City. He might cross the Raritan River to Paulus Hook and cross directly into New York City. He could take the army northeasterly to Perth Amboy and cross to Staten Island and on to New York City. He could move more directly east and farther to Sandy Hook and cross over to New York from the little peninsula there, protected by the rugged heights at Navesink. He didn't make the choice right away but instead set out across central New Jersey. Secretly, he harbored hopes that the Continental Army might give him a fight that he could then decisively win, thus turning circumstances back in his favor and gaining him the martial glory he sought.

> And I was, moreover, not altogether without hopes that Mr. Washington might be tempted by his superior numbers and many other advantages to measure his strength with me in the field... For, though I was prepared to expect from such a multitude every obstruction

which their numbers and knowledge of the country might enable them to give me in so long a march, yet I had so full a confidence in the spirit and discipline of the troops I led that I had little doubt respecting the issue of a general and decisive action with them. I had, therefore, only to guard against the enemy's catching the little triumph of some partial blow, which the unavoidable length of my line of carriages and the several strong defiles I had to pass through might possibly expose me to.[6]

Just as Washington was in the dark as to where the British would march, Clinton was unsure of the rebels' reaction.

Charles Lee

By June 8, Washington was sure that the British were going to evacuate soon and Clinton would take the main army overland to New York. Baggage wagons moving to the Delaware and large bodies of troops moving to board ships and to the Delaware crossings confirmed his suspicions. Still, there were many questions about what the British planned. Turning his mind to a matter closer at hand, Washington sent Martha back to Mt. Vernon on the 9th.

One of the many things that Washington found needing his attention was the return of his second in command, Charles Lee. With his long legs on a thin body, he was a gangly figure that often brought smirks for his physical presence. But Lee probably had more time as a soldier and more varied experiences than any other general in the Continental service.

Lee started as an ensign in the British army at the age of 15, studied in Switzerland, and served as a lieutenant in Edward Braddock's ill-fated expedition on the Ohio in 1755. He served in the Louisburg, Fort Ticonderoga, and Montreal campaigns, and particularly distinguished himself in Portugal fighting against the Spanish. His record as a soldier of fortune was equally impressive, serving as a major general in Poland's army, observing the war between Turkey and Russia, and meeting such luminaries as Frederick the Great and Catherine the Great. He had friends in Parliament and the army.

A vocal Whig, Lee arrived in America as the crisis between colonies and mother country slowly moved toward violent revolution. He was attended by his Italian servant, Giuseppe Minghini, and a pack of dogs led by his Pomeranian, Mr. Spada, often remarking how he enjoyed the company of those dogs more than people. He toured from Boston to Williamsburg and earned a bit of notoriety. People were impressed by his experiences; he was erudite, educated, and an entertaining, if somewhat sarcastic and crude, guest at many homes, including that of George Washington. With a great ego, he was respected by many, able to awe those of limited international and military experience, such as John and Sam Adams. When he first arrived at Cambridge in 1775, the noted historian Mercy Otis Warren wrote of him: "No man was better qualified at this early stage of the war, to penetrate the designs, or to face in the field an experienced British veteran, than general Lee. He had been an officer of character and rank in the late war between England and France. Fearless of danger, and fond of glory, he was calculated for the field, without any of the graces that recommend the soldier to the circles of the polite. He was plain in his person even to ugliness, and careless in his manners to a degree of rudeness. He possessed a bold genius and an unconquerable spirit: his voice was rough, his garb ordinary, his deportment morose."[7] John Adams wrote: "You observe in your Letter the Oddity of a great Man—He is a queer Creature—But you must love his Dogs if you love him and forgive a Thousand Whims for the Sake of the Soldier and the Scholar."[8]

Charles Lee was an enigmatic but experienced officer who was second in command of the Continental Army in June of 1778. His controversial actions continue to fuel debates among historians. *The Miriam and Ira D. Wallach Division of Art, Prints and Photographs: Print Collection, The New York Public Library. "General Charles Lee"*

Lee impressed Congress enough to appoint him third in line to command after Washington and Massachusetts' prickly Artemas Ward. He became the second in command upon Ward's resignation in April of 1776 and served in that role when the army moved to New York in May after the British evacuation of Boston. Congress ordered him to go to Canada to save the critical situation that had developed after the American invasion the previous fall failed. Before he could take command there, however, the British mounted a threat to the Southern colonies that seemed to require his presence there more than Canada. He was ordered to take over command of the Southern Department as it appeared the enemy was moving south toward Charleston.

Lee traveled south, spending much of the time observing militia companies, defenses, and the logistical preparations of the Southern states. The people of Charleston were very happy to see him as they lacked any local commander of his reputation. He gave advice, helped set up batteries, and directed fortification work, but most of the preparations to repel the impending attack had been completed by the time he arrived. His important contribution to the defense was boosting morale. Colonel William Moultrie of the Second South Carolina Regiment said: "General Lee appeared from the northward, and took command of the troops; his presence gave us great spirits, as he was known to be an able, brave, and experienced officer, though hasty and rough in his manners, which the officers could not reconcile themselves to at first: it was thought by many that his coming among us was equal to a reinforcement of 1000 men, and I believe it was, because he taught us to think lightly of the enemy, and gave a spur to all our actions."[9]

During the actual battle for Charleston on June 28, 1776, Lee did little to direct the defensive battle that resulted in a defeat for the His Majesty's forces under the command of Admiral Peter Parker and Sir Henry Clinton. Lee spent less than 15 minutes on Sullivan's Island, the center of the battle, directing a few guns and watching the cannonade. Finally, he told the local commander: "Colonel, I see you are doing well here, you have no occasion for me, I will go to town again."[10] With the defeat of the British fleet, Lee was given much of the credit for the victory.

After a brief flirtation with the idea of Lee leading an expedition into Florida, Congress decided that Lee was no longer needed in the South and he was recalled to join the Continental Army in New York City, where Clinton had sailed with the defeated Charleston force to join forces with Sir William Howe and the main British army. Lee stopped off in Philadelphia to lobby Congress to protect him financially, should some economic misfortune befall him.

In his role as second in command in the disastrous New York campaign, Lee had relatively little direct impact on the events that ended in Washington's crushing defeat and retreat across New Jersey into Pennsylvania. He frequently criticized the decisions of the commander in chief, particularly after the loss of Fort Washington with over two thousand men and significant amounts of equipment. Separated from Washington with a third of the army during the commander in chief's ignominious retrograde from New York, Lee broadly interpreted his discretionary orders and dallied about northern New Jersey without threatening the British or reinforcing the main body, despite Washington's increasingly serious entreaties to join him. He felt he could do better than anyone else, if given total control, writing to a congressman, "such a total want of sense pervades all your counsels that Heaven alone can save you. Inclosed are some hints. I could say many things—let me talk vainly—had I the powers I could do you much good—might I but dictate one week—but I am sure you will never give any man the necessary power—did none of the Congress ever read the Roman History?"[11]

In addition, Lee wrote several letters to others critical of the commander in chief's ability. There was nothing unusual about officers complaining about their superiors, but in at least one case, Washington read one of these letters. His aide, Joseph Reed, had written critically of Washington: "General Washington's own Judgment seconded by Representations by us would, I believe, have saved the Men & their Arms, but, unluckily, General Green's Judgt was contrary this kept the General's Mind in a State of Suspense till the Stroke was struck. Oh! General—an indecisive Mind is one of the greatest misfortunes that can befall an army. How often have I lamented it this Campaign."[12]

He inadvertently opened a return letter from Lee to Reed: "I received your most obliging, flattering letter—lament with you that fatal indecision of mind which in war is a much greater disqualification than a stupidity or even want of personal courage—accident may put a decisive blunderer in the right—but eternal defeat and miscarriage must attend the man of the best parts if cursed with indecision."[13] Washington no doubt understood that there was criticism of his leadership, but the knowledge that his second in command and his aide were involved in such talk must have struck the commander in chief hard. He let Reed know of his knowledge in a letter to his aide a few days later. The note did not betray the general's feelings concerning his aide's indiscretion.[14]

When Lee finally responded to Washington's directive to join the main army, disaster struck. Lee ordered his men into camp near Basking Ridge and moved himself with a small retinue just outside of camp. On December 13, 1776, British Dragoons swooped down and captured him. Luckily, his detachment marched without him to join Washington in time for the important battles of Trenton and Princeton. Lee would spend over a year as the guest of the British in New York City, hated by many British officers who wanted to execute the former British officer as a traitor.

Sir William Howe, as British commander in the colonies, initially was one who wished to try Lee for treason, but ultimately had to be satisfied that Lee had technically resigned his commission in the British forces before the start of hostilities. Lee hardly suffered during his internment. He socialized and interacted with many British officers, some of whom had served with him previously. With so much time on his hands, he sent Congress a letter encouraging them to open negotiations with the British. Circumstances changed when American forces captured British Major General Richard Prescott for the second time on July 10, 1777. It was arranged that Prescott would be exchanged for Lee.

Lee was gracefully greeted at Valley Forge on April 23, 1778, by Washington and his staff, with bands playing and all the pomp the American army could muster. Lee was escorted to the Potts House for a great welcoming meal. After the meal, he was invited to stay with the commander in chief and his "family" in the Potts House. He quickly made an impression, especially on Mrs. Washington and the other wives, by spending much of his time fornicating with a British soldier's wife in a room at the rear of the house. Upon the liberated general's arrival at Valley Forge, Dr. James Thacher gave a description of him: "General Lee was rather above the middle size, plain in his person even to ugliness, and careless in his manners even to a degree of rudeness; his nose was so remarkably aquiline, that it appeared as a real deformity. His voice was rough, his garb ordinary, his deportment morose. He was ambitious of fame without dignity to support it."[15] As quickly as he arrived, two days later he went to York, Pennsylvania, where Congress was sitting, to give a report on how to win the war and lobby for a promotion to lieutenant general.

During his brief visit at Valley Forge, Lee formed a negative opinion of the army. He told the commissary of prisoners, Elias Boudinot, "That he found the Army in a worse situation than he expected, and that General Washington was not fit to command a Sergeant's Guard."[16] Lee, again the army's second in command, felt that much of the problem lay with Congress as well as Washington: "Inter nos [Latin: Between ourselves] the Congress seem to stumble every step—I do not mean one or two of the Cattle, but the whole Stable—I have been very free in delivering my opinion to 'em—in my opinion General Washington is much to blame in not menacing 'em with resignation unless they refrain from unhinging the army by their absurd interference."[17] Due to his parole, he could not officially rejoin the army until May 20, missing out on an opportunity to reacquaint himself with the newly trained army and its officers.

Upon his return to Valley Forge, he alienated many of his new comrades. Congress demanded that all officers take an oath of allegiance to the United States and denounce any former loyalties. Lee was asked to do so upon return to the army. When presented with the Bible for the oath, he quickly removed his hand and flippantly stated, "As to King George, I am ready enough to absolve myself from all allegiance to him; but I have scruples about the Prince of Wales."[18] His vigor in the pursuit of liberty and the American cause had never been in question but now only a nervous round of laughter met his comment. He eventually agreed to take the oath.

While in captivity, Lee missed many important events that had changed the army that he returned to in the spring of 1778. While he was a prisoner, Washington and the army had fought in the major actions at Brandywine and Germantown, skirmished in places like Cooch's Bridge and Barren Hill, and suffered together through the winter at Valley Forge. Lee did not observe the ceremonies celebrating the treaty with France on May 6 that demonstrated the army's new skills. He had not participated in or truly observed the training sessions of Baron von Steuben. Many of the senior officers were new to him. The officers who had been easily awed or swayed by his grandiose strutting and opinions earlier in the war were now changed, having their own experiences and mature opinions based on battles fought while Lee was in captivity. Many of the men he knew were simply gone; some had been killed or wounded, and over one hundred officers resigned during the stay at Valley Forge. Unlike Washington, who spent much of each day riding around the camp, conversing with officers and enlisted men as well as observing camp conditions and training, Lee did little to familiarize himself with the army.

Washington had spent the difficult winter in camp with his men, getting to know them and his subordinates intimately. But Lee missed out on the bonding experience. He was now a stranger to many, lacking the feelings of comradeship shared by those who had fought and suffered over the last 15 months. Unlike the inexperienced officers he had encountered during the early years of the war, the veteran officers were no longer easily influenced and failed to share his high opinion of his own abilities. He was an outsider but still considered himself essential to the Continental Army: "I am well and hope always shall be well with General Washington—and to speak again vainly I am persuaded (considering how he is surrounded) that he cannot do without me."[19]

Lee sent Washington an interesting letter on June 15, outlining his ideas about the upcoming campaign and giving Washington advice about the army in general. Despite intelligence from Philemon Dickinson and other sources indicating at least a partial British move across New Jersey, Lee was convinced that the British had other plans in Pennsylvania. Although he did not know many of the young officers well, Lee also complained that many of them were not familiar with their divisional structure or commanders. Now, just as the army was about to march, Lee wanted to institute a new structure to alleviate such a problem. Some of his ideas had been previously discussed with Congress and any others that would listen during the second in command's recent visit to Philadelphia. After reading the note, Washington courteously replied, thanking Lee but also subtly making note of Lee's previous free giving of advice. "I shall be always happy in free communication of your Sentiments upon any important subject relative to the Service, I only beg that they may come directly to myself—the custom which many Officers have of speaking freely of things & reprobating measures which upon investigation may be found to be unavoidable is never productive of good, & often of very mischievous consequences."[20]

Council of War

After obtaining Lee's unsolicited advice, Washington decided to get a more formal opinion, calling a council of war on June 17 to determine the general officers' ideas as to what course of action the Continental Army should take when the British left Philadelphia. There was no doubt now that the last of Clinton's army was leaving the city soon. Reports from Dickinson, Maxwell, and other detachments gave Washington a pretty good idea of Clinton's intentions to leave by both ship and land. The marching of soldiers to embarkation points, the loading of ships, and the fortifying of the Delaware crossing confirmed some type of British overland march and its general direction. Troops loading on ships in the Delaware indicated a partial move by sea. These factors gave Washington reason to pause. He gave the officers five questions and asked for their opinions in writing:

> Whether any enterprise ought to be undertaken against the enemy in Philadelphia, in their present circumstances?
>
> Whether this army should remain in the position it now holds, 'till the final evacuation of the city or immediately move towards the Delaware?
>
> Whether any detachment of it shall be sent to reinforce the Brigade in the Jerseys, or advanced towards the enemy to act as occasion shall require and endeavor to take advantage of their retreat?

If the army remains on this present ground till the enemy quit the city, and if they march, through the Jerseys towards Amboy, will it be practicable, from the obstructions they may probably receive, from the troops already there, in conjunction with the Militia, to arrive, in time, with this army, to give them any material interruption? Will it be prudent to attempt it, or not rather more eligible to proceed to North River, in the most direct and convenient manner, or secure the important communication between the Eastern and Southern states?

In case such measures should be adopted, as will enable this army to overtake the enemy on their march, will it be prudent, with the aid, which may reasonably be expected from the Jersey Militia, to make an attack on them, and ought it to be a partial or a general one?[21]

The officers left the meeting to ponder and then write down their opinions, not knowing that Clinton had nearly completed his evacuation. Still, their answers would provide Washington a gauge of his generals' opinions on the ensuing campaign. There were six major generals and nine brigadier generals at the meeting, including Charles Lee. Each of them brought different experiences and abilities. These were the men who would lead the army in the next campaign and the council gave them a chance to be part of the decision-making process. After three years of war, Washington knew each of them with varying degrees of familiarity.

Nathanael Greene, as previously noted, held the post of quartermaster general, having served with distinction alongside the commander in chief throughout the war's initial campaigns. Dr. Benjamin Rush described Greene: "Genius supplied him the place of a learned education. He was active and intelligent, but thought more than he felt, and hence he was said to be more qualified for the cabinet than the field. His temper was gentle, and his manners engaging. He was beloved and respected by all that knew him."[22]

Major General William Alexander, Lord Stirling, fought in every major engagement with Washington's army before Valley Forge. A wealthy New Jersey landowner who served during the French and Indian War, Stirling went to Scotland to claim his family title in 1759. Although he was able to convince Scottish officials of the claim, the House of Lords of Britain refused to accept the opinion of the Scots. Nevertheless, he called himself the Right Honorable William, Lord Stirling, for the rest of his life. A brave officer in the field, he was prone to drink and often in poor health due to that fondness. Dr. Albigence Waldo wrote of him: "Major General Lord Stirling, is a man of a very noble presence,—and the most Martial Appearance of any General in the Service—he much resembles the Marquis of Granby—by his bald head—& the make of his face—and figure of his Body—He is mild in his private Conversation, and vociferous in the Field."[23] He was a division commander at the time of the council of war.

Major General Benedict Arnold attended the conference essentially as a general without a command. A former businessman and trader, Arnold was a fighting general who had a string of battlefield exploits matched by few others. Starting at Fort Ticonderoga, he fought many engagements on Lake Champlain, at Quebec, at Valcour Island, during the British raid on Danbury, Connecticut, and in the Saratoga campaign. Wounded in Canada and at Saratoga, he walked with a painful limp and was without a command due to the injury. His fierce disposition alienated many people. He had many admirers, including Washington, but equally had his many detractors. The commander in chief eagerly waited for his return to action, writing Arnold in January:

> May I venture to ask whether you are upon your Legs again—and if you are not, may I flatter myself that you will be soon? There is none who wishes more sincerely for this event than I do, or who will receive the information with more pleasure. I shall expect a favourable account upon the subject. And as soon as your situation will permit, I request that you will repair to this Army, It being my earnest wish to have your services the ensuing Campaign. In hopes of this, I have set you down in an Arrangement now under consideration, and for a Command which, I trust will be agreeable to yourself & of great advantage to the public.[24]

Major General Marie Joseph Paul Yves Roch Gilbert du Motier, Marquis de Lafayette, attended the council as a division commander. He led the ill-fated expedition to Barren Hill a few weeks before. Only 20 years old at the time, the red-haired young Frenchman was eager for martial glory. Born into a wealthy, aristocratic, military family, he was a child when his father died fighting the British, and Henry Clinton, at the battle of Minden in 1759. Lafayette enlisted in the army at age 13, served in no field command but did go through several of the French army's summer maneuvers and had a long experience of peacetime army life before coming to America. The youthful nobleman became enraptured with the American cause for idealistic reasons as well as a thirst for glory that could not be satisfied in France. He purchased a ship to come to America and disobeyed the French king's orders not to leave. Congress, having dealt with so many foreign officers seeking employment and rank, at first rudely dismissed him. Congressman James Lovell met him outside the Pennsylvania State House where Congress was meeting and snarled at him: "It seems that French officers have a great fancy to enter our service without being invited. It is true we were in need of officers last year, but now we have experienced men and plenty of them."[25] Appealing to Congress through fellow Mason President John Hancock, and offering to serve as a volunteer officer at his own expense, altered opinions. A captain of dragoons in France, he joined Washington in the fall of 1777 as a major general without command. Meeting

Lafayette during a visit to Philadelphia on August 5, 1777, Washington took a liking to the zealous young aristocrat immediately.

As an aide to Washington, Lafayette learned the ways of fighting in America and to speak English. Despite being a staff officer, he was wounded at Brandywine when he went to help rally the right wing at that great battle. After Brandywine, Washington lobbied Congress for a field command for Lafayette:

> I would take the liberty to mention, that I feel myself in a delicate situation with respect to the Marquis Le Fayette. He is extremely solicitous of having a Command equal to his rank, & professes very different Ideas as to the purposes of his appointment from those Congress have mentioned to me. He certainly did not understand them. I do not know in what light they will view the matter, but it appears to me, from a consideration of his illustrious and important connections—the attachment which he has manifested to our cause, and the consequences, which his return in disgust might produce, that it will be adviseable to gratify him in his wishes—and the more so, as several Gentlemen from France, who came over under some assurances, have gone back disappointed in their expectations. His conduct with respect to them stands in a favorable point of view, having interested himself to remove their uneasiness and urged the impropriety of their making any unfavorable representations upon their arrival at home, and in all his letters has placed our affairs in the best situation he could. Besides, he is sensible—discreet in his manners—has made great proficiency in our Language, and from the disposition he discovered at the Battle of Brandy Wine, possesses a large share of bravery and Military ardor.[26]

He performed well during a raid in Gloucester County, New Jersey, in November of 1777 but narrowly escaped disaster during the Barren Hill reconnaissance. He earned the friendship of many officers through his eagerness for the American cause. Dr. James Thacher described his pleasing personality: "His manners being easy, affable and engaging, he was particularly endeared to the officers and soldiers under his command; they admired, loved, and revered him as their guide and support when in peril, and their warmest friend when in perplexity and trouble… His very soul burned with the spirit of enterprize, and he manifested a disinterestedness and devotion to the cause of freedom, ever to be admired and applauded by a grateful people."[27]

The last major general at the council was the Baron von Steuben. He was eager for the upcoming campaign as it would put his training to the test. His position with the army was still inspector general in charge of training. He was one of three major generals, Lafayette and Arnold the others, who had not served in action with Charles Lee. He would serve as an additional officer on Washington's staff when the army left Valley Forge.

A staff officer at the council of war was Brigadier General Henry Knox, the chief of artillery. Missing two fingers on his left hand due to a gunshot

Henry Knox was a self-taught artilleryman who did yeoman service throughout the Revolution. The American artillery was especially well served at Monmouth. *Gilbert Stuart George Washington Bicentennial Commission. National Archives NAID: 532858 Local ID: 148-GW-800 Photographs and other Graphic Materials Covers: 1931–1932*

accident, Knox was a large man who had started the war as a bookseller in Boston. He had a pleasing personality that earned him the friendship of everyone he met, a French officer describing him as "a man of understanding, a well-formed man, gay, sincere, and honest; it is impossible to know, without esteeming him, or to see without loving him."[28] Prior to the war he had served in a militia company of artillery. During the siege of Boston, he served as both an engineer and an artilleryman. In December of 1775 he went to Fort Ticonderoga to bring back urgently needed cannon. The 300-mile journey added 58 guns to the army's stockpile and earned Knox fame in the army. He commanded the artillery effectively at Trenton, Assunpink Creek, and Princeton. He established an artillery school at Springfield, Massachusetts, in 1777. His artillery performed admirably at the defeats at Brandywine and Germantown. George Washington, who became a friend, described him to

Congress as an officer, "who has deservedly acquired the character of One of the most valuable Officers in the service, and who, combating almost innumerable difficulties in the department he fills, has placed the Artillery upon a footing, that does him the greatest Honor."[29]

Brigadier General William Smallwood also attended the council. He commanded the First Maryland Brigade composed of four Maryland and one Delaware regiments. Stocky, with a florid complexion, he was described by a young woman who met him during the winter of 1777–78: "The General is tall, portly, well-made; a truly martial air, the manner of a gentleman, a good understanding and a great humanity of disposition constitute the character of Smallwood... We had the pleasure of the General and suite at an afternoon tea. He (the General, I mean) is most agreeable; so lively, so free, and chats so gaily that I have quite an esteem for him. I must steel my heart! ... I declare this General is very, very, entertaining, so good natured, so good humor'd and yet sensible I wonder he is not married."[30] A well-educated plantation aristocrat, Smallwood had served in the militia during the French and Indian War. At the start of the war, his regiment proved to be well trained and had earned an excellent combat reputation. He was wounded at the battle of White Plains.

Another of the brigadier generals was John Paterson, sometimes spelled Patterson. Big, strong, full of energy, Paterson was a lawyer from Massachusetts when the war began. He organized his own regiment, one of the first units in the lines outside Boston after Lexington and Concord. His brigade commander praised him in a letter to John Adams: "A Good Officer of a liberal Education, ingenius and Sensible."[31] An active, aggressive leader, he and his men repelled an attack on Lechmere Point on November 9, 1775. After taking his regiment to Canada and suffering through the disastrous campaign, he rejoined the main army in time to fight at Trenton and Princeton. Returning to the Northern army, he fought during the victorious Saratoga campaign. Afterwards his brigade of four Massachusetts regiments returned to the main army and spent the winter at Valley Forge.

Brigadier General Enoch Poor commanded a brigade made of New Hampshire and New York regiments. A member of the New Hampshire provincial council when the war began, he served with his 2nd New Hampshire Regiment in the siege lines outside Boston. Sent to assist the faltering Canadian Expedition, he fought in many of the actions during the retreat from Quebec and his regiment was decimated at the battle of Trois Rivieres on June 8, 1776. When he returned to the main army in September of 1776, Horatio Gates lauded Poor's contributions in the North: "Col. Enoch Poor of New Hampshire and Col. John Paterson of Massachusetts are also deserving officers, worthy the notice of Congress."[32] He fought at both Trenton and Princeton before being sent with a brigade to the Northern Department in July of 1777. He fought at Freeman's Farm and Bemis Heights during the Saratoga campaign. After his men returned to the main army, they were part of Lafayette's near disaster at Barren Hill.

Commanding the 1st Pennsylvania Brigade was Anthony Wayne. He was also acting commander of Benjamin Lincoln's Division in the latter's absence. A surveyor from Pennsylvania, Wayne was well educated and wealthy. He served in the colonial legislature and local committee of safety before hostilities began in 1775. His first action was at the battle of Trois Rivieres on June 8, 1776. During the retreat from Canada, he frequently commanded the entire army or other substantial commands as others died, were wounded, or resigned. Soldiers found him a strict disciplinarian with a colorful vocabulary. Officers found him arrogant but brave. He also fiercely guarded his reputation, writing to Horatio Gates during a squabble over seniority: "I shall with the utmost composure retire to my Sabine field, where love, where peace, and all that a man can wish fondly, wants my return. I never will submit to be commanded by the men who I commanded yesterday. I may be wrong, but I have Custom and prejudice in my favor, and a pride common to a soldier, that will not be easily eradicated."[33] Despite threatening to resign over lack of promotion and respect, he returned to the main army and led a brigade at the battle of Brandywine on September 11, 1777. A few days later his detachment was tasked with maintaining observation of the British army but was surprised and routed in the night action called the Paoli Massacre. He was criticized for the battle and only regained some of his fighting reputation with his part in the battle of Germantown on October 4, 1777.

Commanding a Virginia brigade was William Woodford. A wealthy Virginian, Woodford had served with Washington during the French and Indian War. Attractive, with a crooked smile, he was commander of the 2nd Virginia Regiment when the war began. Despite frustration over seniority in the Virginia line, he set to work intensely training his men. He led a group of men that drove off a British attack on Hampton, Virginia, on October 25, 1775, and played a crucial role in the defeat of the British at Great Bridge on December 9, 1775. The commander of the colonial forces in that engagement, Robert Howe, wrote: "Of my friend, Colonel Woodford, it is almost needless to speak, but I cannot avoid expressing that I received from him every assistance which conduct and spirit could give me."[34] While serving with the army in New York, Woodford resigned his commission when he felt slighted about seniority. He returned to the army and was wounded lightly at Brandywine. He led his brigade in the battle of Germantown a few weeks later.

One of the generals at the council had an unusual background for a fighting man. John Peter Gabriel Muhlenburg was the son of an immigrant German Lutheran minister. As a youth, Muhlenburg was sent to Germany to study and learn business. After a short time learning the merchant trade, he ran off to join a British regiment that was assigned to America. Upon release from service, he returned to Pennsylvania and became a Lutheran minister. Moving to Virginia, he was also ordained as a minister by the Church of England as all ministers in that colony were required to be ordained by the Anglican Church. Representing his district in the Shenandoah Valley, he served as a member of the House of Burgesses. A member of his local committee of safety and the provincial Congress, he trained local militia until appointed as commander of the 8th Virginia Regiment. His regiment was part of the defenses of Charleston in the British attack on June 28, 1776. Charles Lee complimented Muhlenburg and his men: "Muhlenberg's regiment was not only the most complete of the province, but I believe of the whole continent. It was not only the most complete in numbers, but the best armed, clothed and equipped for immediate service."[35] He fought at Brandywine and Germantown. A cultured, erudite man, he was described by a fellow officer as "tall, strikingly handsome, and courtly."[36]

Connecticut's Jedediah Huntington commanded four regiments from his home state at the time of the council. Diminutive in size, he was well educated and a leader in Whig politics. A militia officer at the beginning of the war, he marched his men to Cambridge to take part in the siege of Boston. During the battle of Long Island, he was sick and took no part in his regiment's actions. His brigade missed the battles of Brandywine and Germantown, and then settled in with the main army at Valley Forge. His brigade went from 1290 men in December to 440 in March due to sickness and desertions. He exhibited his care for his men when he wrote: "…fighting will be far preferable to starving: my Brigade are out of Provisions… I am exceedingly unhappy in being the Bearer of Complaints to Headquarters. I have used every Argument my Imagination could invent to make Soldiers easy, but I despair of being able to do it much longer."[37] He had the least combat experience of any general at the meeting.

Louis Lebegue Duportail, the commander of the army's engineers, was also at the council. From a wealthy and titled French family he attended the school for engineers at Mezieres in 1762. After a career in the French army, he was one of the first four officers recruited by Benjamin Franklin to aid the fledgling United States. A handsome man with a thoughtful-looking face, he was appointed the senior engineer for the Continental Army on July 8, 1777. He helped organize and construct fortifications around Philadelphia and Valley Forge. Respected by Washington, he provided the army with skills and experience not found in the 13 states. Washington told the president of Congress: "It is but justice to General Du Portail to observe, that I have a high opinion of his merit and abilities; and esteem him not only well acquainted with the particular branch he professes, but a man of sound judgment and real knowledge in military science in general."[38]

Washington knew them all personally. All were veterans of battles from Charleston to Canada. Their wealth of experiences ensured that Washington received the different perspectives he needed to make plans for the upcoming campaign. Calling the council also fulfilled the Congressional mandate to meet with his officers when major decisions were to be made.

Each of the generals responded with a written reply to Washington's questions. Several were in favor of harassing the British on their march. Another group, led most forcefully by Lee, felt that no action should be attempted, and the British should be allowed to march unmolested to New York. The feelings of the majority were expressed in Huntington's written answer: "If a great Degree of Caution has marked the Tenor of your Excellencys Conduct hitherto, & you have won by Delay—no Risque should be run at this Stage of the War, when the general Complexion of our Affairs at Home & abroad is more promising than ever—One hazardous Enterprise might ruin the fair prospect."[39]

The replies to Washington's questions uniformly urged caution but reached no consensus, so Washington publicly tabled the idea of an immediate attack. But personally, he felt some sort of offensive action against the British should be taken. Keeping his options open, Washington decided that the Continental Army would leave Valley Forge and shadow Clinton's army. The next day he issued the order to begin the march while instructing Colonel Henry Jackson to prepare his Massachusetts regiment to move into and occupy Philadelphia.

Having decided to wait and see what Clinton decided to do, there were many reasons for Washington to remain optimistic about the outcome of the new campaign. His army had gained experience from the battles the previous fall, it had survived an awful winter, and had been rigorously trained by the Baron von Steuben; the French were fully in the fight, the question of adequate supplies was being solved, and the British were in retreat. Despite his generals urging caution, the summer did indeed hold promise for the leader of the rebellious Americans and his army.

Philadelphia

On June 18, acting on information from a local man, Captain McLane's American scouts crept carefully into Philadelphia, fanning out through the deserted streets. A few local citizens drifted out to observe the wary soldiers. For the most part, the former rebel capital was clear of Crown forces. The scouts found a small party of British stragglers on Second Street and a slight skirmish occurred. No one was injured and 33 British soldiers were captured. Sifting through the remainder of the city, McLane could see that the British had indeed left. He sent one of his horsemen to Washington with the news.

The detachment withdrew to the north end of the town and waited to escort the new commander of Philadelphia, Benedict Arnold, into the city. Unable to take the field with Washington's army due to the battlefield injury sustained at Saratoga that hadn't yet healed, the man some believed to be the Continental Army's best field commander moved into Philadelphia to oversee its liberation. Soon after McLane declared the city secure, Arnold arrived in the city with Colonel Stephen Moylan's dragoons and Colonel Henry Jackson's Additional Regiment.

Even before Arnold arrived, civilians trickled, and then flooded, from the countryside into the dirty and looted town. Over six hundred buildings had suffered major damage during the British occupation. The streets of the liberated city were strewn with discarded items that the Loyalists or retreating British troops could not take with them. Some houses, like that of Benjamin Franklin, had many items stolen by those who had stayed there during the past winter. Many of the churches that had been centers of opposition to the king's policies had been turned into barracks or stables or severely damaged through vandalism and neglect. Just as the Carlisle Commission had dealt a blow to Henry Clinton's plans for glory, the dreadful British occupation had dealt a blow to the Crown's hopes for reconciliation. The poor conduct of the occupiers had done nothing to encourage the Americans to reconsider their opposition. On the contrary, it had only steeled their resolve to continue the fight.

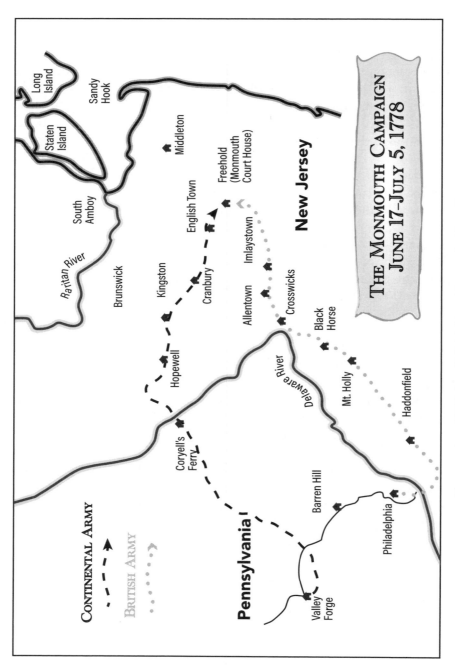

The campaign of 1778 from Philadelphia to Monmouth. *Megan Dacus*

CHAPTER 3

Across New Jersey

Into New Jersey

On the northern perimeter of the Valley Forge camp was Sullivan's Bridge, 12 feet wide with split logs laid across pilings driven into the Schuylkill River bottom, built by General John Sullivan's troops near Fatland Ford. On the sunny morning of June 19, George Washington and his staff clattered across the Schuylkill at Sullivan's Bridge, escorted by 50 mounted members of the commander in chief's personal guard. The well-mounted horsemen turned northeast and headed for Coryell's Ferry on the Delaware. For the commander in chief, the eagerly anticipated 1778 campaign was at long last underway.

Washington and his party were not the only ones that left the sprawling camp that day. Two divisions also moved out of Valley Forge, those of Charles Lee and Anthony Wayne. Marching at a modest pace, the divisions arrived at Coryell's Ferry the next day and secured the crossing site for the remainder of the army. A second crossing site at Howell's Ferry was also secured.

The remaining divisions of the army, those of the Marquis de Lafayette and Lord Stirling, followed by the train of supplies and camp followers, crossed over the Delaware during the next two days. Unlike the dashing and well-dressed British that had set out across New Jersey a few days previously, the Continental troops were poorly dressed in comparison, with few of the soldiers completely clothed in proper regimental uniforms. Most had not received uniforms or material for making uniforms since the previous fall. But they marched with a new step, displaying a professionalism born of experience and the training of Baron von Steuben. The Continentals marched with a purpose and the determination of men who had been turned into proficient soldiers. They showed the eagerness of men involved in a pursuit: they were chasing the British, a new situation welcomed by the Continental Army. Above all, they were relatively well-fed, adequately equipped, and healthy.

Many women, some with children, straggled along with the army. Washington had made allowances for these women; a number were allowed to follow each regiment and receive a half ration in return for such work as nursing, laundry, or sewing. The women walked; they were not allowed to ride in the army's few wagons. Typical among these women was Mary Hays, wife of barber William Hays, a member of a Pennsylvania company of artillery commanded by Captain Francis Proctor. She would follow her husband, as many of the women did, right into the upcoming battle and perform the duties of an artilleryman.

The Continental Army took two days to complete its crossing of the Delaware. Once across the river, Washington determined to stay northwest of the British until their destination was clear, north toward Amboy or east to Sandy Hook. If the Crown forces attempted to turn on him, Washington could easily move into northern New Jersey where the terrain was more rugged and he could put himself in a good defensive position. No matter which route Clinton chose, the terrain and conditions on the march would be the same for both armies: over relatively flat terrain, through good farm country. The weather would be equally tough on the soldiers of both armies with hot, humid days, interrupted in the afternoons by thunderstorms that turned the dusty, loamy soil into mush. Paradoxically, to the continued discomfort of the marching soldiers, the roads quickly dried out and sent forth dusty cloud the following morning. It was a typical summer in New Jersey, great for growing crops. But for many troops who had been relatively inactive in Philadelphia or Valley Forge for several months, the march was a rude introduction into the harsh realities of campaigning.

Across New Jersey

Clinton's slow-moving army reached Haddonfield, New Jersey, on June 19. He waited for his garrison from Billingsport to join him and then set out across the country toward the coast.

Clinton set his order of march as they marched from Haddonfield toward New York City. He divided his army into a pair of divisions under two capable commanders, Lieutenant General Charles, Lord Cornwallis, and Lieutenant General Wilhelm von Knyphausen. Clinton was influenced in his choice of marching order by the presence of the New Jersey militia and Continentals of Maxwell in front of the British, between them and their goal of New York. Clinton placed Cornwallis up front with the bulk of his best infantry: the Grenadiers, Guards, Hessian Grenadiers, 3rd, 4th, 5th Brigades of British infantry, and the Queen's Rangers. The logistics train and bulk of the artillery followed as part of Knyphausen's division. Knyphausen followed with the 1st and 2nd British Brigades, the Loyalist regiments, and two German brigades with some light troops and cavalry. In total, Clinton could muster about 14,000 men.

British Order of Battle[1]

Sir Henry Clinton, Commander in Chief

First Division Lt. Gen. Charles, Earl Cornwallis

Hessian Grenadiers Brigade—Col. Heinrich von Kospoth
      Regiment von Linsing—Lt. Otto von Linsing
      Regiment Lengerke—Lt. Col. Georg Lengerke
      Regiment Minnigerode—Lt. Col. Friedrich von Minnigerode
Guards Brigade—Brig. Gen. Edward Matthew
      1st Guards (Coldstream)—Col. John Trelawney
      2nd Guards—Lt. Col. James Ogilvie
3rd Brigade—Brig. Gen. Sir Charles Grey
      15th Foot—Lt. Col. Joseph Stopford
      17th Foot—Lt. Col. Charles Mawhood
      1st Battalion, 42nd Highland—Lt. Col. Thomas Stirling
      2nd Battalion, 42nd Highland
      44th Foot—Lt. Col. Henry Hope
4th Brigade—Lt. Col. James Webster, acting commander
      33rd Foot—Lt Col. James Webster
      37th Foot—Maj. James Cousseau
      46th Foot—Lt. Col. Enoch Markham
      64th Foot—Maj. Robert McElroth
5th Brigade—Maj. Gen. Alexander Leslie
      7th Foot—Lt. Col. Alured Clarke (Fusiliers)
      26th Foot—Lt. Col. Charles Stuart
      63d Foot—Lt. Col. William Meadows
Grenadiers
      1st Grenadiers—Lt. Col. William Meadows
      2nd Grenadiers—Lt. Col. Henry Monckton
Rear Guard
      Queen's Rangers—Maj. John Graves Simcoe
      Queen's Rangers Dragoons—Maj. John Graves Simcoe

1st Light Infantry—Lt. Col. Robert Abercromby
16th Dragoons—Maj. Francis Gwynne

Second Division—Lt. Gen. Wilhelm von Knyphausen

Flank Guards
      17th Dragoons—Lt. Col. Samuel Birch
      2nd Light Infantry—Maj. John Maitland
      40th Foot—Lt. Col. Thomas Musgrave
Jaeger Detachment—Lt. Col. Ludwig von Wurmb
      Mounted Jaegers—Capt. August von Weedon
      Jaegers—Maj. Ernest von Bruenschenk
      Chasseurs—Capt. Carl von Cramon
1st Brigade—Maj. Gen. James Grant
      4th Foot (King's Own)—Maj. Sir James Murray
      23rd Royal Welsh Fusiliers—Lt. Col. Nesbit Balfour
      28th Foot—Lt. Col. Robert Prescott
      49th Foot—Lt. Col. Henry Colder
2nd Brigade—(Commander unknown, thought to be Smith)
      5th Foot—Maj. George Harris
      10th Foot—Lt. Col. Francis Smith
      27th Foot (Innskilling)—Lt. Col. Edward Mitchell
      55th Foot—Lt. Col. Cornelius Cuyler
Stirn's Brigade—Major Gen. Johann Stirn
      Leib—Col. Friedrich von Wurmb
      Donop—Col. David von Gosen
Loos' Brigade—Col. Johann von Loos
      Regiment Alt Lossberg—Col. Johann von Loos
      Regiment von Knyphausen—Maj. Johann von Stein
      Regiment von Woellworth—Col. Wolfgang von Woellworth
Guides and Pioneers—Capt. Simon Fraser
Roman Catholic Volunteers—Lt. Col. Alfred Clifton
1st Bn Maryland Loyalists—Lt. Col. James Chambers
2nd Bn Pennsylvania Loyalists—Lt. Col. William Allen
New Jersey Volunteers—Lt. Col. John van Dike
2nd New Jersey Volunteers—Lt. Col. John Morris
Bucks County Light Dragoons—Lt. Walter Willet
Pennsylvania Dragoons (3 troops)—Capt. Richard Havenden
2nd Regiment Volunteers of Ireland
Caledonian Volunteers

The long columns of British and German troops provided a diverse and colorful panoply of military might: the red coats of the British, the green of the Queen's Rangers, the blues and greens of the German regiments, cantering troops of dragoons; men wearing tall bearskin caps, mitred helmets, tricornes, light infantry caps, the crested helmets of the dragoons, or the distinctive bonnets of the Highlanders. It was an impressive spectacle. In and throughout the column were well-dressed officers with the gold-braided uniforms of the best military fashions of Europe. Among the marchers were Americans who had volunteered to serve the Crown during the British occupation of Philadelphia. It had been hoped that up to ten thousand Loyalists would volunteer for the provincial regiments, but the numbers were disappointing, with only about a thousand marching with the British army. Some groups were not even regiments, just a company or two. They included such units as the Roman Catholic Volunteers, the Maryland Loyalists, Pennsylvania Loyalists, Bucks County Light Dragoons, Pennsylvania Dragoons, 2nd Regiment Volunteers of Ireland, and the Caledonian Volunteers. As they were locally and recently raised, their usefulness in battle was doubted by the British generals. On the march, the Loyalists were placed with Knyphausen's division to help defend the baggage.

The British column moved slowly, ponderously, across New Jersey, tied down by its long baggage train. In addition to wheeled vehicles towing artillery, there were over 1,500 wagons that stretched the column out to almost 12 miles and left it vulnerable to attack. Considering the army rarely moved more than 12 miles, usually less, in a day, it was possible that the rear of the train was leaving a bivouac just as the head of the column was entering the campsite for the next evening.

American militia and New Jersey regulars under "Scotch Willie" Maxwell shadowed the column and there were frequent small clashes. Philemon Dickinson sent Washington daily, sometimes twice daily, reports of British progress and the terrain they encountered. Bridges were torn down and small gaggles of Americans constantly followed the British and German column, occasionally exchanging fire with British flank guards and then running away.

Throughout the march, the same heat, stifling humidity, and rain that affected the Americans also took its toll on the British and Hessians, who were encumbered with heavy packs, wool uniforms, and accoutrements. Dickinson reported to the commander in chief that, "A Hessian Deserter this moment came in, an intelligent fellow, he say's, the reason of their marching so slow, is the weight of their Baggage—I suppose plunder."[2] Much of the Loyalist and military baggage was loot from Philadelphia. It was difficult for the infantry, slogging along the alternately dusty and muddy road. Pushing carts and wagons through the sandy, often wet, soil was even more exhausting to the teamsters, camp followers, and artillerymen. The march was relatively quiet, the rattle of equipment and squeaking of vehicles' wheels forming the background to the soft, plodding sounds of thousands of marching feet. The men were too tired and hot to converse, and the countryside provided few amusements.

What few diversions there were would come from the people residing along the route of march. Unfortunately, previous negative encounters in earlier campaigns with the Hessian and British soldiers and their female camp followers, combined with new instances of pillaging and looting, had made the local population sullen, surly, and uncooperative. Livestock were driven into hiding, valuables concealed, and barns locked up when the royal column approached. The locals were often unwilling to trade or sell fresh food to the passing troops. The New Jersey militia threw roadblocks of felled trees across the British line of march, destroyed bridges, and occasionally traded shots with British flankers and foragers. In response to this lack of cooperation and their frustration with the many obstructions from the American militia, the British and Hessians plundered and destroyed the locals' property indiscriminately, especially if they knew it was owned by rebels. Two houses in Evesham, the ironworks near Mount Holly, and the home of Israel Shreve, a Continental officer, were burned by the passing soldiers.

Desertion was a major problem for the British by the time they arrived at Mount Holly on June 20. So many were deserting that Clinton decided on a lesson. In one of the many skirmishes with local rebels, several militiamen had fallen into British hands. One proved to be a former member of the British 28th Regiment. The luckless young man, serving as a drummer for the colonists, was hanged and left by the side of the road. The example failed miserably: most of the army either didn't see the swaying body or didn't care. The number of desertions, especially among the German troops, failed to slacken. Benedict Arnold reported 70 British deserters arriving in Philadelphia on June 21.[3]

On that same date, Washington was enjoying the hospitality of local man John Holcombe in his tall stone house. The commander in chief entertained thoughts of possibly engaging the enemy, writing Arnold: "We intend, as soon as things are in a train to move towards them and to avail ourselves of any favourable circumstances that are offered."[4] He used similarly aggressive words in a letter to Henry Laurens: "As soon as we have cleaned the Arms and can get matters in train, we propose moving towards Princeton, in order to avail ourselves of any favourable occasions that may present themselves of attacking or annoying the enemy."[5] Dickinson encouraged the commander in chief's aggressive spirit by advising him that instead of merely harassing the enemy he could use the militia to "fall on the rear of the enemy."[6] Governor William Livingston encouraged aggressiveness in a letter to Charles Lee forwarded to Washington: "I think for the good they do, we ought rather to hang on their rear, & drive the rascals thro' the state as soon as possible."[7]

The last of Washington's army crossed the Delaware at Coryell's and Cooper's Ferries on June 22. Washington ordered all excess baggage to be dropped off with the tents. Sick and injured troops remained with the equipment while the army continued marching. Most of the Americans had little excess baggage and they were not encumbered by heavy regimental coats and full packs like their British counterparts. The divisions were reorganized, with Lee commanding the "Right Wing" and Lord Stirling leading the "Left Wing." The Marquis de Lafayette led a reserve "wing" consisting of two Maryland and two Virginia brigades. Excluding Maxwell's New Jersey troops and Dickinson's New Jersey militia, Washington had over 12,000 men.

Washington remained with Holcombe until the morning of June 23. The bulk of the army reached Hopewell on the same day. That night he stayed with John Hart, a signatory of the Declaration of Independence. The next morning the army moved to the north of the British columns, near the rough country of upstate New Jersey. Washington sifted through the reports from locals, his cavalry, Maxwell, and Dickinson, trying to decipher Clinton's intention of going either to Sandy Hook, Elizabethtown, or to Perth Amboy before crossing into New York.

Clinton knew that Washington was to his left rear and split his army into two parallel columns on June 23 to use different roads and speed up movement. Cornwallis' division, containing most of the elite infantry, moved to the northern flank on the left, closest to Washington's path. Knyphausen's division, with the wagons and supplies, veered to the right, more to the south. "I had also in view by this move to draw the enemy down from the hilly country, in the hopes that an opportunity might offer of getting a fair stroke at him before I finally took my leave," Clinton wrote explaining his choice. "For, though the principle of my march was unquestionably retreat, I wished to avoid every appearance of a precipitate one."[8]

Near Crosswicks' Creek, west of the village of Crosswicks, Cornwallis' column ran into a group of American militiamen that didn't melt away when confronted but instead traded gunfire with the approaching redcoats. They held up the British just long enough for others to set up on the other side of the creek. The Americans then crossed the watercourse and destroyed the bridge behind them. Major John Graves Simcoe's Queen's Rangers splashed through the water and scattered the locals with a few wounded on both sides. Artillery was necessary to dislodge other, more obstinate, Americans at the Friends' Meeting House nearby.

Bridges and roads throughout the area were damaged or destroyed by the New Jersey militia, combining with the weather to further slow the ponderous British columns. Militia general Dickinson described the skirmish on June 23: "Unexpectedly, the Enemy made their appearance, about six O Clock this Evening, on the other side the Drawbridge—I take this to be, their advanced party, consisting of about seven, or eight hundred Men this is the Column, whh I mentioned to your Excellency, that was advancing on the Bordentown road—but from the best intelligence, their main body, lays on the Allentown road—they were busily employ'd in pulling down a Barn, to rebuild the Drawbridge, but our Artillery & Musketry, effectually put a stop to their Operations, for this Eveng—I have taken the necessary precautions, to prevent a surprize—& to'morrow, shall dispute the passages with them, unless they out flank us."[9]

The action at Crosswicks was repeated the next day at Doctor's Creek, where the militia had torn up the small bridge. After light troops and artillery scattered the hovering militia, the British were forced to construct their own bridge across the watercourse. Though these little streams were no impediment to infantry or even light artillery if a ford could be found, the bridges needed to be maintained or repaired to facilitate the movement of the cumbersome wagon train and heavier guns. Brigadier General James Pattison of the Royal Artillery glumly noted these irritating tactics: "The enemy had all along made some… attempts to obstruct or at least retard our march by pulling up the bridges thrown across small creeks and causeways, and felling timber across the road."[10]

Cornwallis' troops skirmished with the annoying militia while Washington was at Hopewell planning to harass the British even more. The Continental commander detached Daniel Morgan and his light infantry, mostly Virginia riflemen but also 25 men picked from each of the army's 13 brigades, to join Maxwell's New Jersey troops and annoy the British column. Moylan and the Continental horsemen were dispatched to cooperate with Dickinson's militia. On June 23, Washington detached 81 of his own personal guards under Captain Caleb Gibbs to join Morgan. He ordered Morgan "to take the most effectual means for gaining the enemys right flank, and giving them as much annoyance as possible in that quarter—Among the Militia annexed to your Corps, General Dickinson will take care that there are persons perfectly acquainted with the country and roads—so as to prevent every delay and danger which might arise from the want of intelligent guides."[11]

Washington pressed forward with the main army. The slow march of the British warned him that Clinton might be looking for a major engagement. He wrote Dickinson: "If their delay is voluntary it argues a design to draw us into a general action and proves that they consider this to be a desireable [ev]ent."[12]

On June 24 a total solar eclipse took place. Was it an oracle of success for one of the marching armies? A bloody defeat? Whatever the heavenly event prophesied, on this day Clinton made up his mind on his direction of movement. To turn directly north now toward Perth Amboy and across to Staten Island to New York City would require crossing the Raritan River. The army would be vulnerable to the pursuing Continental Army as they crossed such a natural obstacle. Moving northeasterly through South Amboy and Staten Island to New York City would also be dangerous for the army as it moved toward Raritan Bay. This route also necessitated a move through rough terrain in unfriendly areas that had been ravaged by the British in 1776 and 1777. Militia would have plenty of cover to launch hit-and-run raids. Washington coming from the west could attack part of the army split up by terrain or water crossing. Somewhere to the north was the army of Horatio Gates, the victor the previous fall against "Gentleman Johnny" Burgoyne's British column at Saratoga. There were persistent rumors that Gates and his army were hurrying southward to join Washington. One other unknown was the position of the French fleet that was in North American waters. The British commander in chief decided that it would be best to go east to Sandy Hook for his final move to New York City. The rough country around the Hook, a peninsula jutting into the Atlantic Ocean, would make it easy to defend when the ships arrived to take off the army. In addition, the British navy could provide cover as the army moved its rear guard onto the peninsula. An important negative was the lack of knowledge about the whereabouts of the French navy.

His decision made, Clinton sent out additional scouts to observe Washington's advance elements. He also acquired two guides to take him through Monmouth County to the shores of the Atlantic at Sandy Hook. Light infantrymen and cavalry flanked the British column to protect the wagons and give warning of militia attack. Several British cavalrymen were killed near Lewis's Mill that day. Despite little American successes like that at Lewis Mills, the British proved skilled at skirmishing, which was the type of fighting preferred by the American militia. Rarely were the poorly trained and undisciplined militia able to close with the main column.

The redcoats of the light infantry and grenadiers were, for the most part, the best-trained, most enthusiastic, and most physically capable men in the British army. Young officers often requested the appointment to a light infantry company because they knew that was where the action was, and they could make their reputation fighting alongside the light infantrymen. Through training and experience, these tough soldiers adapted to the irregular methods of warfare and were highly successful in their encounters with local troops. Unfortunately for the British, even though they were able to defeat the militia in most of their encounters, they could never destroy the irregulars.[13] The militia simply melted away whenever the odds turned against them.

Another Council of War

Also on June 24, Washington sent the Frenchman Duportail with John Laurens on a special scouting mission. They reported back the same day with a map of the terrain north of the British column. During the day, Washington received a note from Dickinson that indicated the British might want a full engagement: "The whole of General Clinton's movement, since he came into this State, has convinced me of his wish, to bring on a general action—it does admit of a doubt with me—tis the constant language, of the intelligent deserters—I do not mention this as a reason—but his Conduct, carries conviction with it."[14]

A firm believer in the superior position of the civilian government over the military, George Washington assiduously adhered to Congress' directions as commander in chief. Since first taking command outside of Boston in 1775, he followed Congress' instructions to call together councils of war to assess the opinions of his senior officers in matters that might bring action with the enemy or other major decisions, such as choosing Valley Forge as their winter encampment. In the past, this method of sounding out his senior leaders had saved him from some embarrassment, such as deterring him from an unsound attack on Boston in 1775. If anything, he might be considered guilty of lending too much weight to his subordinates' views, such as allowing the continued defense of Fort Washington in 1776 that resulted in a frightful loss of men and materiel. While staying in Hopewell Township, on June 24, Washington sought the opinions of his fellow generals. The meeting that morning coincided with the solar eclipse.

The council meeting was held at the home of John Hart's neighbor, Noah Hunt. In attendance were the French engineer Lebeque du Duportail; Major Generals Lee, Greene, Stirling, Lafayette, and von Steuben; and Brigadier Generals Henry Knox, Enoch Poor, Anthony Wayne, William Woodford, John

The Council of War held on June 24 started the events that led to the battle of Monmouth. The officers pictured, from left Duportail, Steuben, Poor, Knox, Stirling, Lafayette, Scammell, Washington, Paterson, Scott, Wayne, Greene, Woodford, and Lee, would lead the battle that ended in British defeat. *The Miriam and Ira D. Wallach Division of Art, Prints and Photographs: Print Collection, The New York Public Library. "Council of war at Hopewell, PA"*

Paterson, and Charles Scott. It was essentially the same group that had met on June 14 with Arnold, Smallwood, Huntington, and Muhlenberg absent. Charles Scott was the only officer present who had not attended the June 14 conference. In holding his council of war, Washington was dealing with men he was extremely familiar with. For the first time in the war, Washington would command a force of experienced and well-trained officers and enlisted men. There were some new recruits but the bulk of the army that would take the field were of better quality than previously.

Washington began with a quick evaluation of the situation as to the placement and movement of the British troops, the estimated numbers of the opposing forces, and the status of local militia. Washington then asked the assembly to advise him as to which of three courses of action to follow:

> Will it be advisable for us, of choice, to hazard an action?
>
> If it is, should we do it, by immediately, making a general attack upon the Enemy, by attempting a partial one, or by taking such a position, if it can be done, as may oblige them to attack us?

> If it is not, what measures can be taken, with safety to this Army, to annoy the Enemy
> in their march, should it be their intention to proceed through the Jerseys.
> In fine, what precise line of conduct will it be best for us to pursue?[15]

Each officer was allowed to voice his thoughts. Opinions varied, with the well-articulated ideas of Charles Lee placed in the forefront. He convincingly advocated that the British be allowed to retreat, unmolested, to New York. The recent treaty with the French was a good opportunity to sit back, wait and see, Lee argued. Soon supplies and soldiers would arrive from their new ally that would allow greater freedom of action. Lee spoke strongly about the abilities and numbers of the British, painting a gloomy picture of a battle between the inept, inexperienced Americans and the more professional Germans and British. Lafayette remembered that: "Lee very eloquently argued that we should provide a pont d'or [bridge of gold] for the enemy to reach New York: that British negotiators were discussing possible reconciliation with Congressional leaders; that the British had never been so disciplined and as strong."[16] To many of the assembled officers, Lee's comments were derogatory toward both them and their Continental soldiers. Yet most of those present agreed with Lee that a general attack "will not be advisable."[17]

Despite the apparent unanimity that no general attack was advisable, that was not the end of the conversation. Lafayette led a group that felt the Continental Army had never been stronger and that to allow the enemy to retreat with impunity was disgraceful. The generals were at all points on the scale between Lee and Lafayette with no possibility of consensus. The majority was opposed to a general attack, but many felt some type of action should be undertaken. The give and take was frustrating to Alexander Hamilton, who was writing down the recommendations for Washington. Hamilton said of the meeting: "The General unluckily called a council of war, the result of which would have done honor to the most honorab[le] society of midwives, and to them only."[18]

Although the proceedings advised against a general attack, the aggressive members of the council, Wayne and Lafayette among the more vocal, were gratified when it was suggested that an additional force of 1,500 men would join the advance guard to "annoy" the British columns, with even Lee concurring. Hamilton put the results into writing and all present signed them except Wayne, who held out for a more aggressive action. Wayne took the time to write out a long explanation of why he failed to join the others. Although he was not in favor of a "General Action," he felt a stronger, more aggressive force of up to three thousand men should be added to the harassing forces and that a major general be placed over the entire force.[19]

Charles Scott would command a small detachment of picked men, taken from each brigade, to act as light infantry and annoy the British. *The Miriam and Ira D. Wallach Division of Art, Prints and Photographs: Print Collection, The New York Public Library. "Ch. Scott"*

Washington received the recommendations of the council, and he accepted them. As the army lacked a permanent corps of light infantry to provide the 1,500 men to "annoy" the British, he placed Virginian Charles Scott in command of fifteen hundred "picked men" drawn from the brigades that would join Maxwell to act as light infantry in harassing the retreating British column.

Most European-style armies had some type of specialized infantry for screening, skirmishing, and patrolling. Such German units were called "Jaegers." The British army included 10 companies in every regiment, one being a company of light infantry, one of grenadiers, and the other eight companies being called hat men or regular infantrymen. The grenadiers and light infantry were the elite of each regiment. They were usually the fittest and best troops of the regiment, and many officers transferred from their own regiment to join the light infantry or grenadiers of another regiment. These companies were often taken from their parent regiment to form a separate battalion consisting only of the light infantry or grenadiers of the army. Clinton was marching with four such units, two battalions of light infantry companies and two battalions of grenadiers.

Washington ordered Charles Scott to organize and command a force like one of these specialized battalions. Scott's force was made up of "picked" or "chosen" men, consisting of about 80 men from each of the regiments of a single brigade and forming one light infantry detachment. Veteran Colonels Joseph Cilley, Mordecai Gist, Richard Parker, and Lieutenant Colonel William Butler were chosen to command the light infantry detachments formed from their different brigades. Scott also took four pieces of artillery and a detachment of cavalry under Lieutenant Colonel Anthony White. Scott was a Virginian who had served with Washington in the French and Indian War. He served ably in the Philadelphia campaign but had been accused of insubordination by the disgraced Major General Adam Stephen after Germantown. No charges were ever filed, and Washington showed his confidence in Scott with the appointment to the command of the "picked men." He would tell a member of Congress later that Scott was "a good Man, & a brave & intelligent Officer."[20]

In sending Scott out to join the advanced guard, Washington ordered: "You are immediately to march with the detachment, under your command towards Allen Town, in order to fall in with the enemy's left flank and rear, and give them all the annoyance in your power. You will carefully collect intelligence as you advance and govern your motions accordingly; and you will take every precaution for the security of your detachment consistent with the objects it is intended to promote. You will cooperate as far as may be proper with the other troops in the neighbourhood of the enemy. You will keep me continually and punctually advised of every occurrence, that happens, either with respect to the enemy, or yourself."[21] Scott's troops would fall in with Maxwell's brigade on the left, and Morgan on the right.

Even with the dispatch of the additional light troops, Washington couldn't hide his disappointment in the results of the council. He felt the British were vulnerable, encumbered as they were by baggage, in the open country of central New Jersey, and that it would be more difficult to attack them if they reached the more rugged country near the coast. Washington was not alone.

Nathanael Greene, frustrated with the results of the council, urged an attack on the enemy's rear guard by militia, Scott's light infantry, Morgan's detachment, and Maxwell's New Jersey Brigade, with the main army close by for support. He wrote Washington a note using the morale of the country and the army as reasons for attempting some action: "If we suffer the enemy to pass through the Jerseys without attempting anything upon them, I think we shall ever regret it. We are now in the most awkward situation in the World—we have come with great rapidity until we got near the Enemy and then our courage faild us and we halted without attempting to do the enemy the least injury." He concluded: "The people expect something from us, and our strength demands it."[22]

The results of the officers' meeting also failed to satisfy young Lafayette. He met with other officers who urged more troops be sent to attack the British with the main army in a position to aid the attackers if necessary. In a note to Washington, he stated that he spoke specifically for von Steuben and Duportail, who wanted to speak up but were hampered by their lack of ability to express themselves in English. He told Washington, "I am Clearly of the opinion, that a chosen corps of two thousand five hundred or at least two thousand Selected men ought to have been Sent or are to be Completed towards the enemy's left flank or rear—not to Scout as Some Say, but to attack any part of the english army or of theyr baggage as will furnish a proper opportunity…" He continued to make his point, using the word "attack" repeatedly with the emphasis on the rewards of the attack, "of even beating those tremendous grenadiers if they fight with them."[23]

In view of these opinions voiced after the council, on June 25 Washington decided to send forward another 1,000 men under Anthony Wayne. They would join with Scott, Maxwell, Dickinson, and Morgan to "annoy" the rear and flanks of the British army. If they became embroiled in a larger battle, Washington and the main body would be only a short distance away in support. Instead of Wayne taking his own brigade, Washington followed the policy that had been used in organizing Scott's detachment and gave Wayne a "picked force" of men from various brigades. Wayne had picked men from Ebenezer Learned's brigade under Colonel James Wesson, men from Poor's brigade under Colonel Henry Beekman Livingston, and a detachment under Colonel Walter Stewart. Two cannons under Captain Thomas Seward supported them. The instruction of Steuben at Valley Forge would be tested as units were organized into new detachments. Would they be able to operate together?

George Washington's continued reinforcement of the troops harassing Clinton's columns indicated that he wanted some sort of action. He knew that the enemy was being pressed by militia at various points. He also knew that he had detachments on each side of the enemy columns and to their rear. He had a clear picture of Clinton's dispositions as Dickinson, Moylan, and others gave him information on the enemy's progress. Typical was the report of Colonel Henry Jackson, who had been sent by Benedict Arnold from Philadelphia to follow the British: "Their Rear move'd about 9 O.C. this Morg from Rechleys Town—they march'd in two divisions. the right towards Walls Mill1 & the Left towards Allen Town."[24]

While the officers debated what strategy to follow, the militia and New Jersey Continentals continued to peck away at the British. Major Joseph Bloomfield of the 3rd New Jersey noted one day's action: "25. June. 1778. This night I lay with…50 Contl. Soldiers & 40 Militia on Taylor's heights within a quarter Mile of Clinton's Main-Army. Fired upon & alarmed them several times in the night, and in the morning followed their rear. Capt. Voorhees party took 15 Prisoners & had several skirmishes with the Jagars. Took three Jagars myself Prisoners when I was reconnitreing within sight of the enemy's rear."[25] Washington sent his aide, Alexander Hamilton, with the Baron von Steuben to confirm the direction of the enemy movement. Washington began formulating in his mind the route of the enemy based on the excellent intelligence he was receiving from locals, Moylan, Dickinson, and Maxwell.

With the latest reinforcements, the size of the advanced corps had reached over 4,500 men, not including Dickinson's militia or Morgan's men. Washington, as Anthony Wayne had suggested, felt that a senior officer should take command and coordinate the different detachments if a chance presented itself to engage the long enemy column. Naturally, Charles Lee as second in command was the senior officer and should command this sizable force. Washington offered Lee the command but the enigmatic general quickly refused. Lee was unenthusiastic about the whole idea of attacking the enemy's rear guard. He still felt, as illustrated by his position at the earlier council of war, that the British should be allowed to proceed unmolested to the coast. Washington would have to choose someone else. Lee felt "pleased to be freed from all responsibility for a plan he was sure would fail."[26]

Rebuffed, Washington settled on the young Marquis de Lafayette as the commander for the advanced corps. Lafayette was loyal, dynamic, and always in search of glory. Washington passed over his friend Nathanael Greene, who was acting in a staff position as quartermaster general, and his next senior commander, Lord Stirling, for reasons unknown. Greene was on staff at the time, although he had been promised field command if a battle were imminent. Possibly Washington believed that Stirling was not physically capable of an independent command due to his poor health caused by an overindulgence of alcohol. Stirling talked to Lee about being passed over but the two agreed not to raise the subject with Washington and to let Lafayette command the advanced forces.

At first glance, his youth and short time in America made Lafayette an unusual choice. But as an aide to Washington, he had learned the ways of fighting in America and to speak English. He was aggressive and wanted to be in on the action, demonstrating his eagerness on several occasions. Despite being a staff officer, he was wounded at Brandywine on September 11, 1777, when he went to help rally the right wing during that great battle. Upon recovery from his wound, he led raiding expeditions into New Jersey. His personal example in action earned the admiration both of Washington and the men of the army. Congress thought enough of his abilities to have made him commander of the aborted expedition to invade Canada that was never carried out due to a lack of logistical support.

Lafayette led the unfortunate expedition to Barren Hill on May 20, 1778, where the abilities of his well-trained troops and a lot of luck avoided a disaster. His leadership during the skillful retreat earned him additional respect. Consequently, Washington's friendship, the young Frenchman's wealth and influence in France, and his recent battlefield experience led the commander in chief to give Lafayette command of the reserve wing when the army left Valley Forge. Lafayette demonstrated by his actions, and his note to Washington during the council, a tendency to be more aggressive than some of the other generals that influenced Washington's decision on June 24.

On this June day Washington's instructions to Lafayette were simple: "All continental parties that are already on the lines will be under your command, and you will take such measures, in concert with Genl. Dickinson as will cause the Enemy most impediment and loss on their march; for these purposes you will attack them on occasion may require by detachment, and if a proper opening shd. be given by operating against them the whole force of your command."[27] These were aggressive orders given to an aggressive officer, and Lafayette could be counted on to carry them out.

The knowledge of Washington's army behind them and a sizable militia detachment to the north forced Clinton to reform his order of march to counter these threats. On June 25, Clinton placed Cornwallis' division with the best troops at the rear of the army. Knyphausen moved out of Imlaystown, his troops followed by the long baggage train forming the leading elements of the army. Cornwallis fell in behind as the army marched in a single column across central New Jersey toward Sandy Hook. The heavily laden British and German troops struggled through the heat, although the light infantry with their short coats were a little more comfortable. Much of their baggage was in wagons. The ever-present militia kept them constantly on the alert. On June 25, a foray by some locals was pushed back only after the Jaegers used three-pound cannon to drive off the marauding Americans. That same day Cornwallis used his light infantry to dissuade a force of militia from plundering his own headquarters.

The British troops were losing many friends along the march. Captain Johann Ewald of the Jaegers was disappointed when he found a farm and mill aflame near Bordertown. He had stayed at the home previously and given his word it would not be damaged.[28] The American soldiers who followed the king's columns also saw many examples of the British and German depredations. Connecticut soldier Joseph Plumb Martin was one who saw it first hand: "We had ample opportunity to see the devastation they made in their route; cattle killed and lying about the fields and pastures, some just in the position they were in when shot down, others with a small spot of skin taken off their hindquarters and a mess of steak taken out; household furniture hacked and broken to pieces; wells filled up and mechanic's and farmer's tools destroyed. It was in the height of the season of cherries, the innocent industrious creatures could not climb the trees for the fruit, but universally cut them down."[29]

Oddly enough, Washington had addressed just this sort of looting in his General Orders for June 22: "The Brigadier of the day with the Officers ordered to remain in the Rear will see that every thing is properly conducted there—the Guards kept to their duty and all damage to the fruit trees prevented, of which the whole road hitherto exhibits such shameful Proofs."[30] The wanton destruction by Crown forces, combined with the militia and rebel light troops' necessary destruction of bridges and cutting down of trees to obstruct the British path, made the crossing of armies through New Jersey painful for the inhabitants no matter where their loyalty lay.

Washington understood that the looting and pillaging of homes or property could turn a population against the army. He had warned Charles Lee when the march began: "Be strict in your discipline—suffer no rambling—keep the Men in their Ranks & the Officers with their divisions—avoid pressing Horses &ca as much as possible and punish severely every officer or Soldier who shall presume to press without proper authority—prohibit the burning of Fences—in a word you are to protect the persons & property of the Inhabitants from every kind of Insult & abuse."[31]

The weather continued to follow the pattern of New Jersey in June: hot, steamy days with frequent rain and thunderstorms. The soldiers on both sides had little in the way of comfort and most no longer had tents. To travel more quickly, the American troops had left their tents behind. The British troops loaded their tents on the wagons and left them there to facilitate movement. Most of the troops merely slept on the ground, covered with only "the canopy of heaven for our tent."[32] Some of the soldiers constructed crude shelters called wigwams to keep out the rain or sweltering sun, as Joseph Plumb Martin related: "It was uncommonly hot weather and we put up booths to protect us from the heat of the sun."[33]

Englishtown to Monmouth Court House

The American army camped near Kingston on June 25. While there, Washington was given a present by the governor of New Jersey: a beautiful white horse. Although the commander in chief had several horses, Washington would ride the horse over the next few days. Stephen Moylan reported to Washington that evening the proximity of British troops as well as the terrain: "…the Country is much in favor of light troops thos very bad for horse." Moylan joined Baron von Steuben in a close reconnaissance of the British near "the Court House."[34] With the latest intelligence from Moylan, Steuben, and the local militia, Washington used a night march on the evening of June 25 to gain ground on Clinton and push Lafayette's advanced corps to Cranbury, less than 15 miles from the British.

On June 25 there were nearly five thousand American troops under Lafayette's command closing on the British. As the day wore on, Charles Lee reconsidered his position as to commanding the advanced guard. He approached Lafayette, asking him to give up the command and to intervene on Lee's behalf with Washington. Then he wrote the commander in chief himself:

> When I first assented to the Marquis de Lafayette's taking the command of the present detachment, I confess I viewed it in a very different light from that in which I view it at present. I considered it more proper busyness of a Young Volunteering General than of the Second in command in the Army—but I find it is considered in a different manner. They say that a Corps consisting of Six thousand men [Lee's estimate], the greater part chosen, is undoubtedly the most honourable command next to the Commander-in-Chief; that my ceding it would of course have an odd appearance I must intreat therefore, (after making a thousand apologies for the trouble my rash assent has occasion'd you) that if this detachment does march that I may have command of it… both Myself and Lord Steuben will be disgrac'd…[35]

Oddly, Lee referred to "Lord Steuben," perhaps meaning Lord Stirling.

Washington was obviously irritated with the position he had been placed in. He had been unhappy with his second in command before the latter's captivity. Lee's near insubordination and reluctance to join the main army with his troops in December of 1776 had seriously vexed the Virginian. Then Lee had been so careless as to be easily captured. In the month since Lee's return to the army he had done little to regain the prestige he possessed before his capture. His machinations in Congress, his open correspondence with enemy officers, his lack of respect for the new Continental Army or its officers, his flippancy when taking the oath, and continued, uninvited, and random advice had done little to restore him to his prior place of confidence with Washington. Nevertheless, the Virginian decided to allow Lee to take command.

While Lee pushed to take command of the advance corps, Lafayette moved even closer to Clinton, gaining a position only four miles from the British on June 26. As anxious as he was for action the Frenchman wanted to be sure of the enemy's exact disposition and was reluctant to attack until things became clearer. Fortunately, the leader of the local militia, General David Forman, rode along as a guide for Lafayette. Lafayette also found that the advanced corps had marched too far in a short amount of time and outdistanced its supply columns. He urged Washington to send him rations:

> I will try to meet and Collect as Soon as possible our forces, tho' I am sorry to find the ennemy So far down that way—we'll be obliged to march pretty fast if we want to attak them—it is for that I am particularly Concern'd about provisions—I Send back immediately for that purpose and beg you would give orders to have them forwarded as Speedily as possible—and directed to march fast, for I believe we must Set out early to morrow morning—the Detachement is in a wood, covered by Cranberry creek and I believe extremely Safe—we want to be very well furnish'd with Spirits as a long and quick march may be found necessary, and if general Scot's detachement is not provided it Schould be furnish'd also with liquor—but the provisions of this detachement are the most necessary to be Sent as Soon as possible, as we expect them to march.[36]

Despite the lack of supplies, Lafayette cautiously continued to press forward when the British marched away from him toward Monmouth Court House. He hoped to attack the British in motion: "I would be very happy if we could attak them before they halt for I have no notion of taking one other moment but this off the march—if I Can not overtake them we could lay at some distance and attak to morrow Morning provided they do'nt escape in the night which I much fear as our intelligences are not the best ones; I have sent Some partys out and I will get some more light by them. I fancy your excellency will move down with the army, and if we are at a Convenient distance from you I have nothing to fear in striking a blow if opportunity is offered, I believe that in our present strength provided they do'nt escape we may do Some thing."[37] The Frenchmen was intent on action.

Washington was uneasy because of reports that the British were not moving and might be spoiling for a fight. While Washington did want some sort of attack on the British, it appeared as if the young Frenchman was too eager to engage and Washington warned him about pushing his troops too hard: "Though giving the Enemy a stroke is a very desireable event, yet I would not wish you to be too precipitate in the measure or to distress your men by an over hasty march. The Weather is extremely warm and by a too great exertion in pushing the Troops many of em will fall sick and be rendered entirely unfit for service." Then he followed it up with a note of caution: "I must repeat again my wish that you do not push on with too much rapidity. You may be, in case of Action, at too great a distance to receive succour and exposed from thence to great Hazard. The Troops here are suffering for want of provision, as well as those with you, and are under the necessity of halting, till they are refreshed. Had this unfortunate circumstance not intervened, the severe rain now falling would compel 'em to delay their march for the present."[38]

The commander in chief pushed forward the supplies. He also sent a note concerning a change in command. Even though Lee had informed Lafayette of his intentions earlier, the order was still a disappointment to the young man's hopes for command distinction:

> General Lee's uneasiness on account of yesterday's transaction rather increasing than abating, and your politeness in wishing to ease him of it, has induced me to detach him from this Army, with a part of it, to reinforce, or at least cover, the several detachments under your command, at present. At the same time that I felt for General Lee's distress of mind, I have had an eye to your wishes, and the delicacy of your situation; and have, therefore, obtained a promise from him, that when he gives you notice of his approach and command, he will request you to prosecute any plan you may have already concerted for the purpose of attacking or otherwise annoying the Enemy. This is the only expedient I could think of to answer both your views. General Lee seems satisfied with the measure, and I wish it may prove agreable to you, as I am with the warmest wishes for your honor & glory.[39]

If there were to be "honor and glory" for Lafayette it would be as a subordinate. Charles Lee would command the advance detachments. Washington was taking a chance by changing commanders when he expected some type of action soon.

Frustrated by his second in command's decision, the commander in chief wrote Lee:

> Your uneasiness, on account of the command of yesterday's detachment, fills me with concern, as it is not in my power, fully, to remove it without wounding the feelings of the Marquiss de la Fayette—I have thought of an expedient, which though not quite equal to either of your views, may in some measure answer both; and that is to make another detachment from this Army for the purpose of aiding and supporting the several detachments now under the command of the Marquiss & giving you the command of the whole, under certain restrictions; which, circumstances, arising from your own conduct yesterday, render almost unavoidable. The expedient which I would propose is, for you to march towards the Marquiss with Scot's & Varnum's Brigades. Give him notice that you are advancing to support him—that you are to have the command of the whole advanced body; but as he may have formed some enterprize with the advice of the Officers commanding the several Corps under his command, which will not admit of delay or alteration, you will desire him to proceed as if no change had happened, and you will give him every assistance and countenance in your power. This, as I observed before, is not quite the thing; but may possibly answer, in some degree, the views of both.[40]

With Scott and Varnum's Brigades numbering about nine hundred men, Lee would have over 5,000 troops when he assumed command of the Advanced

Corps. The additional troops were partly as a face-saving move for Lafayette so that it looked like a larger force needed a more senior commander.

Washington, faced with an awkward situation caused by his second in command's change of mind, had to come up with a diplomatic solution. He agreed to allow Lee to take over the advance but told Lafayette that he could continue his own operations. This put the cautious Lee at odds with the more aggressive youth. Nearly every note that passed from the commander in chief or his aides to the advancing units contained the word "attack," but also contained wording that made it plain that they should view the order as discretionary and to press the attack only when there could be some "advantage." As Lafayette had not closed with the British or formed a formal plan of attack, Washington's note was of no consolation to Lafayette. Instead, any attack would have to be led by Charles Lee.

Lafayette received the orders to give up command late on the evening of June 26. The next day, Washington ordered the different commanders of the various advance detachments to meet with Lee when he arrived at Englishtown, about seven miles from Monmouth Court House. Lee arrived at Englishtown with Scott's Brigade under Colonel William Grayson and Varnum's Brigade under Colonel John Durkee. Also included was Colonel Henry Jackson's detachment that had been following the British army in company with Lieutenant Colonel Anthony Walton White's cavalry.

Grayson was a physically impressive man, a well-educated lawyer with family connections in Virginia. He had served previously as an aide to Washington. As a reward for that service, the general sent Grayson home to raise his own regiment. Grayson now commanded a force made up of his own Virginians, plus a detachment of various Virginia regiments under Colonel James Woods, and a regiment of Pennsylvanians under Lieutenant Colonel John Parke. Referred to as Scott's Brigade, its former commander Charles Scott was leading a detachment of picked men.

John Durkee was the epitome of the adventurous American. Originally from Connecticut, he was one of the first settlers in the much-disputed Wyoming Valley of Pennsylvania and was arrested twice by that colony's leaders for trespassing. He founded the village of Wilkes-Barre, naming it after the two distinguished British politicians who were sympathetic to the American cause, John Wilkes and Isaac Barre. A leader of the Connecticut Sons of Liberty before the war, he served in nearly every major engagement of the Continental Army. Durkee commanded a brigade consisting of his own Connecticut Battalion, made up of the remnants of the 4th and 8th Regiments, and the Rhode Island Battalion under Lieutenant Colonel Jeremiah Olney.

The brigade had previously been commanded by James Varnum but he was on recruiting duty in Rhode Island.

Jackson was a Massachusetts man commanding his own regiment and two additional regiments commanded by Lieutenant Colonel William Smith and Major John Tyler. Despite having served since 1775, Jackson had seen little action. With these troops and those of Lafayette, Lee had a force of over 5,000 men and was supported by Dickinson's militia numbering around a thousand more.

On June 26 Clinton ordered a halt not far from Monmouth Court House to allow his tired troops a brief respite before the final push to Sandy Hook and on into New York. He set up headquarters in the Covenhoven House just outside of Freehold, the site of Monmouth County Court House. It was only a short march from there to a low plateau near Middletown where the countryside would be a little more rugged and more difficult for the American army to strike the cumbersome British column. Throughout the day the American light troops continued to harass the British columns as they slowly marched through the fertile New Jersey countryside toward the evening bivouac at the seat of Monmouth County.

Captain Ewald of the Jaegers found himself constantly in battle with militia throughout June 26. Unable to deal with the swarms of Americans, who he termed "riflemen" but were local militia and Maxwell's New Jersey troops, Ewald had to get support from the light infantry. He estimated his losses at over 60, including 20 that fell due to the heat. It took hours for the tired British and German troops with their long trail of camp followers to settle in around the town. The last troops were still setting up their camp as darkness fell at 7:35 pm.

Daniel Morgan's detachment captured 15 grenadiers on June 27. The British troops, apprehended by some of Washington's personal guard, had been caught bathing in a stream during the heat of the day. The same day Moylan's dragoons took five wandering British soldiers closer to Freehold. Large numbers of British and Hessian soldiers, tired of heat, rain, marching, war, and the service in general, continued to desert. Washington noted that at least 420 deserters had arrived in Philadelphia by June 27.[41]

About noon that day, Washington rode forward and met Lee at Englishtown. Present were some of the principal leaders of the advanced corps: Lafayette, Wayne, and Maxwell. Washington recognized the British were closing in on the rugged terrain close to the coast and the time to strike was now. The commander in chief gave orders that "...General Lee was to attack as soon as he had information that the front was in motion or had marched off...

that something might be done by giving them a very brisk charge by some of the best troops."[42] To those men who had fought in so many battles with Washington, it was understood that they were to attack when the enemy moved. Washington instructed Lee to call his officers to a second conference that afternoon and discuss Lee's own plan to carry out the attack.

As the meeting broke up, Maxwell was pleased that Washington personally acknowledged him.[43] The tall Virginian indicated that he would have preferred that Maxwell's brigade lead the attack but the New Jersey brigade was composed of too many new 90-day levies and some lacked proper equipment. "Scotch Willie" Maxwell, a nickname he earned due to his accent and propensity for drink, acknowledged Washington's compliment and apology then returned to his troops. Washington rode back to the main body, content to let Lee choose his own order of battle and course of action in carrying out the instructions of the commander in chief.

Upon returning to the main body, Washington gave orders that the troops be prepared to move out as soon as intelligence indicated the departure of the British from Monmouth Court House. The last units of the advanced corps closed up on Englishtown; Maxwell and Wayne's men had been trailing the British columns on the Allentown–Monmouth Court House Road and had to change their axis of advance to meet the others.

Lee called together his subordinates for a short meeting that afternoon. Lee didn't wait for all of his junior leaders to arrive and began the officers' call without several of them. Daniel Morgan and Dickinson were not present, and Charles Scott only arrived after the other detachment leaders left. Once Lee started, he was frustratingly vague about what lay ahead and stated that because of the lack of good intelligence he would make no plans that evening but wait to see how things developed. Oddly, he told the officers not to worry about the chain of command and follow orders as given. Lafayette was essentially the second in command of the advanced corps but was left with no direct responsibility. Lee was unfamiliar with most of the commanders, leaving him uncomfortable. His subordinates, equally unfamiliar with Lee, were excited about the prospect of battle but also uncomfortable with the lack of a clear chain of command and Lee's lack of concrete plans that might have helped with the communication between the various units. Lee did not reveal his intentions or what the objective of the next day's action would be. He also did not visit any of his units or conduct a reconnaissance of the route he would take the next day or of the enemy's positions.

Lee sent Washington a note giving his position and where he thought the British were. He complained of a lack of cooperation from the locals—"The people here are inconceivably Stupid"—and requested "two or three (if They can be spared) active well-mounted light Horse Men."[44] His new command was large and spread out, and he found it difficult to communicate with his various detachments with his small staff.

Upon returning to his brigade, Maxwell was met by Major Richard Howell of the 2nd New Jersey. Howell's twin brother was dying, and he requested leave to go see him the next day. Maxwell, with his most gruff look and voice, gave the young officer permission to go but insinuated that Howell would miss the upcoming battle, vaguely questioning the man's courage. Embarrassed, Howell declined the leave and went back to his regiment.

During the march from Valley Forge, a constant flow of letters passed between Dickinson and Washington, keeping the commander in chief informed of both British movements and the position of the militia and light units. The Virginian constantly prompted Dickinson about details. In addition to Dickinson's militia, the Continental cavalry under Colonel Stephen Moylan also kept a close watch on the British.

Moylan sent a report to Washington at 9:00 pm the night of June 27: "I am just come from Longstreets hill. I sent an officer Since sunset close in to the Lines and from his report, with my own observation there was no appearance of a movement, I sent an officer on the Middletown & Shrewsbury roads, who makes the Same report, I will be out before the Sun, & if any thing new you will hear it from Sir your most ob. H: St."[45] Washington still did not know if the British would remain in place or move out of Freehold the next morning.

Moylan added one last bit of information with a report at 11:30 pm when he informed Washington that "every thing looks in the Same Situation as yesterday at Freehold, we took three prisoners whom I send to your Excellency, they Say it is the opinion which prevails in their Camp, that they will march to morrow morning for So. Amboy."[46] The captured soldiers' information seemed in error as the British the past several days had been moving toward the coast at Sandy Hook and not northward toward South Amboy.

Washington slept that night confident there would be some sort of attack the next morning. Soldiers arriving late that night at Englishtown tried to get some sleep. There was another thunderstorm on the night of June 27, heavier than the night before. For the hot troops, the evening gave them no respite, as the wind died away and the air cooled very little after the rain.

Just after midnight back on June 24, Washington had detached portly Baron von Steuben with several aides to check the position of the British forces. Since then, the Baron had followed doggedly along behind the slow-moving enemy columns, sending back frequent reports about the movements of the

British. On the evening of June 27 and early morning of June 28, von Steuben, with young John Laurens and several other aides, moved to a position within pistol shot of the enemy near Monmouth Court House. They rode carefully around the various British bivouacs long enough to know that the great army was bestirring itself and preparing to move out. As the baron completed his reconnaissance, several British dragoons left their camp and made after him at a gallop. Von Steuben realized the better part of valor was to retreat, fired his two pistols at the approaching British, and rode off so fast that he lost his hat. Winded and bare headed, the German gave Washington a last-minute report of the British positions and the local terrain.

Opening Shots

Among the troops preparing for action on Sunday, June 28, was the Connecticut lad, Joseph Plumb Martin. When Martin and his comrades were awakened and told to drop their packs in preparation for the day's events, one of the officers noted that the men seemed eager for battle and he brought them a dose of reality: "Now," he said to us, "you have been wishing for some days past to come up with the British, you have been wanting to fight,—now you shall have fighting enough before night."[47] Martin and the others dropped haversacks and waited for the order to move out; the sick and injured would guard their belongings

Clinton had his men moving before four in the morning on Sunday, June 28, 1778. He wanted to get Knyphausen's column into the rugged Navesink country past Middletown as soon as possible. He deployed dragoons and the Queen's Rangers as a screen to his rear. Like any other day since leaving Philadelphia, they found the annoying American militia was active early.

It was appropriate that the first shots of the battle were from New Jersey militiamen on their home soil. Shortly after 4:00 am steady, dependable Philemon Dickinson led his militia in a move that approached the British pickets. A landowner with refined taste, Philemon was the brother of John Dickinson, the writer of the pre-war pamphlet "Letters from a Pennsylvania Farmer" that had awakened many colonists to the crisis in government. Aristocratic by nature, Philemon had been an ardent Whig before the war and served almost continuously in the militia since the beginning of the conflict. A lawyer, he had never practiced law but was living comfortably on his estates when the war interrupted his near idyllic life. As a militia general, he was known to be an active commander with a great deal of experience, particularly renowned for an action in January of 1777 in which he led a body of New Jersey militia in an attack on a British foraging party near Somerset Court House that sent the raiders home without their plunder. His militia, often supported by Maxwell's Continental New Jersey brigade, had skirmished the last two years with British and Tories who were raiding and pillaging New Jersey. He was a man to be reckoned with.

With Clinton's first move, Dickinson sent word to Washington and Lee that the British were moving from Monmouth Court House:

> ¼ past 4 OClock A.M.
> Dear Sir   June 28th 1778 [Monmouth, N.J.]
>   A Major who was on duty last night informs me, that the Enemy are in Motion— marching off—

Dickinson's aggressive nature came through in the postscript:

> I am moving down two or three hundred Men to amuse & detain them—& have parties out to gain Intelligence—shall take down the whole of my troops, as soon, as they can be collected—a second Express from the Mill Picket informs me, they moved as early as 4, OClock.[48]

The note gave Washington the information he needed to begin moving the main body.

During the morning, small groups of militiamen fanned out around the British in search of intelligence or to trade shots with British and German skirmishers. Some came in close to the baggage train near Briar Hill northeast of the court house and succeeded in scaring horses and overturning some wagons before they were chased off. This attack reminded Clinton of the vulnerability of his wagons and his mission to bring them all to New York. Many of the small militia scouting parties withdrew after making contact, joining up with Dickinson and the bulk of the militia along a rail fence near a small cluster of buildings called the Parsonage Farm.

The Hunterdon Light Horse militia approached the court house itself and encountered mounted members of the Queen's Rangers. When the militia horsemen fled west along the road toward Englishtown, the British horsemen followed closely behind, but were in turn brought to an abrupt halt when they encountered the main body of militia infantry along a fence. The helmeted horsemen fell back into ranks of the Light Infantry and Queen's Rangers of the British rear guard. Unfazed by the show of local strength, the Light Infantry came up and outflanked the New Jersey men, forcing the militia to give way. They did not go easily, halting to fire at the advancing redcoats, and then scurrying off before firing again. The militia stopped as the first of Grayson's Continentals from the advanced corps appeared to bolster their ranks. With the appearance of militia cavalry and Continental infantry, the British soldiers retreated to the east to rejoin the main column. As the redcoats moved out, the first of Lee's advanced corps was moving down the twisting road that ran along Perrine Ridge to cross the West Ravine. With the approach of the American advanced guard, skirmishing was at an end. It was time for the main armies to meet.

American Order of Battle

Commander in Chief—Gen. George Washington
4th Continental Dragoons—Col. Stephen Moylan
Commander in Chief's Guard—Capt. Caleb Gibbs

Advanced Corps Commander—Maj. Gen. Charles Lee
Advanced Corps Assistant Commander—Maj. Gen. Marquis de Lafayette
Grayson's Detachment (Scott's Brigade)—Col. William Grayson
      Virginia Detachment (4, 8, 12 VA)—Col. James Woods
      Patten's Additional Regiment—Lt. Col. John Parke
      Grayson's Additional Regiment—Grayson
      Two guns—Capt. Thomas Welles
Durkee's Detachment (Varnum's Brigade)—Col. John Durkee
      Connecticut Battalion (4/8 CT)—Durkee
      Rhode Island Battalion (1/2 RI) Lt. Col. Jeremiah Olney
      Two guns—Capt. David Cook
Wayne's detachment—Brig. Gen. Anthony Wayne
      Wesson's Detachment of Picked Men—Col. James Wesson
      Stewart's Picked Men—Lt. Col. Walter Stewart
      Livingston's Picked Men—Col. Henry Beekman Livingston
      Two guns—Capt. Thomas Seward
Scott's Detachment—Brig. Gen. Charles Scott
      Cilley's Picked Men—Col. Joseph Cilley
      Gist's Battalion—Col. Mordecai Gist
      Butler's Picked Men—Lt. Col. William Butler
      Parker's Picked Men—Col. Richard Parker
      Four cannon
New Jersey Brigade—Brig. Gen. William Maxwell
      1 NJ—Col. Matthias Ogden
      2 NJ—Col. Israel Shreve
      3 NJ—Col. Elias Dayton

4 NJ—Col. Ephraim Martin
    Somerset County Light Horse—Lt. Col. Anthony White
    Two cannon
Jackson's Detachment—Col. Henry Jackson
    Jackson's Additional Regiment—Jackson
    Lee's Additional Regiment—Lt. Col. William Smith
    Henley's Additional Regiment—Maj. John Tyler
9th Pennsylvania—Col. Richard Butler
Morgan's Detachment—Col. Daniel Morgan
    Rifle Companies from the 6, 7, 8, 11 Virginia and 1, 4, 12 Penn
    Light Companies from 1 and 2 NC
    Picked men, 1 officer and 25 enlisted from the 13 brigades
    Washington's Guard, 2 officers and 80 enlisted
    Monmouth Militia
New Jersey Militia—Brig. Gen. Philemon Dickinson

Right Wing—Maj. Gen. Nathanael Greene

Woodford's Brigade—Brig. Gen. William Woodford
    3/7 Virginia—Col. William Heth
    11/15 Virginia—Lt. Col. John Cropper
Clark's Detachment—Col. Thomas Clark
    1 NC—Col. Thomas Clark
    2 NC—Col. John Patten
Poor's Brigade—Brig. Gen. Enoch Poor
    1 NH—Col. Joseph Cilley (detached)
    2 NH—Col. Nathan Hale
    3 NH—Col. Alexander Scammell
    2 NY—Col. Philip van Cortlandt
    4 NY—Col. Henry Beekman Livingston (detached)
Huntington's Brigade—Brig. Gen. Jedediah Huntington
    2/5 Connecticut—Col. Philip Bradley
    1/7 Connecticut—Col. Herman Swift
1st Maryland Brigade—Brig. Gen. William Smallwood
    1 MD—Col. John Hawkins Stone
    3 MD—Col. Mordecai Gist (detached)
    5 MD—Col. William Richardson
    7 MD—Col. John Gunby
    Delaware Regiment—Col. David Hall

2nd Maryland Brigade—Smallwood
    2 MD—Lt. Col. Thomas Woolford
    4 MD—Col. Josias Carvil Hall
    6 MD—Col. Otho Holland Williams
Muhlenberg's Brigade—Brig. Gen. Peter Muhlenberg
    1/5/9 VA—Maj. Thomas Marshall
    1 VA State—Col. George Gibson
    2 VA State—Col. Gregory Smith
    German Battalion—Lt. Col. Ludowick Weltner
Weedon's Brigade—Col. Christian Febiger
    2 VA—Febiger
    6 VA—Col. John Gibson
    10 VA—Col. John Green
    14 VA—Col. William Davies

Left Wing—Maj. Gen. William Alexander, Lord Stirling
1st Penn. Brigade—Col. William Irvine
    1 PA—Col James Chambers
    2 PA—Col. Henry Bicker
    7 PA—Irvine
    10 PA—Col. George Nagel
2nd Penn. Brigade—Col. Francis Johnston
    1 NY—Col. Goose van Schaick
    4 PA—Lt. Col. William Butler (detached)
    5 PA—Johnston
    11 PA—Col. Richard Humpton
3rd Penn Brigade—Col. Robert Magaw
    3 PA—Col. Thomas Craig
    6 PA—Lt. Col. Josaih Harmer
    12 PA—(unknown)
    Malcom's Additional—Lt. Col. Aaron Burr
    Spencer's Additional—Col. Oliver Spencer
Glover's Brigade—Brig. Gen. John Glover (detached, commanding West Point)
    1 MA—Col. Joseph Vose
    4 MA—Col. William Shephard
    13 MA—Col. Edward Wigglesworth
    15 MA—Col. Timothy Bigelow
Learned's Brigade—Col. John Bailey, senior officer
    2 MA—Col. John Bailey

8 MA—Col. Michael Jackson

9 MA—Col. James Wesson (detached)

Paterson's Brigade—Brig. Gen. John Paterson

10 MA—Col. Thomas Marshall

11 MA—Col. Benjamin Tupper

12 MA—Col. Samuel Brewer

14 MA—Col. Gamaliel Bradford Brown

Artillery—Brig. Gen. Henry Knox (detached to support various units)

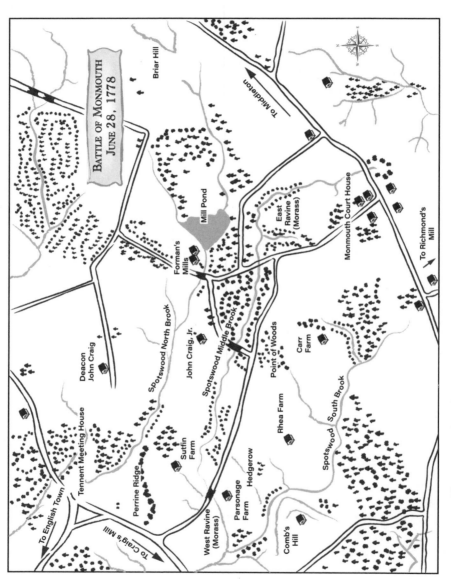

BATTLE OF MONMOUTH
JUNE 28, 1778

Briar Hill

To Middleton

Mill Pond

Forman's
Mills

East
Ravine
(Morass)

Monmouth Court House

To Richmond's
Mill

Deacon
John Craig

Spotswood North Brook

John Craig, Jr.

Spotswood Middle Brook

Point of Woods

Carr
Farm

Tennent Meeting House

Perrine Ridge

Sutfin
Farm

Hedgerow

Rhea Farm

Spotswood South Brook

To English Town

To Craig's Mill

West Ravine
(Morass)

Parsonage
Farm

Comb's
Hill

The area around Freehold, New Jersey, the site of Monmouth Court House. *Megan Dacus*

CHAPTER 4

An Imminent Battle

Englishtown to Monmouth Court House

The dusty road from Englishtown to the seat of Monmouth County winds through typical New Jersey farm country; fertile fields under cultivation broken by scrub pines, orchards, and patches of wild woods. Some of the farms grew grains such as corn, wheat, and rye. Originally Scottish and Dutch farmers had settled Monmouth County but now most were of English ancestry and there were a few African slaves. Typically, women tended gardens as well as the chores connected with the colonial homes such as rearing chickens, making butter, mending or making clothes, and providing food for their families. It was a scenic, pleasant ride along the Elizabethtown–Freehold Road for George Washington and his staff.

The main road heads three miles southeast until it forks at the Freehold Meeting House (referred to as the Tennent Meeting House after the name of the last two pastors), one fork going northeast to South Amboy, the other south to Craig's Mill. The terrain is generally sandy soil often broken by small streams or creeks. Taking the road south to Craig's Mill, there is a hook to the southeast around low Perrine Ridge; passing the ridge it continues to Monmouth Court House. From the Tennent Meeting House to Monmouth Court House is nearly five miles. Just past the ridge, the road moves through low ground to a small causeway or bridge that crosses a sluggish stream, the Spotswood Middle Brook or Weamaconk, and then wanders up a small rise toward Monmouth Court House. The low area between Perrine Ridge and the small incline, wet and marshy even in summer, is referred to as the West Ravine or the West Morass.

The brook turns just after the causeway and parallels the road until just north of the court house, where it turns south and forms the East Ravine. Just north of the Tennent Meeting House is another creek, Spotswood North Brook or McGellairds, that roughly follows the same course of the Middle Brook until it runs into the mill pond by Forman's Mill almost directly north of Monmouth Court House. There is also Spotswood South Brook, sometimes referred to as the Wemrock, which forks off the Middle Brook not far from the causeway, passes the slopes of Comb's Hill to the south and parallels the Middle Brook to a position near the Baptist Meeting House southwest of Monmouth Court House.

From the Tennent Meeting House to Freehold, the road makes its way through farmland, rich enough to entice many Hessians to desert, interrupted by small woods or orchards. Like many counties in rural New Jersey, the names of the farms and points of interest reflect the residents of the neighborhood. The Parsonage Farm, just past the West Ravine as the road goes east, was the home of the pastor of the Tennent Meeting House. The Rhea Farm was next, rented by William Wikoff, Jr., and then the Carr, or Ker, Farm. North of the Spotswood Middle Brook was the John Craig Farm—the Craigs were a typical family with several farms in the area. Comb's Hill sat on the land of Comb's Farm, and Perrine Farm gave its name to the nearby ridge.

The road follows the course of the Spotswood Middle Brook, near the Carr Farm crossing another ravine, often referred to as the Middle Ravine. Eventually it turns south just past the Carr Farm to enter the village of Freehold. The small town was the seat of Monmouth County and site of the county court house. A small cluster of dwellings grew up around the court house and the village there was often referred to simply as Monmouth or Monmouth Court House. Freehold had been the county seat since 1715. There were about 40 buildings in the area but aside from the court house the only major edifice in the vicinity was St. Peter's Episcopal Church. The court house itself was an unimposing wood structure. In the village the road splits, one fork leading southwest toward Allentown whence the British had approached Monmouth and the other northeast past Briar Hill toward Middleton and on to Sandy Hook. It was on the latter road that the British began to move in the early hours of June 28.

To the east and northeast of the village lay flat land bordered on the north by the mill pond of Forman's Mill and trees along a branch of the Spotswood North Brook. Just east of the town was an extension of the Spotswood Middle Brook that flowed through another gully called the East Ravine or, because of its soggy, wet nature, the East Morass.

The Situation

Clinton's army continued moving after the rear guard rebuffed the militia advance earlier that morning. Clinton's mission was clear. He was to take his troops, the refugees, and wagons to Sandy Hook. He was also willing to give battle to the Americans but only if he could do so without endangering his logistics train and the Loyalists from Philadelphia.

The bulk of the Washington's army, around 7,000 men in all, was camped near Englishtown. He had a good idea of the strength and position of the British army thanks to the reconnaissance of Steuben, Moylan, and the various militia leaders. Washington also believed his orders were understood: Lee was to attack the British rear guard as it moved, and he would bring up the rest of the army if the action became too involved for Lee's 5,500 troops. The subordinate commanders of Lee's detachment knew only that Washington wanted an attack. Lee's intentions were less clear: were they to go straight at the British, try a flanking movement, or continue the pursuit as they had been doing the past few days merely harassing the British?

Lee Moves

Advised by Washington to keep a close watch on the British to prevent a surprise attack by the redcoats, Lee agreed that it was prudent. He sent a note by Lieutenant Colonel Fitzgerald, Washington's aide who had delivered the message, that he expected the British to turn on him to "make a stroke at them."[1] The excitement of a possible battle was almost palatable as the various officers dashed back and forth delivering their messages.

Late on the evening of June 27 Washington sent another message to Lee fearing that the British might get away before they could be engaged. He instructed Lee to start a party forward to contact the British and to coordinate with Morgan's detachment in an attack on the British after they began to move. Lee received the note about 1:00 am on Sunday, June 28, but it was not until 3:00 am that he ordered Grayson's detachment to move out to contact the enemy, both to prevent being surprised and to maintain contact with the British column when it began to move. Grayson immediately awakened his men with drums beating and officers gathering their companies. Lee sent the light horseman on to deliver Washington's message to Dickinson and Morgan.[2]

Militia scouts noticed the movement of British troops as soon as the redcoats began their march. Dickinson had reported the progress of the British from the court house area to both Washington and Lee. Grayson's troops, ordered to maintain contact with the British rear guard, had been unable to procure proper guides. David Forman finally stepped forward to provide local intelligence and lead the column. Waiting on guides consumed time and when Grayson's detachment finally moved out it was about three hours after being awakened. Meanwhile Dickinson's report that the British were moving had arrived and

Lee ordered the entire advanced corps to move out. The slumbering soldiers were jolted out of their stupor by the shouts of their leaders and the roll of the drums. Companies formed up, turned into regiments or detachments and prepared to march. Any of the troops that still had their packs and coats left them behind as they knew the pattern of weather and anticipated a hot day that the warm morning presaged. Those troops that were injured or sick remained in place to guard any remaining personal baggage.

Washington's main body, camped about three miles from Lee's advanced corps, was also moving. Now that he was sure the enemy was on the march, and unsure if Dickinson had informed Lee about the British movement, the commander in chief sent Lieutenant Colonel Richard Meade with the news. Meade repeated Washington's earlier instructions for Lee to attack as soon as possible and he would bring the main body up to support him. The message emphasized the attack but also left the mode of advance to Lee according to circumstances.[3] Meade arrived as Lee's troops were beginning to move.

Lee's lack of clear directions plagued the advanced corps in the early morning darkness and prevented a timely departure. Maxwell's brigade, composed of many inexperienced troops, was supposed to be at the tail of the column but found itself moving out in front of Wayne and Scott's men. Maxwell had to pull his men out of line and then wait for the others to pass. Jackson's detachment was also out of line, cutting in at the rear of Scott's men, further slowing the process. Not knowing many of his subordinate officers by sight, Lee had to depend on others to direct the various detachments into position. Lee was taken aback when he was informed by his own aides that the British had not left their encampment.

There was more confusion when a horse trotted up bearing Lieutenant Colonel Benjamin Walker, one of von Steuben's aides, who indicated that the British army was indeed moving. Although the British army had a large baggage train and the various detachments would take hours to get moving, Lee hesitated. Confused about British intentions and afraid that part of the British army was turning on him, he ordered the advanced units to halt. Lee knew the approximate position of the British around Monmouth Court House but did not move into a position to personally observe them. He was aware of the British disposition of their best troops at the rear of their column supported by cavalry.

Meade delivered his message from Washington at this point, emphasizing that Washington wanted an attack, and the main army was moving to support Lee's advance. Pushed by Meade's persistence, Lee ordered the troops to resume their march.

Things were further complicated by rumors that the British had feigned their movement to draw on the Americans and then steal a march around the right, southern flank, to get in between the advanced guard and Washington's main body. The leaders of the various detachments were also unsure what the day's objective was. Lee had not indicated if they were to attack or merely continue the pursuit of the British. With the stops and starts of the early hours, it was unclear if they were even to pursue the British.

Lee, still not sure that the entire British army was leaving, hesitated, and split his command. Instead of following the others to the east, Lee ordered Maxwell's New Jersey Brigade to take the fork of the road at the Perrine Farm toward the south and Craig's Mill, to prevent the British attempting a flanking movement to the south as the advanced corps continued along the road to Monmouth. Maxwell had not marched far when he received new orders. Lee decided that the entire British army was indeed leaving the Court House and the New Jersey Brigade needed to get back on the main road to follow Lee's column. Exasperated, Maxwell turned his brigade of bewildered men around and rejoined the main column.

Dickinson met Grayson's advancing column just past the West Ravine. The militia leader gave Grayson a quick account of his earlier skirmish with the British. It was the appearance of Grayson's detachment that had helped drive away the enemy rear guard earlier. Dickinson also pointed out the lay of the land with an emphasis on how poor their present position was. If they continued, the mushy morass and brook would be to their rear with only the small causeway to cross the brook if threatened by the British. Essentially the advance was channeled between the two lines of the Spotswood Brook, the Middle and South creeks forming a barrier on each flank if the Americans continued along the road to Monmouth Court House. Dickinson was not sure all the British were moving off and cautioned that it might be a trap. Grayson acknowledged the warning and continued, following orders, advancing over the bridge and up the slope. Facing him there were the men of Colonel John Simcoe's Queen's Rangers and the green-clad British moved back as Grayson formed his Virginians and deployed a cannon. Grayson followed the British closely but cautiously.

Lee and Wayne arrived a few minutes later and Dickinson also updated them. Dickinson cautioned against a quick advance; he was still unsure if the entire enemy force had left. Lee, who had an amiable dislike for Dickinson, equivocated. The two exchanged thoughts and it was obvious that Lee was not happy with the conflicting reports about British movements. Dickinson believed that the advanced corps should not move past the West Ravine until the situation was clearer, repeating the fact that the ravine would form an impediment in their rear if the British flanked them. More confusion resulted from reports of a body of unknown troops to the north of the Middle Brook. John Durkee's men were sent to check out the possible enemy force, but they found the strangers to be only a large body of militia under militia general Frederick Frelinghuysen. Lee ordered this group of local soldiers to outpost the road to Craig's Mill, fulfilling the mission he had originally given to Maxwell earlier to watch their right flank.

One of the most experienced officers in the Continental Army, Anthony Wayne would be in most of the action throughout June 28 at Monmouth. *The Miriam and Ira D. Wallach Division of Art, Prints and Photographs: Print Collection, The New York Public Library.* "*Brigr. Gen. Anthony Wayne*"

The column marched on slowly, moving in fits and starts as each new rumor reached Lee. He contemplated the situation until Lieutenant Colonel John Laurens, who had been with von Steuben, appeared and told Lee that the entire enemy force was indeed in motion. With the situation somewhat clearer, Lee acted. He ordered Wayne to take command of Grayson, Jackson, and Colonel Richard Butler's 9th Pennsylvania, and advance with the intent to attack the British. Colonel Eleazer Oswald took four cannons and joined Wayne. Lee gave Wayne no other instructions and did not inform his other subordinates of his intentions. More confusion ensued as Jackson and Butler's men were farther back in the column and were forced to pass through several other regiments to join Grayson. The order of march was now Wayne leading his three detachments, followed by Durkee commanding Wayne's original command of Wesson, Stewart, and Livingston's "picked men," then the brigade of Charles Scott, also made up of "picked men," and finally Maxwell's New Jersey brigade bringing up the rear.

Throughout these actions, Lee's demeanor reflected a calm, cautious general. He seemed in no hurry and did not appear in a rush to battle. The serpentine column of Americans, about five thousand fighters, most of them having discarded any regimental coats and now dressed in their shirts and small clothes only, slogged wearily through the morning heat, passing through the area between the Spotswood South Brook and the Spotswood Middle Brook. Somewhere in front were Simcoe's green-coated Rangers. Twice the column stopped and prepared to deploy as rumors reached Lee that the British had turned and were attacking. These false reports slowed progress and it was after 9:00 am by the time Lee arrived in view of Monmouth Court House.

Out in front, Butler's men moved toward the village of Freehold, driving away some British cavalry near the town. The bulk of the advanced corps soon arrived. Lee had the men wait in the shade of a point of woods north of the village; some munched on their rations in the shadows, while Lee, Wayne, and several officers rode toward the British to get the lay of the land.

Lee ordered Wayne out on the plain, close to the British rear guard, to the east of the ravine and personally moved to a position to observe the British and the terrain. Lee looked over the ground; a ravine to his rear, the village of Freehold with the court house on his right, and an orchard near a wood-covered stream to his left. He could see the small mound of Briar Hill rising next to the Middleton Road three miles northeast of Freehold, and near it a few hundred red-coated infantry and cavalry who appeared to be milling around but moving toward the left and the leading American troops. Lee initially intended that Wayne would move through the village to the right, entice the British, and then Lee would cut them off by moving north of the village between the British rear guard and its main body. Instead, when the Americans under Wayne—Butler, Grayson, and Jackson—arrived just north of Monmouth Court House they veered to the left across the base of the East Ravine and into the cool of the woods to the north past Foreman's Mills and its pond, parallel to the Middleton Road facing the British across the plain. Lee decided to alter his plans. He allowed Wayne to continue to the left.

As Wayne's men moved out, Jackson didn't follow, holding his men back and keeping them in the shade. He reported to Lee that his men were short of cartridges, having only 13 or 14 per man. For some reason they did not have the 40 cartridges the other regiments had. Lee told him to have his sergeants go to the other detachments ahead and take one round from each man. Once they had their allotment of ammunition, it was a hard march for Jackson's men to rejoin Butler's detachment at the front. It was the second time that day that Jackson had to rush his troops from one place to another and the soldiers, not used to the pace of marching, were tiring easily in the late morning sun. They moved lethargically into the woods, catching up with Butler near the Middleton Road.[4]

Moving into a position to attack the retreating British, Wayne's men passed an orchard and some trees to face the British. Charles Scott and his men passed the East Ravine and slipped in behind Wayne. Maxwell brought his brigade into some woods to their right rear. For some reason Lee failed to bring the rest of the advanced detachment on line with Wayne. He did not order Wayne or any other commander to press the attack now as the British were moving.

Lee had a good view of the British and the terrain. About five hundred enemy infantry and several hundred cavalrymen were in view. The main body of the British army was on the road to Middleton somewhere off in the distance. Eleazer Oswald arrived on the scene, unlimbered his guns, and brought them across the East Ravine. He set them up on the edge of an orchard to the right rear of the rest of the advanced guard and prepared to open fire on the redcoats.

British Movement

During the morning, while Lee was closing on the British, Clinton's army was well on its way to Middleton and Sandy Hook. Cornwallis and his division moved out last that morning. They comprised the bulk of British combat

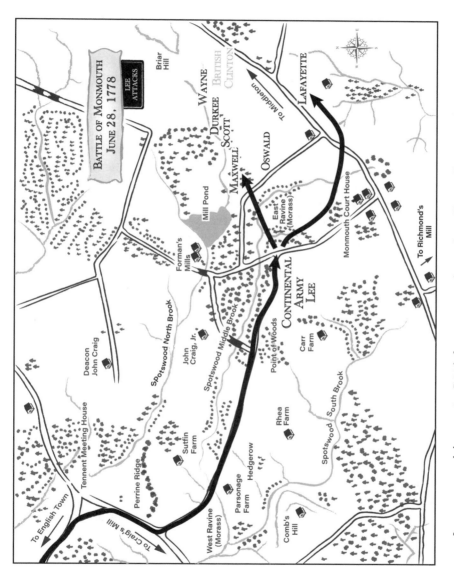

Lee moves toward the retreating British forces to engage them and possibly cut off a rear guard. *Megan Dacus*

power: three infantry brigades, Foot Guards, and the Hessian and British Grenadiers. Clinton himself stayed near the rear guard, made up of the elite First Light Infantry, Simcoe's (Queen's) Rangers, and the 16th Light Dragoons. Militia dogged the heels of the British with short, sharp fights that were loud and smoky but caused few casualties.

During the morning movement some of the British left Freehold in a minor orgy of violence, setting some buildings on fire, killing a few cattle, stealing furniture, and committing random acts of vandalism. Even Clinton's presence did little to dissuade the destruction. A local resident complained after seeing his home burned: "John Benham's house and barn they wantonly tore and broke down so as to render them useless. It may not be improper to mention that my own and Benjamin Covenhoven's houses, adjoined the farm and were in full view of the place where Clinton was quartered. In the neighbourhood below the court house they burnt the houses of Matthias Lane, Cornelius Covenhoven, John Antonidas and one Emmons…"[5] Except for the vandals, the British moved out quickly and efficiently. Clinton directed the order of march essentially as before: Cornwallis' division, containing the best of the British troops, provided a rear guard while Knyphausen's division led off protecting the logistics train. Militia swarmed around the column, wounding and capturing several men near the wagons and forcing the German general to deploy men to check the offending locals. It was difficult to guard so long a train of wagons, carriages, and livestock. Knyphausen was forced to position two artillery pieces atop Briar Hill and a full brigade of troops was deployed to support the guns. It was only through these precautions that Knyphausen was able to drive away the pesky militia, but the threat of irregulars disrupting the baggage column influenced the British command throughout the rest of the day.

Advanced Corps

Anthony Wayne deployed his men along the woods on the banks of the Spotswood North Brook that extended east from the Mill Pond. Wayne, a surveyor before the war, was a man with a fierce disposition and physical makeup that made him aggressive and eager for action. After the "Paoli Massacre," Wayne and his men regained some of their reputation with a solid performance in the defeat at the battle of Germantown but even that brave action was marred by an incident that involved another American unit firing on Wayne's men in a thick fog. Wayne's conduct in the upcoming battle could do much to redeem his reputation.

Wayne, commanding Jackson and Butler, kept them moving toward the retreating enemy, staying near the woods along a creek bed. Just behind was Grayson's detachment. Wayne had no doubt as to the instructions from Washington to attack, but he was unclear how Lee wanted him to proceed. A small body of cavalry of the Somerset County militia cantered along with them just outside the woods. Maxwell and Scott were just to his rear but instead of pushing the two detachments on to support Wayne, Lee ordered them to halt.

Clinton Acts

Clinton was aware he must protect his baggage and issued orders for Knyphausen to proceed with the wagons toward the heights of Navesink. All morning Clinton had been lingering near the rear guard. He had seen the militia and ordered out covering parties to discover if the Americans were moving around his flanks with anything more than militia. He had also seen the head of Grayson's column pushing toward Freehold. That had not bothered him initially because he estimated the advancing Americans at less than one thousand. Just before 10:00 am, Henry Clinton, who had displayed his tactical skill at several previous battles in the Revolution, began to form a clear picture of what was happening and what he must do. He determined that the Americans were deploying regulars in force toward his rear and sensed an opportunity. He quickly went to Lord Cornwallis and determined to strike the rebels with the flower of the British army.

Clinton welcomed a general engagement and eagerly accepted the opportunity for a chance to destroy the rebel army and possibly achieve a victory that could end the war. He quickly formulated a plan. He ensured that the long train of wagons continued toward Sandy Hook, protected by Knyphausen's men. Then he would turn Cornwallis' Division and strike Wayne's detachment, the Americans closest to him. To keep the Americans from making any flanking attacks he would launch his own flanking attack. While engaging Wayne's men, he would send a detachment to his left, southeast, toward Freehold. Orders were issued; the well-trained British regulars executed the movement to the rear with alacrity. It would take time for him to turn around all of Cornwallis' division and Clinton knew he had a severe handicap. Unlike Washington's ragged army, Clinton was burdened with a long logistics train.

The realization for Henry Clinton and the British troops that they faced the Continental Army, or a large portion of it, was a satisfying thought. After the long winter of inactivity in Philadelphia, the escape of the "Boy" Lafayette at Barren Hill, the sad experience with the Carlisle Commission, and the ignominious retreat from Philadelphia, here was a chance for the soldiers take out their frustrations on the rebels and settle things with the bayonet. Even though he was initially outnumbered by Lee's five thousand men Clinton didn't wait for his orders to reach the bulk of his men. He reformed the rear guard, deployed artillery, and gave the order for his cavalry to charge a group of militia horsemen that appeared to be covering the enemy forces.

Wayne

Farthest forward of Wayne's detachment were Colonel Richard Butler's men. Butler, a physically strong Irishman from a family of gunsmiths, led the 9th Pennsylvania consisting of about 300 men. A soldier in the French and Indian War, Butler was one of five brothers in Continental service (his brother William commanded a picked detachment in Scott's command), and was a seasoned veteran who had been in service since the beginning of the conflict. His men

Colonel Richard Butler led the advance that engaged the British rear guard. *The Miriam and Ira D. Wallach Division of Art, Prints and Photographs: Print Collection, The New York Public Library.* *"Richard Butler"*

were partially covered by woods and screened by the local horsemen of the Somerset County Light Horse under Lieutenant Colonel Anthony White. Grayson's detachment was arrayed to the rear of Butler near Freehold. Aligned to their right rear were the men of Jackson's regiment. They could see in the distance to their front the British soldiers along the road and the smartly dressed dragoons cantering about.

It was about 10:30 am. The British horsemen drew up in ranks and then wheeled about, moving toward the militia cavalry. The horses picked up speed, faster and faster, charging directly at the New Jersey horsemen. White's militia horse fled, discretion being the better part of valor when facing the excellently trained and equipped Imperial riders, uncovering the muskets of Butler's men. There was a rhythmic plodding sound as the British horsemen neared the American line and a background noise of the snapping of muskets from dismounted dragoons providing a covering fire for the advancing horsemen. The helmeted dragoons abruptly reined in and stopped short as they discovered the lines of Continental infantrymen partially hidden in the trees in front of them. Some discharged their pistols while others prepared to continue their charge. Pistol balls passed through Butler's position, and few of the balls sailed through Jackson's troops coming online with Butler. The pistol fire had no effect on the Americans. With a loud crash, American muskets broke the Sabbath's calm, concealing the firing line in smoke as their musket balls emptied British saddles. Riderless horses continued towards the Americans for a few yards, stopped, and milled around for a few moments, then turned and joined the cavalrymen who had been repulsed. Several dragoons fired a few parting shots at the solid line of American infantrymen, but the horsemen then retired. Smoke drifted away as Butler's men prepared for the next wave of attackers, teeth biting through cartridges as they reloaded. Their noses bloodied and pride bruised, the British cavalry contented themselves by retreating out of range.

Wayne was excited, his blood was up, and his troops mirrored his spirit as they now advanced slowly toward the British. The American line moved forward and to their left, buoyed by the fact that the magnificently dressed British cavalry had been repulsed, but the rebels were held back by Lee's order to merely fix the enemy's attention. Now the British would face the bayonets of a thousand American soldiers. A sense of excitement filled Wayne as the Pennsylvanian led his men toward the British rear guard: he was sure his men would garner glory today. Detecting an opportunity, he sent a message asking Lee to bring up the rest of the advanced guard to attack the British. Unfortunately for Wayne, Lee had other ideas.

Wayne's troops, idling in the open, came under fire from a pair of 3-pounder cannon near the Middleton Road. Wayne took his men off amongst the nearby woods to help screen them as they moved to their left. It appeared as if there was only a small force of the enemy, less than a thousand, covering the retreat of the British on the Middleton Road. To Wayne's rear, Eleazer Oswald's guns were making loud popping sounds as they fired solid shot at the British formations. Oswald, an obstinate, opinionated man who quickly made friends or enemies, held his ground as the British artillery tried to silence his guns. Lee sent Durkee's detachment to protect the guns and they took casualties from the British cannon fire, losing several wounded. Durkee himself fell, severely wounded in the arm. His wound proved to be so serious that he had to turn over command to Lieutenant Colonel Jeremiah Olney. Durkee was not the only one injured. A soldier ran up to Captain Stephen Olney of the Rhode Island Battalion and said "Corporal - - - - is killed." Olney coolly replied, "Never mind, he has paid the last debt."[6] The New Englanders pulled back into cover and left Oswald's guns in the open.

Lee, at the Court House

Lee was delighted at his prospects. Viewing the battlefield before him, he saw only a few outnumbered British soldiers; most were already on the march to New York. To Lee, the picture before him was inviting. He remarked to Colonel Grayson that, "by God he would take them all."[7] To the left was a wood and a stream, on the plain before him were redcoats clustered around the road leading toward the northeast and the rest of the British army, and to his right was an open area to the east of Monmouth Court House. Off in the distance was Briar Hill. Unfortunately, he failed to move up and take more direct command of the efforts of Wayne's troops on the left. Instead of pushing Scott and Maxwell up to support Wayne, Lee stayed near the village. Scott and Maxwell did not close on Wayne but remained behind and to the right of Wayne.

It was about 11:00 am. Lee had missed the opportunity that Washington had intended when he gave the original orders. Washington's orders before the battle had emphasized an attack but with discretion if the attack might be under unfavorable conditions. With the rebuff of the enemy cavalry, Lee had a chance to push forward his full force. He didn't. Rethinking his options, he felt that such an attack would just push the British rear guard back into their main body or bring the main body back to support the rear guard. Either of these options would have satisfied the spirit of Washington's intention that an attack was made. Briefly, Lee thought he would ride to the left to supervise the action there but changed his mind and remained near Freehold. Lee missed an opportunity to observe the situation on the left personally. His lack of aides to communicate and observe proved to be an important handicap.

Instead of acting quickly to support Wayne's men, Lee decided on a more difficult maneuver that would take time. In doing so he gave up the initiative to Clinton. Every minute Lee spent redeploying his troops, Clinton was pushing more of Cornwallis' troops toward Freehold. The Americans would spend a great deal of time trying to set up their new maneuver while Clinton was already moving.

Lee had originally anticipated immediately moving a detachment to the left of Wayne via Forman's Mill and attacking the retreating British from there. Now he decided to push in a different direction. He chose to use Wayne to hold the attention of the British and then push a force around the British left, southern, flank. Hopefully, Wayne and the Americans to the north, on the British right, would maintain their position in the woods and keep the attention of the enemy. Wayne was to keep moving but not to press: "rather affect shyness rather than confidence, lest the appearance of vigor should give the enemy reason to think we were in force."[8] They would fix the enemy in place.

Lee decided that Lafayette would lead a detachment and push southeast toward the enemy left. Lafayette pulled the men of James Wesson, Walter Stewart, and Henry Beekman Livingston from the line and led them toward the village and the British left flank. The time lost in doing this proved a mistake. While Lee took time to inform Lafayette and the Frenchman organized his detachment, the British moved along the Middleton Road across the front of the idle detachments of Wayne, Grayson, Jackson, Scott, and Maxwell.

Lec sent messengers out to the various brigades to inform them of his intentions, but word did not get to many of the regiments due to a lack of aides. Lee was frustrated with the lack of mounted men he could use as messengers and wished he had a troop of dragoons to help spread the word. At this point James McHenry, one of Washington's aides, approached Lee and asked if there was any message for the commander in chief. Lee spoke in a positive tone, sure of what he was saying, briefly describing the position of the British and then telling McHenry: "Inform his Excellency… that the rear of the enemy was composed of 1500 or 2000 men; that he expected to fall in with them and had great certainty of cutting them off."[9] This was the first news that Washington had of the action.

Even as Lee slowly pushed Lafayette to the right, the British moved more quickly to cover that flank. Not long after McHenry left, Captain Nicholas

Gilman, assistant adjutant, appeared and told Lee he had seen the retreating enemy. He too was going back to report to Washington. Was there a message he could take to the commander in chief? Lee calmly informed him to: "… tell him they have attacked the rear guard of the enemy and… were in hopes of cutting them off." Gilman whirled and rode back along the road until he found Washington and the main body passing the Tennent Meeting House. The message was slightly premature, and hopeful, as Lee had yet to attack. Washington's view of the battle was colored by the messages of McHenry and Gilman. There appeared to be no need to hurry the main body.

Lee watched Lafayette move his detachment southeast toward the enemy left. Meanwhile, Wayne's troops continued to move east along the woods, not attacking but maintaining the attention of the British as instructed by Lee. The detachments of Scott and Maxwell were in the woods on the left near Wayne. Durkee's men, now commanded by Giles Russell of the 4th Connecticut, were tucked into the woods between Scott and Wayne. Oswald's guns soon found themselves the only Americans between Lafayette and Scott as those detachments moved right and left.

At that moment Washington was moving with the main body around Perrine Ridge. From the messages he had received it appeared that the British were in full retreat and Lee was making some sort of attack. His goal of taking some sort of action before the British reached New York appeared to be fulfilled.

British Counterattack

More of Clinton's men appeared as Lafayette made his move. The Queen's Rangers and 1st Light Infantry lined up to screen Wayne. Cornwallis was directed with the remainder of his division to flank the American center, Durkee and Oswald. In doing so they mirrored Lafayette's movement. At least 10 pieces of artillery fired at the various rebel formations, sometimes with such unpleasant closeness that Henry Jackson thought the enemy was targeting him personally. During these actions there were few casualties. Along the Middleton Road, Cornwallis worked to turn his 6,000 men about to face the Americans. Clinton could not initially use his entire force because of the harassment of his baggage train by the militia groups, who were never in great strength but omnipresent all day.

Lee

Like two great arms, the Americans appeared to reach around the rear guard of the British, Wayne on the left and Lafayette moving around to the right. Because of the terrain, Lee was able to observe his two wings in action, although he lost track of his farthest units in the woods along the creek to the left. Everything was going according to plan; his five thousand troops would soon bite off and maul what appeared to be the two-thousand-man British rear guard.

Surveying the field, Lee became hesitant, for even as troops under Lafayette crossed in front of him to attack the British left, more British soldiers were appearing in the distance, including more cavalry. It appeared as if the entire British army was turning about and might challenge his plan, their cavalry in particular moving ominously off to the right of the court house. He summoned Lafayette and the two heatedly exchanged views. The eager Frenchman wanted to continue with the original plan, gain the British flank and attack the enemy, even if a few more enemy troops appeared. Washington and the main body were only a little way off. But Lee began to waver.

Lafayette's detachment moved through the village and continued to the east. To Lee, still reluctant, it appeared as if the British were gaining strength and he recalled the prowess of British troops. Lafayette disagreed. Lee was showing that his absence as a prisoner and the time he left the army to mingle with Congress in Philadelphia had prevented him from getting to know his American soldiers or his officers as well as he knew the British officers with whom he had spent 17 comfortable months. He had a lack of confidence in the abilities of the Americans and overconfidence in the abilities of the British. But Lafayette was determined: the redheaded Frenchman argued that a chance must be taken. Lafayette told Lee that the British had been defeated before and it could happen again.

Exasperated but not entirely convinced, Lee acquiesced and the American troops under Lafayette continued their move past the village of Freehold, then executed a fine left wheel just as they had been trained by von Steuben that previous winter. Livingston and Wesson were just east of the court house itself and Stewart's men on the right of the Middleton Road, all facing toward the approaching British. Less than 600 yards separated the two forces, Lafayette with his back to the court house. They were close enough to suffer from British artillery, losing several men. One of those wounded was Colonel James Wesson, formerly commander of the 9th Massachusetts but now in command of one of the detachments of "picked men." He was carried from the field and replaced by Marylander Nathaniel Ramsey.

Washington's aide John Laurens observed the interaction between Lee and Lafayette. He asked for a report on the action, offering to take it back to Washington. Lafayette, excited and eager for the glory of the battle, was calm enough to think that Lee needed help and requested the aide to tell Washington to move up as fast as possible.

Lee calmly watched his plan slowly unfold as he had directed. Scott and Maxwell had crossed the Spotswood Middle Brook, entered the trees, and were moving to face the British right with Wayne. Lafayette's men were approaching the British left. At the moment it all seemed to be going in the Americans' favor, but Lee didn't like the way the British kept moving toward the open ground on his own right with a large number of cavalry. Daniel Morgan, with his 800 men, was off the American right, in perfect position to help cover that flank, but Lee did not contact Daniel Morgan.

Morgan remained at Richmond Mills about three miles to the south of Freehold. oblivious to the developing battle. He had received a cautionary message from Washington earlier that morning: "As your Corps is out of supporting Distance I would have you confine yourself to observing the motions of the Enemy—unless an opportunity offers of intercepting some small Parties—and by no means to come to an Engagement with your whole Body unless you are tempted by some very evident advantage… but the orders are repeated to guard against accidents."[10] Washington also sent orders to Lee instructing him to contact Morgan to let him know "what parts they have to act."[11] Lee sent word to Morgan at 1:00 am on June 28, instructing him to attack the following morning, which, as noted above, Morgan misinterpreted as the morning of June 29.[12]

During the tense minutes while Lafayette was moving into position, Eleazer Oswald's guns had been consistently firing, inflicting only a few casualties on the British but keeping the enemy at arm's length. One of his guns was damaged by enemy fire and several men were casualties; the rest of the gun crews were slowly exhausted from the working of the hot guns in the increasingly warm day. Oswald noted that he was running short of ammunition and his supply was behind the East Morass. He couldn't get more ammunition across the ravine, so he decided to fall back past the East Ravine to resupply at the caissons.

Oswald informed Lee of his intention and Lee agreed to the move. The general would use Scott's men to cover the area in the battle line that Oswald had vacated. He sent several messengers with orders for Scott to hold the position formerly covered by Oswald's guns. Unfortunately, none of the messengers could find Scott and he never moved back to replace Oswald.

Butler's men held their position in the woods to the British right. Butler, Grayson, and Jackson's men used the cover of a small depression out of sight of the rest of the advanced corps. Wayne's two cannon fired away at the British, dull crumps signaling each shot, but they were more an irritant than a threat. British artillery fired back with more accuracy and effect in a virtual cacophony of loud sounds, encouraging the Americans to remain under cover. Wayne sent

American artillery at the battle of Monmouth performed excellent service. Eleazer Oswald ably led sections of cannon in the early part of the battle, during the retreat and at the hedgerow. *New York Public Library, Lossing, Benson John (1813–1891), 1863*

several messengers back to Lee to request reinforcements. The messengers either received no straight answer or were treated dismissively. Wayne worried about the buildup of British to his right and a lack of reinforcements. Washington had expected them to attack but Wayne continued holding in place without any guidance other than to threaten the British. Where was the attack?

Charles Scott and William Maxwell were just northeast of where Oswald's guns had been positioned. Moving along the woods and advancing towards the British, Scott's men never reached a position close enough to come to grips with the enemy. As the detachment moved near the edge of the woods, Scott saw something he didn't like as they moved into the open. He noticed large numbers of British appearing along the Middleton Road heading toward the village, yet that wasn't what bothered him. What confused him was the sight of Oswald's artillery leaving the line and heading back behind the ravine. In addition, he could not see Wayne's men to his left as they had taken cover in woods. With no one on the right or left, it appeared as if Scott and Maxwell, located just to the rear of Scott, were alone without orders. Scott's only contact with Lee was a brief conversation with Lee's adjutant who had no new orders for him. Scott talked to Maxwell and pointed out the lack of direction and the apparent lack of support for their detachments. He decided to fall back to the woods near the East Ravine and get some direction. Scott halted his advance and ordered his men to move to their rear into some trees. Confused, the detachment moved off by regiments and lost some of its order. Maxwell tried to follow Scott's movement, but he was confronted by the deep ravine of the morass and forced toward the right flank and Lafayette's men.

As his detachment moved out into the open just east of Monmouth Court House, Lafayette sensed something was amiss. Some units on the American left seemed to be moving without direction. Some detachments appeared to be withdrawing and there was no communication among the various leaders. Lee's failure to communicate his intentions combined with misunderstandings as commanders were thrown together with picked men from different brigades and were often not sure of the proper chain of command. The last-minute appointments of Wayne and Lafayette added to confusion.

To add to the chaos, British artillery continued to throw solid shot at the Americans. A new group of British, the entire Second Infantry Brigade and the horsemen of the 17th Dragoons, were moving toward Lafayette's right, attempting to gain that flank. Lafayette ordered his men to halt and move to their right rear to refuse the flank to the British seeking the open ground on that side. Even as the detachment began to deploy, an officer appeared from Lafayette's left with the news that General Scott was retreating. Within a few minutes, he received orders from Lee to use the buildings in the village of Freehold around the court house as cover. Lafayette instructed his men to do so, falling back toward the shelter of the buildings.

During these moments of confusion, Major John Clark, a clerk who had offered his services to Washington as another messenger, arrived with a message from the commander in chief to Lee: "…to annoy the Enemy as much as possible as in his power, but at the same time proceed with caution and take care that the Enemy don't draw him into a scrape; that I have information the Enemy's rear have left Monmouth, have ordered the troops with me to throw off their Packs, and will march to reinforce him." Lee was at a point of uncertainty and replied; "I shall not advance a foot further, my men are fatigued excessively and it would be sacrificing them to pursue."[13] The choice, to advance or pursue, was no longer possible for Lee. The initiative had passed to the British.

The confusion caused by the lack of clear command is illustrated by the case of Colonel Stewart, who had started out under Wayne's command that morning. Now Stewart's men formed the extreme right flank of Lee's advanced detachment under the command of Lafayette. In just a short time, Stewart was given direction from Lafayette to move to the right, received contrary orders from two different aides, another from Lee himself, from another aide, from Lee again, and finally from Lafayette to move into the village. For the soldiers, not to mention their commander, it was chaotic.

Feisty Anthony Wayne found himself almost beyond the British rear guard as the American forces echeloned toward their right rear, anchored on Freehold. Wayne had been following his orders, slowly moving left to entice the enemy but not to push them. Grayson was in view of Briar Hill and wanted Jackson to join him but Jackson demurred, keeping his men in a defile for protection. At this point Wayne had Grayson and Butler way out in front of the rest of the American army. Wayne took a quick look across the plain that separated him from the court house to his right rear and saw a startling picture. The men of Lafayette's detachment were changing position, moving back to the court house. Oswald's artillery, which had been supporting the present position, was moving back across the East Ravine. To add to his concern, it appeared as if Scott and Maxwell, who were supposed to be supporting him, were now disappearing back into the woods to his right rear. To him it looked as if most of the other troops of Lee's advanced corps were withdrawing just when the British were increasing their numbers to his front and to his right. If this were the case it would leave his men alone on the flat ground northeast of the court house with little room to escape; a creek bordered by woods to their left, to their rear a ravine difficult to cross, and increasing numbers of British to their front. Wayne didn't panic but instead sent Colonel Benjamin Fishbourne to find General Lee to ask for more troops. As a precaution Wayne pulled Butler's men back toward the rest of his detachment, under cover. At this point none of Lee's subordinate commanders, Lafayette, Wayne, Maxwell, or Scott, estimated the enemy at more than two thousand infantry and a few hundred cavalry.

Maxwell and Scott's men continued their retreat into the woods and were soon out of sight of those troops on the right. The two commanders conferred together about what was happening. Oswald had pulled back over the ravine. They couldn't see any troops to their left and it appeared those of Lafayette on the right were in retreat. The British troops in front of them were firing their artillery and maintaining their position while others were moving in strength toward the rebel right, past the village toward Lafayette. They had received no word from Lee about any changes in disposition, but it appeared that the rest of the Advanced Corps was moving backward. Scott thought it was best they retreat before the British cut them off from the road. He ordered his men to head west, moving across the John Craig farm between the Middle and North Brooks. Maxwell watched Scott's retreat and, believing that he would be the only detachment on the east side of the ravine, ordered his men to move across the ravine and gain the road, with cannons going first to prevent their loss. Scott and Maxwell on their own initiative were taking over 2,000 soldiers from the field, and in doing so, they pulled the foundation out from under any plans, however improvised, Lee still had.

The men with Lafayette looked to their left and saw Americans, probably Scott or Maxwell, moving to the rear. Oswald's guns, seeking their ammunition wagons, could be seen falling back to the west. Durkee's New Englanders had disappeared from the center of the American position. To many of the men on the right and left it appeared as if the troops on the other flanks were falling back even though neither side had suffered many casualties.

Colonel Henry Jackson started to retreat but one of his subordinates, the commander of Lee's Additional Regiment, Lieutenant Colonel William Smith, thought they should wait for orders. Smith was an old veteran, a graduate of Princeton, who had served in the battles around New York and been wounded at Harlem Heights. His advice seemed sound, and Jackson agreed to wait. They were in a small gully and relatively well protected, so Jackson allowed Smith to go and find General Lee for directions. Smith never found Lee but one of Lee's aides found Jackson and gave him permission to pull out.

No one knows who gave the first order, or if there were any orders, but by 11:30 am most of the detachments began moving back. Scott was first, followed by Maxwell and Jackson. Lafayette began his movement as an extension of his withdrawal toward Freehold. Russell, leading Durkee's detachment, fell in with Oswald's artillery as they moved back along the main road.

Watching the crumbling of his detachments, Lee ordered those units near him to withdraw. He found he could not communicate with all his forces consistently as most of his aides were now on foot. Two members of his staff, his adjutant and a French volunteer, were astride exhausted mounts. He did not, and probably could not, tell any of his subordinate commanders where they were going; instead, he allowed the crumbling line to carry him farther and farther away from the court house. Only a few men had been killed or injured and except for Butler's repulse of British horsemen and Oswald's cannonade the Americans had been involved in very little fighting. They had suffered only a few casualties from the steady British artillery fire. Lee briefly thought that perhaps Lafayette's men could use the little village of Freehold as a defensive anchor but closer inspection of the village revealed that most of the buildings were made of wood and would provide little protection against the British artillery. He ordered Lafayette to move back but the orders were unnecessary as the detachment was already in motion to the rear.

Lee was unsure about his northern, left, flank. Would the redcoats move around his left and get between him and Washington? He was unaware of the position of Scott's brigade or Wayne's detachment. He was unsure of where to set up a defense and unsure of the positions of his subordinates. Instead of sending word to Washington and asking for immediate support, he allowed the collapsing situation to dictate his actions. As the detachments began moving backward, he did little to stop them or give them concrete orders. He failed to inform Washington of the change in the situation but more importantly, he failed to inform Wayne of what he planned to do. Wayne was stuck out on a limb and never received direct orders to retreat.

To the men of the various regiments, the short clash with the British and aimless wanderings were tiring. By the time the retreat began, it was late morning with the sun already high in the sky and the temperature soaring. It would remain in the 90s throughout most of the day and the only solace the Americans could take was that it was just as warm for the British. Joseph Plumb Martin felt as if he were in a "heated oven" and "it was almost impossible to breathe."[14] Luckily there were many streams and watercourses around the battlefield but that did not prevent heat casualties. Artillerymen at their cannon went to their hot work, some of them running to nearby water holes for buckets of water to wet the sponges used to clean out the guns as well as for the refreshment of thirsty gunners, matrosses, and bombardiers. Infantrymen fell out from their regiments when passing a pool of water to satisfy a thirst that seemed unquenchable. Men collapsed alongside the road, and some died.

Wayne was confused. He wanted to get at the British and had repeatedly asked for reinforcements to attack the British instead of toying with them. Now it was obvious he was without support in a position to the north and east of the British main body. A messenger from Daniel Morgan appeared now when everyone seemed to be pulling back. Unable to find Lee, the man asked Wayne if there were any new orders. Wayne looked around and told the man to tell Morgan that they were falling back to a new position and the "Old Wagoner" should do what he thought was best. Then Wayne, with only Grayson and Butler's men, headed for the rear. Most of the other regiments filed back along the road they had taken previously. Butler followed the same route that Scott's detachment had previously taken, moving west through the avenue formed between the North and Middle arms of the Spotswood Brook, passing by Craig's Farm toward the Sutfin Farm. Frustrated, John Laurens thought, "I have been in several actions; I did not call that an action, as there was no action prior to the retreat."[15]

Morgan

About three miles to the south of Monmouth Court House, near Richmond's Mill, was Daniel Morgan and his light infantry, including a detachment of Washington's Life Guards. Morgan heard some firing but for some reason the tough old campaigner didn't move his troops. Perhaps there was some type of distortion due to the terrain but the sounds of a full-scale battle never reached him in such a way as to cause alarm. Washington had explicitly given him orders to cooperate with Lee's advance corps but Morgan didn't contact Lee and Lee's only order was confused by its timing. Lee's message on the night of June 27 indicated the army would attack the next day. Unfortunately, the message didn't reach Morgan until early in the morning of June 28 giving him the impression the action was to take place the following day, June 29. Morgan tried to contact Lee but his aide could not find the general and only managed to reach Anthony Wayne after the advanced detachment began its retreat. Morgan took no action. How Morgan did not respond to the sounds of battle, especially the artillery duel between Oswald and the British guns, is hard to understand. Morgan's force may have been in an acoustic hollow, unable to hear any battlefield sounds. This is unlikely, as eight hundred men spread out over a large area would not all be affected by the same anomaly. Perhaps he was frozen by Washington's words of caution. Strangely Lee did not contact Morgan and one of the best field commanders in the Continental Army, with hundreds of its best troops, took no part in the morning battle near Monmouth Court House.

Retreat

Unhurried, Washington was riding near the Tennent Meeting House. The advanced force, as far as he knew, was engaged in cutting off a part of the British rear guard. Without word from Lee, he made no extra effort to push the main body of the army forward.

Forced to retreat, Lee decided to look about for a place to form up to cover the withdrawing units. He ordered Lafayette to pull back behind the

East Ravine, a little late as the American troops had left the village and were already headed west, having suffered few casualties and fired just a few shots. The British cavalry was not far away, maintaining contact. The bulk of the Americans crossed the East Ravine and headed back along the dusty road and fields towards the Tennent Meeting House.

Near the Carr Farm, Eleazer Oswald turned his guns to slow the advancing British. Oswald was a late arrival to America, coming from England in 1770. He had taken part in the capture of Ticonderoga and Benedict Arnold's famous march to Quebec, where he was taken prisoner. Exchanged almost a year later, he became a lieutenant colonel in the 2nd Continental Artillery commanded by John Lamb. Oswald had fought alongside Arnold again during the Danbury Raid in 1777 and won a reputation as a cool artilleryman. Outspoken and afraid of no man, Oswald gathered guns from the retreating detachments to form a line just east of the Carr Farm. With 10 cannons, he settled in for a few minutes of explosive disagreement with the British, giving the retreating Continental columns time to put distance between them and the oncoming redcoats. After firing enough shots to keep the British at arm's length, the guns limbered up, moved back to a slight rise, and repeated the procedure.

William Maxwell, the aggressive New Jersey commander, was frustrated by the day's events. Starting with the early morning mistake in the order of march and continuing until this point at midday, his men had marched and countermarched with little obvious purpose. They had covered three miles to the Tennent Meeting House, a mile and a half on a wild goose chase toward Craig's Mill, retraced their steps back toward the meeting house, and finally three more miles to pass over the East Ravine. His brigade had only been in position on the plain above Monmouth Court House for a short time when Scott began the retreat that Maxwell had followed. Now, as he crossed the East Ravine, he found Lee and asked him for orders. Lee ordered him to move to the woods along the right. When Maxwell pointed out there were already troops there and his men were far to the left, Lee changed the order and Maxwell was told to stay on the left. Once in position on the left, Maxwell's men could cover any move by the British on the road toward Forman's Mills.

Charles Lee now viewed the situation with some alarm and considered where to set up a defensive line. He briefly thought about defending the west side of the East Ravine, but decided against it and sent the French engineer Duportail to see if the ground further west near the Carr House was a more defensible position. Duportail, the chief of the Continental Army's engineers and a graduate of the French engineer school at Mézières, galloped off to check out the possibilities. The position was slightly elevated, protected by the Spotswood South Brook on the right and the Middle Brook on its left. Numerous scrub trees and brush covered both flanks for protection against cavalry. With his experienced eye, and knowledge of the capabilities of the Continental troops, the Frenchman felt it would to be sufficient to rally the troops and hold the British until the arrival of Washington with the main body. Duportail returned to Lee and informed the general that indeed the new position would serve its purpose. Lee asked Lafayette to form a line there. The British would be limited in the number of men they could employ after passing Freehold, when the branches of the Spotswood Brook funneled them into a channel with frequent woods that would break up their formations. Stewart and Livingston began organizing the position at the Carr Farm with Oswald's omnipresent guns. Lee went with Duportail to make a final decision.

After giving it more thought, Lee concluded that the location did not provide the tactical advantages it first appeared to have and countermanded his order. Talking it over with Duportail, he pointed out a small rise to their front that might be used by British artillery to dominate them.[16] Lee also thought the position would be easily outflanked, ignoring the obstacles formed by the south and middle tributaries of the Spotswood Brook. The troops continued their retreat to the west along the road and in the fields between the Middle and North Spotswood Brooks. After briefly firing at the pursuing British, Oswald dispersed the battery of 10 guns back to their original detachments, and then joined the westward exodus. Lee also rode on to the west across the field, unaware as to the locations of many of his formations.

Lieutenant Colonel Richard Kidder Meade, one of Washington's aides, rode up on his black mare after riding through several retreating formations, and inquired about the situation. Lee could not provide any message for Washington, even when repeatedly pressed. Meade left Lee and headed for the court house to try and see what was happening. Unfortunately, this detour delayed his return to the commander in chief with the news of the retreat. Lee did not think to send someone to alert Washington to the change in the situation.

The rush of the withdrawing regiments and detachments was not panicked but lacked any overall control. Lee occasionally tried to organize the retrograde as soldiers shuffled by him along the road, kicking up clouds of dust that only made the day more miserable. He made sure the artillery of Oswald was supported when the cannon stopped to fire at the pursing British. Some tired and thirsty soldiers hurried along, some trotted, and others stopped frequently to look behind them. Annoyed, Lee thought they were retreating in disorder as if every man was his own commander. Fortunately, the British did not press them too closely. The British cavalry, probably due to their earlier rebuff, kept out of musket range but maintained visual contact with the withdrawing Americans.

While he occasionally directed small groups of troops to move or deploy, Lee was unable to control the entire advanced corps and his personal presence had no overall effect on the troops; he failed to inspire or motivate them. He was simply another officer on the march away from the enemy. Young John Laurens received a note from Washington at this point that requested a situation report. Laurens inquired of Lee how he should reply. Lee didn't give an answer and again missed an opportunity to notify the commander in chief that the advanced corps was falling back.[17] Based on what information he had, George Washington believed that a great victory was in the offing.

CHAPTER 5

Retreat?

Afternoon—The Retreat

American regiments were marching slowly in retreat, flags drooping, panting soldiers seeking an easy way west. Hot, covered in dust, the Continentals lacked overall direction, their immediate leaders following the most recent orders or their own discretion. While the entire advanced force was in confusion, individual detachments, even those of picked men who had recently been thrown together, maintained their unit cohesion and stayed in formation. Cantering nearby were the colorful dragoons and elite infantry of the British engaged in what for them seemed to be just another fox chase. To them it was similar to the many previous battles in which they had seen the backs of their opponents. No one, from private soldier to general, in either army knew where it would end. The confusion of battle is not always the result of cannons or other weapons firing with their loud noise and shrouds of blinding smoke or the exhaustion of marching to and fro in hot weather: this battle was an example of confusion also caused by a lack of effective leadership.

After finding that the Middle Ravine near the Carr House was not a good position, Charles Lee looked around for a position to get his men under control and organize them. A local officer, Captain Peter Wikoff, was consulted on where such ground might be found. Wikoff pointed out a nearby house where the British had started the day. Lee pointed out that the enemy was too close and there was no time to occupy that position. Wikoff then suggested that Comb's Hill was the dominant ground over this battlefield, towering above Perrine Ridge and the surrounding countryside. Unfortunately, he noted, the marshy ground covered by trees at its base would make it difficult to get the division up its steep slope. The boggy ground around the creek at its base would have to be planked with wood to get the artillery across and would leave them vulnerable to attack during the crossing.

Finally, Wikoff pointed out some trees that would provide shade on the slopes of Perrine Ridge. Looking over the ground with his professional eye, Lee agreed the gradually sloping ridge farther west appeared best, protected by bodies of water on its front and flank. Lee ordered Wikoff to proceed back to the causeway over the Middle Brook to direct troops over into a position out of the sun. There were plenty of senior officers around, including Lafayette, but Lee chose to send a very junior officer to organize the retreating soldiers once they reached the West Ravine.[1]

Scott's men, and Butler's detachment, weren't retreating along the road but were moving through the avenue between the Spotswood Middle and North Brooks, passing the Craig and Sutfin Farms, out of sight and control of Lee. A relatively junior officer, Wikoff was to direct the troops to rally on the west side of the West Ravine. But who would organize them once there? In the morning Lee had used Wayne and Lafayette to lead troops in important movements but he failed to send a senior officer to organize the withdrawing troops once they reached the West Ravine.

Lee noted confusion among the regiments in his vicinity. Watching the retreating troops, he was worried that some of the regiments weren't closed up, and there were gaps between the detachments in each brigade. There was little he could see that could be done but he felt that it was dangerous to march in such a "broken line."[2]

Maxwell met with Lee and was told that the division was retreating. Returning to his men, Maxwell found they were retreating in good order along the main road. Colonel Israel Shreve, who had local connections and was familiar with the terrain, told Maxwell that Wikoff had come by and passed on orders from Lee telling them to move back across the West Ravine. Maxwell halted the brigade long enough for Shreve to move the cannon ahead and cross the ravine first, then the rest of the New Jersey troops followed. One regiment remained on the east side of the watercourse to cover the bridge.

Moving across the fields of Rhea's Farm, south of the road, were the guns of Captains Cook and Seward, still under the command of Oswald. The New Englanders of Russell and Olney were not far behind, then Livingston, Ramsey, Parker's Virginians, and finally Walter Stewart's detachment. A small group of militia horsemen under Anthony White screened their rear when British dragoons pressed them. Anthony Wayne and the Marquis de Lafayette moved along the column, keeping their troops together while moving to the rear.

Lee ordered Livingston to support Oswald's guns as they fell back. The cannons stopped on a small height north of Combs Hill. Oswald sent six of the cannons back to their parent units and set up with the guns of Captains Seward and Cook. Livingston set up on the nearby hedgerow. Running in a north and south direction, the hedgerow was old and thick, providing protection for troops overlooking the cutaway at the West Ravine. Just arriving on the scene, Brigadier General Henry Knox, the commander of the Continental artillery, sent a messenger ordering Oswald to remain in that position.[3]

Washington

The small gaggle of riders that were George Washington and his staff pressed eastward through the rolling New Jersey countryside, noting the neat farms and orchards with frequent woods that bordered the dusty country road that led from Englishtown to Monmouth Court House. Here and there the ground rose, then fell away again without any major changes in elevation, just a slight ridge or hillock to break the relative flatness of the land. Earlier there had been the sound of gunfire that echoed over the shallow slopes but now only the far-off bark of a cannon could be heard. Washington was closing the distance to the advanced guard and expected that over the next rise or around the next bend he would hear all-out firing of the anticipated battle. He continued to send members of his staff to inquire of the action, but they were not returning with up-to-date information, leaving the commander in chief unsure of the status of Lee's attack.

It was about noon and the lack of battle sounds was eerie. When Hamilton advised him of Lee's initial movement to attack the British, Washington sent Nathanael Greene off to the south to move on the British left flank. The last information from Lee advised the commander of the attack on the enemy's rear detachment. What had happened since? At this point, Washington only knew that Lee was attacking and would soon bag the enemy's rear guard. The rest of the army under Lord Stirling was closing on the West Ravine and would then move on toward the Monmouth Court House.

Passing down slope of Perrine Ridge, and over the causeway, the party of officers' pleasant morning ride was interrupted by the appearance of a local resident. Greeting Washington's party, the man identified himself as Dr. Thomas Henderson, whose home had been torched the day before by redcoats. When asked about information concerning the American army, he informed them that he had been told the advanced corps was in full retreat. Stunned, thinking the statement couldn't be true, Washington queried the doctor further and asked the source of this rumor. The doctor turned and pointed down the road a little further. A lone young man was ambling along on the road toward the party, apparently a soldier but not dressed in any uniform.

Washington stopped the youth who answered the general's inquiries by identifying himself as a musician, a fifer, and stating that the army was in retreat. Washington was dumbfounded: the last he had heard from Lee was a report that the day would soon belong to the Continentals and there had been no other communication since then to contradict that report. After thinking a moment, the perplexed commander in chief ordered the young man to keep the news from anyone he might encounter, or he would be whipped. Visions of past heartbreaks swept quickly through Washington's mind; the panic at Kip's Bay, the surprise and withdrawal at the Brandywine, and the foggy, confused retreat at Germantown. Anger began to grow in the tall general and he ordered one of his aides, Lieutenant Colonel John Fitzgerald, and his secretary, Robert Harrison, forward to see what was happening, even as another local rode up and confirmed the retreat. Harrison and Fitzgerald were among the closest and most trusted members of Washington's military "family," and the commander in chief was confident they would provide accurate information in a calm report. As the two young men rode swiftly off into the glare of the sun, the general's anxious party rode on after them.[4]

The first troops encountered by Fitzgerald and Harrison were those of Grayson. The officers they met had no answer as to who had ordered the retreat or where the enemy was. They had no idea where they were going. Jackson's regiment appeared next but Jackson could give Washington's aides no more information than those they had previously encountered except that he had been ordered to retreat. The two young officers wanted to know more and rode on, encountering various bodies of men. All the soldiers were marching in regimental formations with little straggling but the fatigue of a long day on the march was apparent to Harrison and Fitzgerald.

Moving on, Harrison encountered the dust-covered men of the 1st New Jersey, part of Maxwell's brigade. The commander, Colonel Matthias Ogden, had little concrete information other than the fact they had seen no action but had been ordered to retreat. Clearly showing his disgust, Ogden spat out: "By God! They are flying from a shadow."[5] Every officer in the New Jersey brigade that the pair met had the same answer: they had been ordered to retreat but didn't know why or who had originated the order. Even those who had been ordered to move to the West Ravine were unsure of what to do when they reached that point. Lieutenant Colonel David Rhea told Harrison that he was confused about the retreat and "equally concerned (or perhaps more) that he had no place assigned to go where the troops were to halt."[6]

The first actual news of the British advance occurred when Harrison met Lee's haggard-looking aide, Captain John Mercer, who stated erroneously that the British were only a few minutes behind him. Continuing along the road, Harrison didn't meet the British but instead ran into Maxwell. The New Jersey commander shed no light on why they were retreating and didn't know who had issued the original order to retreat, but said Lee had sanctioned the withdrawal. He knew only that he was to get over the West Ravine. Fitzgerald went nearly to the Carr Farm and found Lee but the two had little conversation, Lee only inquiring about Washington's location. While they chatted, British cavalry approached in the distance and Lee turned his horse to rejoin the retreat.

As he waited for the return of his aides and more information on the advanced corps, Washington approached the Rhea Farm and encountered groups of soldiers. One of these groups consisted of the first regiments of Maxwell's brigade exiting the point of woods east of the bridge over the West Ravine. When questioned, the officers had no clue why they were retreating. Washington looked around and pointed to the height nearby that was Perrine Ridge. He ordered the New Jersey men to place themselves there where they could cover the causeway over the West Ravine. Washington spurred past a hedgerow to find out what was happening. Bewildered, he saw no evidence of battle, no litters carrying wounded or bandages indicating injuries.

The advancing staff, and commander in chief, met whole regiments retreating seemingly without orders. They did not appear to know where they were going or why they were retreating. Beefy Colonel Israel Shreve of New Jersey spoke only in generalities and could give the commander in chief no concrete information except that the men were angry at the retreat. The regiments maintained their unit integrity, but the overall retreat appeared without order or direction. A local officer, Lieutenant Colonel David Rhea, told Washington of his frustrations with the retreat and offered to help the general with his knowledge of terrain. Washington also encountered Captain Wikoff, who was attempting to get troops to move across the West Ravine and rally on Perrine Ridge as ordered by Lee. Wikoff was leading some of Maxwell's troops at that moment and told Washington of his orders. Washington was relieved to encounter an officer who knew what he was supposed to do. A former surveyor and veteran soldier, the commander in chief had already seen the value of the ridge and allowed Wikoff, with Rhea, to carry on.

Despite his anger and frustration, Washington clearly understood that something must be done and done immediately. For years he had watched the army slowly develop, seen their ignoble retreats and their heartbreaking defeats. The Virginia farmer turned professional soldier had watched them fight toe to toe with the better trained and equipped Imperial troops during past campaigns. The tall patrician had watched them stumble and trip their way through von Steuben's evolutions until they had obtained some mastery. Yet he had never given up on them, never lost the optimism that led him to believe they would fight for their cause and each other as well as any men on earth. He was different than Charles Lee; he had faith in his soldiers. He was also a man of action, and he did something that Charles Lee had failed to do: he physically imposed his will on the army.

Near the point of woods along the road, Washington addressed each group of soldiers, each battalion, each regiment, he encountered. The dusty soldiers, tired and thirsty, responded to the explicit direction of a firm hand. He spoke to them, not with hollow exhortations but with firm direction. Like a jolt of electricity, Washington's presence stirred the men immediately and abruptly the atmosphere changed. They recognized his authority and they eagerly responded, many cheering their commander in chief.

Washington gave clear directions to each unit he met. Some of the soldiers were sent farther east toward Englishtown, to rest in the shade and recover from the long morning. The 1st New Jersey remained to cover the causeway over the West Ravine while Maxwell took his remaining regiments with Wikoff into the trees on the lower slopes of Perrine Ridge to find relief from the sun. The commander in chief set to work organizing a position that would serve as a rear guard and allow time for the rest of the army to get up.

One of the last units Washington encountered were the men who had been with Lafayette in the abortive flanking maneuver that morning. In a point of woods nearby out of the sun, Washington set about organizing them for defense. Washington ordered Nathaniel Ramsey and Walter Stewart, as well as the group of Virginians under Lieutenant Colonel James Woods, to prepare their detachments to contest the approaching British. They were to hold on long enough to give him time to bring up the rest of the army, just now deploying on the ridge to their rear. Washington approached Ramsey, the senior officer: "If you can stop the British for ten minutes, till I form, you will save my army!" The valiant Marylander replied, "I will stop them or fall!"[7] Satisfied, Washington moved on, directing Jeremiah Olney's New Englanders to move off the road toward the hedgerow to support Oswald's guns.

The Continental soldiers, well-drilled the previous winter, many of them veterans of past campaigns, followed the orders of the tall man on the white horse quickly and efficiently. The officers also responded with a new level of skill, showing the leavening of past actions, tried in battle, and the harsh conditions of Valley Forge. These were not soldiers who had been defeated by the enemy but merely confused at the abrupt change from advance to retreat and a lack of clear direction. They took heart from the appearance of Washington as he rode back and forth, up and down the road and across the fields as they deployed.

Washington and Lee

It was not long after Washington set about organizing a defense in the point of woods that Charles Lee and his aides rode up, apparently in no hurry and relaxed despite the confusion around them. The commanding general was energetically addressing the men of Lafayette's detachment near a small creek on the Rhea Farm when Washington glimpsed the scarecrow figure of Lee and spurred his horse directly at him, abruptly stopping in front of the surprised general and the tired, sweaty members of his staff. Blue-gray eyes flashing, Washington addressed Lee curtly before the startled general could greet his commander. He brusquely inquired as to why the army was in retreat.

Washington was a man of violent temper, and his tone of voice appeared to shock his subordinate. His direct manner of speech "disconcerted,

An angry Washington met Charles Lee as the subordinate retreated before the British. After chastising his second in command, the commander in chief took charge of the battle. *National Archives, engraving by G. R. Hall (George Washington Bicentennial Commission. National Archives NAID: 532864 Local ID: 148-GW-95 Photographs and other Graphic Materials Covers: 1931–1932)*

astonished, and confounded" Lee. Washington asked about the purpose of the disorganized retreat and the lack of direction in the withdrawing men. Lee, suddenly awakened as if from a stupor, could only mumble about the troops and commanders not following orders. This only infuriated Washington more and he brushed aside the incoherent ramblings to ask for more specific information, but the dumbfounded Lee only sputtered out that the disorder was from disobedience of orders, contradictory intelligence, and the retreat was not by his direction. He blamed Scott and the artillery, as well as other subordinates, for the retreat. Then, paradoxically, he took credit for making such a retreat. Lee suddenly thought that Washington had wanted a full-scale engagement and he tried to tell Washington that he was not in favor of such an action in the first place, to which Washington cut him off and said he shouldn't have asked for the assignment if he wasn't going to follow it through.[8]

It was a spectacle for all to see, the massive figure of Washington astride his great war horse, its nostrils flaring and hooves stomping the ground, and the pitiful, scrawny Lee, dejected and trying to defend himself against the tirade, quieted as his mount idled, the poor animal looking as though it, too, was under verbal attack. Onlookers, various aides, passing soldiers, and commanders, could only watch helplessly. Tench Tilghman, an aristocratic Marylander and one of Washington's favorite aides, could feel the heat of Washington's anger at Lee from a short distance away. Nearby soldiers were amazed at their top commander's outburst, but veterans of Kip's Bay and Princeton remembered a highly animated Washington on those grim occasions, chastising or exhorting troops in need of courage or inspiration as the occasion demanded, often during violent fighting. Thoroughly disgusted, Washington ordered Lee to move away.[9]

Harrison returned as the meeting between the commander in chief and Lee concluded, informing Washington that the British were less than 15 minutes away. Just as he was a man of violent temper, Washington was also a man of immense self-control and he willed himself to forget his anger and return to business. He resumed his directions to Lafayette's detachment and deployed them off the road.

Anthony Wayne also appeared as the confrontation with Lee was ending. His troops were crossing the West Ravine and joining the army assembling on Perrine Ridge. Washington knew Wayne and trusted him. He detailed Wayne to take command of the detachments of Ramsey, Stewart, and Woods in the trees north of the road. The men of Wayne's new detachment were safely into the cover of the woods, as the British troops appeared less than four hundred yards away.

Lafayette had arrived with Lee, not far from the vociferous encounter between the two generals, and remained to see the results of Washington's actions. The troops responded, not necessarily to his voice or the words that he said, but to Washington's physical presence. The commander in chief demonstrated a magnetism that could only be termed charisma. It was something that could not be taught in military schools; it was natural. Washington had exhibited this trait from the time of his defeats and experiences back in the French and Indian War through the first three years of the present war. Lafayette saw Washington's intervention as decisive: "General Washington was never greater in battle than this action. His presence stopped the retreat; his strategy secured the victory. His stately appearance on horseback, his calm dignified courage, tinged only slightly by the anger caused by the unfortunate incident in the morning, provoked a wave of enthusiasm among the troops."[10] Lafayette had been near Lee throughout the early part of the battle and near Washington later, so it was easy for him to see the glaring difference in the impact of the personal leadership between the two commanders.

Washington turned his attention to helping Livingston's men south of the road. The New Englanders of Durkee's detachment, now under Russell, a veteran Connecticut soldier who had fought in Lord Dunmore's War way back in 1774, went into position at the hedgerow near the Parsonage Farm to support Livingston and some cannon placed there under Lee's orders. Terribly weak, the defenders consisted of only a few hundred of Lieutenant Colonel Jeremiah Olney's Rhode Islanders and Russell's own Connecticut men.

Grayson's men were put into line on the slope of Perrine Ridge with the 2nd New Jersey. The 1st New Jersey was just east of the causeway on a slight rise near the Parsonage Farm guarding the causeway. Temper now cooled, Washington was near that position when he again noticed the cowed figure of Lee among the troops east of the causeway. Lee was still the second in command of the army and Washington calmly asked him if he would take charge here, in an exposed position at the hedgerow, until he could bring up the rest of the army.

"Will you, sir, command in that place?" Washington gestured toward the small rise where he had assembled several detachments behind the hedgerow.

"I will!" replied Lee emphatically, beginning to recover himself at the prospect of vindication. Washington continued:

"Then I will expect you to check the enemy immediately." Washington looked directly at his deputy, searching for a positive response.

"Your command will be obeyed, and I will not be the first to leave the field," Lee replied defiantly. One of the nearby aides, impetuous young

Alexander Hamilton, became caught up in the dramatic moment and wanted to stay, also.

"I will fight to the death!" the exuberant Hamilton blurted out, to which Lee gave only a disgusted look. Unlike Lee, who clearly saw the difficulty of the position, Hamilton seemed overcome with martial emotion.[11]

Lee finished the dispositions at the hedgerow and prepared to meet the oncoming British. It would not be an easy assignment—the few regiments placed by Washington against the best of the British army, led by Lord Cornwallis, among the best of the British generals, and overseen by Clinton, one of the brightest of the British commanders. The individual British soldiers had been in this position before, chasing defeated and dispirited American soldiers. The morale of these British soldiers, the finest His Majesty had, was at its highest: grenadiers, guards, light infantrymen, and veteran line regiments, they were the cream of the British army. They smelled blood. Lee knew his task would not be a simple one but Hamilton could only see the opportunity for personal glory.

Just after leaving Lee to contest the British advance, Washington was approached by a messenger from Daniel Morgan. The army was in full retreat and Morgan was essentially out of the picture. Morgan didn't know what was going on and his earlier inquiry to Anthony Wayne had been met with a somewhat sarcastic answer about fending for himself. Washington had sent a messenger through Nathanael Greene on the right flank to Morgan but the message had not reached him. Washington advised Morgan: "I have just received your Letter by the Dragoon—as your Corps is out of supporting Distance I would have you confine yourself to observing the motions of the Enemy—unless an opportunity offers of intercepting some small Parties—and by no means to come to an Engagement with your whole Body unless you are tempted by some very evident advantage—Genl Greenes Aide de Camp has already written you to this effect—but the orders are repeated to guard against accidents."[12] Washington was not in any position to support Morgan's detachment now that Clinton's entire force was between Morgan and the main army.

Earlier, Scott's detachment had retreated through the corridor formed by the sluggish little Spotswood Middle and North Brooks before crossing the West Ravine. At the Sutfin Farm, Colonels Joseph Cilley and Richard Parker put their men into shade along the lower slopes of Perrine Ridge. Scott and the rest of his detachment, Mordecai Gist and William Butler's men, continued on to the rally point west of the Tennent Meeting House on the road to Englishtown. Morosely marching in to join them were the disappointed men of the New Jersey Brigade, who had marched over more territory that day than any other detachment without engaging in any major part of the day's action. Their officers, Maxwell, Elias Dayton, Israel Shreve, and Ephraim Martin, were all dedicated veterans and had seen plenty of action but were now merely bystanders with hundreds of tired and hot men.

The Point of Woods

At the point of woods north of the road on the Rhea Farm, Wayne took personal command of the detachments of Walter Stewart, Nathaniel Ramsey, and the Virginians under James Woods. They were all veteran officers, as good as any of the British officers in the field. Woods was an intelligent and accomplished man who had served as a negotiator for Virginia in the Treaty of Fort Pitt before the war and experienced a great deal of the present war. Stewart, a Pennsylvanian who had fought in every battle the Pennsylvanians had participated in, was a former lawyer and often referred to as "the handsomest man in the American army."[13] Marylander Ramsey had replaced James Wesson who was wounded earlier in the battle. Ramsey was another veteran; he had been in the army since 1776, participating in the battle of Long Island and the battles around Philadelphia, and lately was commanding the 3rd Maryland Regiment. They were experienced officers, and their men were "picked" from their respective brigades.

Wayne tucked the three detachments into the point of woods along the road for cover. The pursuing British were not far off and in just a few minutes the oncoming ranks of the Foot Guards were within musket range of the American position. The British had not been able to pursue quickly due to the heat. Caked with dust mixed with sweat, the redcoats were tired but ready to fight. British officer William Hale described the march to contact: "…a march I may never again experience. We proceeded five miles in a road composed of nothing but sand which scorched through our shoes with intolerable heat; the sun beating on our heads with a force scarcely to be conceived in Europe, and not a drop of water to assuage our parching thirst; a number of soldiers were unable to support the fatigue and died on the spot. A Corps of the 43rd Grenadiers, who had by some means procured water, drank to such excess as to burst and expired in the utmost torments. Two became raving mad, and the whole road, strewn with miserable wretches wishing for death, exhibited the most shocking scene I ever saw."[14] Officers were not exempt from thirst and Hale offered to pay an enlisted soldier for water when his own ran out.

Nervously waiting in the shade of the woods, Wayne's men allowed the British column to close within musket range. At Wayne's signal, the three American detachments opened fire on the oncoming British of the Foot Guards. Startled, the elite British soldiers quickly reacted by deploying in the open just off the road and facing the Americans in the woods. After the surprising first volley, the British exchanged several volleys with the Americans, Brown Bess and Charleville muskets pouring out lead as each side loaded and discharged. Flags waved in the still air as more red-coated troops from the First Grenadiers joined the battle. The firing was heavy and there were casualties on both sides. Among those badly wounded was good-looking Walter Stewart. Dragged from the scene by some of his men, he would live to delight young women another day.

Walter Stewart was called the most handsome man in the army, an "Irish Beauty." He was grievously wounded at the point of woods. *The Miriam and Ira D. Wallach Division of Art, Prints and Photographs: Print Collection, The New York Public Library. "Walter Stewart"*

Gun smoke hovered over the woods. Outnumbered at least two to one, the American resistance could not last long. With the Spotswood Middle Brook to their rear and more British troops arriving each minute, threatening to cut off their retreat to the bridge over the West Ravine, Wayne made a dramatic decision. Not content with merely fleeing from the enemy, Wayne ordered the small American force to charge the advancing British. The Americans burst out of the wood, using their bayonets as von Steuben had instructed them, crashing into the elite British soldiers. Men clubbed, clawed, and stabbed each other in vicious personal combat. Fighting was hand-to-hand but it didn't last long, as the Americans once removed from the woods into the open were charged by the British dragoons and splintered into small groups.

Washington's young aide John Laurens was slightly injured when his horse was killed, spilling the young officer to the hard, dry ground. On foot, he joined in the retreat across the causeway over the West Ravine. More British moved up around the Americans, attempting to surround them. British cannons pounded the Americans, making their position too hot to hold. Wayne's charge had created space and he ordered the troops to fall back. They had stalled the British a few minutes, gaining precious time for Lee to prepare his troops at the hedgerow. It also allowed another 30 minutes for Washington's deployment of the main body going into position on Perrine Ridge.

As the remainder of the three detachments began drifting back toward the bridge, redoubtable Nathaniel Ramsey personally rushed at the attacking British cavalry as a one-man rear guard. His horse was knocked down and he was thrown to the ground. Dismounted, he swung his sword at the oncoming British. One redcoat dragoon came in close to shoot Ramsey, but his pistol misfired. Ramsey took the man's horse after wounding the cavalryman with his sword. It was of no use, as several British horsemen surrounded a re-mounted Ramsey. He was cut up badly in bloody close combat that left him again dismounted and lying bleeding on the battlefield, apparently dead. Wayne and the rest of the Americans made it back to cross the causeway over the Spotswood Middle Brook in small groups, covered by Matthias Ogden's New Jersey troops just on the other side.

Sensing victory, the British swarmed after the retreating Americans.

The Hedgerow, Part One

Lee's judgment and abilities as a leader and commander may have been suspect but he was a brave soldier, and he prepared his mixed force to face the oncoming redcoats. Just as the men of the various regiments found new life after meeting Washington, so did Lee. Energized, Lee began to organize the regiments of Livingston and Stephen Olney that had been stopped by Washington, and formed them to face the oncoming British.

Lee also encountered Lieutenant Colonel William Smith's men of Jackson's detachment. He ordered them to fall in along the hedgerow, but Smith complained that his men were exhausted and were following orders to retreat. Nevertheless, Lee ordered him to join the defense at the hedgerow. No sooner than Smith began following Lee's directions, Jackson showed up and demanded to know why Smith's men were not following his orders. Rejoining Jackson's detachment, Smith noticed Lee in an animated conversation with Jackson. The detachment stood firm until Washington arrived and told him to put the detachment into some trees out of the sun. When Jackson heard these orders, he led the whole detachment not just the few hundred yards Washington had allowed but all the way to Englishtown.

Lee noted the small knoll near the hedgerow with Oswald's four cannon. Livingston, previously ordered by Lee to support Oswald's guns, took up a position along the hedgerow. After Olney's regiment was detailed by Washington to join them, Lee moved the infantry several times to put them in the best position to protect the artillery, leaving gaps to allow the artillery to fire through the infantry.

The British advance from the point of woods was disorganized and fragmented, facing the new line of resistance formed by Jeremiah Olney and Henry Beekman Livingston backed by the guns of Oswald. The Continentals were determined, experienced men; the gentlemanly Livingston an aristocrat from New York and Olney a staid Rhode Islander who had served with distinction during the devastating Hessian defeat at Red Bank in October of 1777. On the little knob dominating the road were Cook's two pieces and the two guns of Thomas Seward personally directed by Oswald.

The first British to face them were the horsemen of the 16th Dragoons, who foolishly tried to assault Lee's position, which was protected by the thick hedgerow atop a slight elevation just east of the Parsonage Farm. The red-coated dragoons, blasted by the four cannons and massed muskets of the Americans, abruptly stopped their advance, and drifted to the right of the American line. For the second time that day, British cavalry had suffered a serious setback. Even as the horsemen moved away, more British troops appeared through the dust and smoke. The Americans faced the men of the 1st and 2nd Grenadiers, who rushed at them after hurriedly forming, led by Henry Clinton himself.

Historically, the original soldiers who were called grenadiers were the strongest and most skilled soldiers in an infantry regiment, picked for their ability to throw the heavy and cumbersome hand grenades. The use of grenades had fallen out of fashion, but each British regiment still included a company of grenadiers who were used more as elite infantry when the grenadier companies of several regiments were formed into battalions.

On June 28, 1778, the battalions of grenadiers, looking threateningly tall in their trademark bear skins, advanced in double ranks straight at the American line led by their fearsome bayonets. Behind the hedgerow were mostly veteran Americans who were picked from their parent regiments much as the grenadiers. They calmly waited behind the twisted wood and foliage of the hedgerow. The redcoats rushed on to reach the hedgerow and the Americans opened fire. Grenadiers staggered and fell but the long red lines pressed forward. Before the smoke had completely cleared, more lead ripped the line of redcoats and they faltered, falling back temporarily.

Despite the terrific fire, the grenadiers resumed their advance toward the American line. The Americans traded volleys with approaching British infantry, dropping many, but the grenadiers marched on as though they were machines, urged on by Clinton who rode amongst them, waving them forward with cries of "Charge, Grenadiers, never heed forming!"[15] They broke ranks on Clinton's inspiration, losing all organization and plunging through the rebel fire like fierce animals intent on their prey. Lieutenant Hale, in the 2nd Grenadiers, noted how the attack was so rushed that officers lost control of their men: "… it was no longer a contest for bringing up our respective companies in the best order, but all of the officers as well as soldiers strove who could be foremost."[16] At the hedgerow they fought fiercely, often hand-to-hand. Olney led his men from cover in a bayonet charge that temporarily stopped the British but only for a moment. The grenadiers had to be reformed and Clinton's exasperated aides pulled their leader out of the fire.

Irritated by Clinton's intervention, British officers reformed the solid ranks of the well-drilled grenadiers. The redcoats attacked again; the fierce fire of the defenders met them again. The tired, hot, and frustrated British were not to be denied at this point, led by the brave men of the 2nd Grenadiers under Colonel Henry Monckton. A well-liked and dedicated soldier, he was the fourth son of the First Viscount Galway. His older brother, Robert, was also in the colonies as an engineer. Handsome, erudite, and a prolific gambler, Monckton had enjoyed his entertaining stay in Philadelphia the previous winter. He also had a reputation as an able and veteran soldier who had been wounded at Long Island and again at Brandywine. A child of privilege and education, Monckton now faced provincial regiments commanded by the sons of merchants, farmers, and mechanics.

Here at the hedgerow, the finest of Great Britain met the finest of Britain's colonies. It was grenadiers led by aristocratic officers, soldiers with a storied history and intimidating reputation, against men who were no longer the farmers and mechanics of Lexington and Concord. The grenadiers were the picked men of the British infantry regiments. They faced Americans that were tough, experienced soldiers led by hard and equally experienced officers with their own legacy of battle. These were men who had marched through snow and ice in Canada, survived smallpox in putrid camps, retreated in agony from New York, through New Jersey, into Pennsylvania, lost battles at Brandywine and Germantown, defeated Burgoyne at Saratoga, and now stood along a hedgerow in formations taught at the bidding of a gifted European drill master.

Courageous and determined, Monckton led the advance. He pressed his men forward in another assault on the American position. The Continentals fired, reloaded, and fired again. Paper cartridges were bit open, primed; loads rammed home; and the weapons belched forth their lead missiles into the oncoming ranks of scarlet-coated grenadiers. The unwavering British soldiers shrugged off their fatigue and the effects of the heat as they came on silently, enduring the musket and cannon fire, until they were only a few yards from the hedgerow. Smoke enveloped them as they replied to the deadly American fire with their own and then they charged, Monckton at their head shouting "Forward to the charge, my brave Grenadiers!"[17] The veterans responded and plunged on toward the equally tired and hot Americans.

Blasts of musket fire pounded the advancing grenadiers; some of the Americans were able to fire off 10 shots during the action. Screams and shouts filled the air despite the dry throats from the heat and biting of cartridges. Cannon poured grape across the gallant grenadiers, and their glorious colonel, as the battle closed to hand-to-hand. Back and forth went the two sides, men clawing and stabbing each other or smashing each other with musket butts. British Dragoons moved to flank the hedgerow and, despite the fire of the American cannon and renewed musketry, it was apparent that sheer numbers of British would overwhelm the few hundred Americans. Alexander's Hamilton's horse had been injured and he was thrown. Slightly hurt, the emotional young aide walked back across the bridge well before Lee. Pressed by increasing numbers of British, Lee finally had to order the remnants back across the creek. The Americans slowly gave way and headed for the bridge over the Middle Brook. There was no rout, there was no panic as the men of Olney and Livingston finally drifted across the causeway or forded at shallow portions of the brook.

The last soldiers across were Olney's detachment and the cannons. Cantankerous Eleazer Oswald refused to leave the battlefield, trying to hold off the entire force of desperate British with his field pieces and a few infantrymen even as others around him faded away and redcoats swarmed after him. Brigadier General Henry Knox darted forward and told Oswald that he was ordering him to fall back across the ravine, but Oswald still refused to order his artillerymen to retire. Only after Knox told him that Lee had ordered the retreat did Oswald allow the gunners to take their guns across the bridge amid shouts and gunfire from the redcoats following them.

During the action at the point of woods and along the hedgerow, Washington was busy putting Lord Stirling's troops into positions along Perrine Ridge behind the New Jersey regulars around the causeway. The various regiments combined their attached cannon into one grand battery on the lower slopes. Colonel Edward Carrington, a Virginian friend of Washington, took control of the battery. The guns opened fire with solid and grapeshot at the redcoats closely pursuing the Continentals falling back across the Western Ravine. Some British tried to force their way into the procession of retreating Americans, one British officer chopping at the Americans with his sword as they splashed into the creek. The grenadiers pressed after the fleeing Americans through the creek or over the bridge, only to be met by blasts of fire from Carrington's massed cannon and the New Jersey troops on the other side of the ravine. Leading his men past the hedgerow and down toward the brook, Monckton was mortally wounded by a ball of grapeshot that struck his heart. He fell in front of his troops. Soldiers from both armies attempted to retrieve his body but rebel artillery kept the British away, and the precipitous withdrawal of the Americans precluded any of them from taking possession of the gallant colonel's remains.

Washington was everywhere, accompanied by his personal slave Billy Lee, moving from one regiment to another, often in range of British guns. The commander of the 1st Maryland, Otho Williams, noted that "our Great good general in person led the fight and was the whole time exposed to the fire of the Artillery."[18] The 1st and 2nd New Jersey Regiments, the arriving brigades of Lord Stirling, and the line of American cannons on the west side of the ravine covered the withdrawal of the last Americans and dissuaded the British from trying to assault across the ravine on or around the causeway. The men at the point of woods and the hedgerow had bought precious time, more than half an hour, for Washington to organize his forces along Perrine Ridge.

True to his word, Lee was the last to cross over to the west bank. Lee reported to Washington that the last of the advance corps had crossed the West

During the afternoon the battle raged around the hedgerow near the Parsonage and the slopes of the Perrine Ridge. *The Miriam and Ira D. Wallach Division of Art, Prints and Photographs: Picture Collection, The New York Public Library. "Battle of Monmouth"*

Ravine and were falling back toward Englishtown. Lee expected Washington to address the earlier sharp words that had been directed at him, but Washington only acknowledged Lee's recent courageous efforts and curtly ordered him to go back toward Englishtown where many of the advanced corps troops were resting and reorganizing. Lee would remain in command there until relieved by Baron von Steuben.

Nathanael Greene and his troops had taken a position on the American right flank along high ground with William Woodford's Virginians, a battery of artillery under Lieutenant Colonel Chevalier Antoine de Mauduit Du Plessis, and some militia. Major Rhea was sent by Washington to assist in locating the best position to cover that flank. Rhea's intimate local knowledge led him to take Greene to the brow of Comb's Hill. Du Plessis set up a battery of four cannon that overlooked the hedgerow and the retreating Americans.

It was a little after noon when the main body of the Continental Army passed the Tennent Meeting House and met Washington. The commander in chief ordered Lord Stirling to place his troops directly into line of battle along Perrine

Ridge. The Continental regulars peeled off and took up positions to cover the valley before them, anchored on the slopes of the ridge and the meandering Spotswood North Brook. The Connecticut brigade of Jedediah Huntington, a Massachusetts brigade, and William Irvine's Pennsylvanians were posted along the dominating heights. Stirling ordered his artillery to form up under Edward Carrington near the base of the hill, ultimately forming a line of cannon of various sizes, 12 in number, which dominated the Sutfin Farm to their direct front and the height above the bridge across the Spotswood Middle Brook. These were the guns that had covered the retreat of Lee's rear guard and killed Colonel Monckton. The 1st Pennsylvania Brigade was positioned just west of the brook in woods to cover the bridge over the watercourse.

The heat was extraordinary. For the fifth day in a row, the temperatures were in the 90s, with high humidity to match the scorching heat, and the soldiers of both armies suffered; many died. The men were not the only ones to suffer. Washington was forced to bring forward his faithful chestnut mare as the beautiful white horse recently given to him by Governor Livingston

General David Forman was another militia officer who provided yeoman service during the battle as a guide for the Continental Army and an advisor to General Washington. *Crayon drawing by James Sharples in Charles Forman.* Three Revolutionary Soldiers, *Cleveland, The Forman-Bassett-Hatch Co., 1902*

perished due to the heat after the terrific exertions of carrying the energetic commander in chief back and forth across the battlefield. David Forman, the local militia leader and Continental colonel, provided Washington with a new mount until the commander's favorite warhorse arrived.

The combination of the heat and brave defense of the Americans at the hedgerow slowed down the main British advance but Clinton had not been idle. A capable tactician, and member of the "German school" of maneuver, Clinton was always looking for a way to flank the Americans. He had been the proponent of a flanking movement at Breed's Hill in 1775, and the architect of the brilliant movement around the American positions on Long Island. This day was no different. As the main body of the army chased Lee's retreating troops, Clinton detached the 3rd Brigade of Infantry, four regiments of foot, under Major General Sir Charles Grey to follow the Americans retreating across the Craig Farm toward Sutfin Farm in the corridor between the North and Middle Spotswood Brooks. He also sent Brigadier General Sir William Erskine with the Queen's Rangers, the Light Infantry, and the German Grenadiers to attempt an attack on Washington's left, or northern flank, by crossing the Spotswood North Brook near Foreman's Mill and pushing toward the Tennent Meeting House. Last, he sent Lord Cornwallis with a detachment to attack the American right. That advance never took place as Comb's Hill lay in his path. Steep hillsides with swampy ground at their base made an attack in that direction impossible.

The Great Cannonade

Stymied by the swampy morass and American fire covering the causeway, Clinton decided to use artillery to force the Continentals facing him across the West Ravine to retreat. Culling cannon from each of the brigades, he organized a gun line consisting of six 6-pounders, two 5½-inch howitzers, and two big 12-pounders. The row of guns, fed by dusty, hot gun crews, spewed shot and shell at the American positions on and around the slopes of Perrine Ridge. The Americans' cannons under Carrington gamely replied with their own fire in what would be a contest of artillery that lasted several hours. Firing and loading cannons was always hot work but on this June day it was oppressively hot. Bombardiers, gunners, and matrosses went to their exhausting work as quickly as they could, trying to silence their opponent's guns and clear out enemy infantry. Cartridges were rammed home, shot loaded, and touch holes fed sparks in a process that fired the solid shot over the terrain between the ridge and the rise near the hedgerow. Closer ranges saw the use of grapeshot. Sponges were dipped into buckets of water drawn in nearby streams or wells and the guns were swabbed out of burning cartridge materiel before the loading process was started all over again.

Smoke hung over the valley between the British guns east of the ravine and the American guns on the slope of Perrine Ridge. The smoke was split again and again by the spitting flame of a gun firing. The rotten-egg smell of gunpowder permeated the air as crews ran back and forth with cartridges and heavy balls to reload. Among Colonel Joseph Cilley's troops at the base of Perrine Ridge was Henry Dearborn. He described the cannonade—"I think it was the finest musick, I ever Heared"—but quickly pointed out its danger: "…however the agreeableness of the musick was very often Lessen'd by the balls Coming too near."[19]

The heat was terrific and members of the gun crews ran to nearby watercourses to fetch liquid relief. Later many soldiers would recall women who performed the chore including one they referred to as Molly Pitcher. Despite the temporary relief from thirst, many of those working the guns dropped, including William Hays, the barber from Carlisle, Pennsylvania, who was working a cannon in Proctor's company. His wife, Mary, had been carrying buckets of water to the gun crews when her husband fell. She dropped her bucket and joined his crew, doing what she could to keep the gun going. Joseph Plumb Martin, with Cilley's detachment along a fence near the artillery, commented on the action: "A woman whose husband belonged to the Artillery, and who was then attached to a piece in the engagement, attended with her husband at the piece the whole time; while in the act of reaching a cartridge and having one of her feet as far before the other as she could step, a cannon shot from the enemy passed directly between her legs without doing any other damage than carrying away all the lower part of her petticoat,—looking at it with apparent unconcern, she observed it was lucky it did not pass a little higher, for in that case it might have carried away something else, and ended her and her occupation."[20] Throughout the day soldiers and their women auxiliaries visited nearby streams or ponds for the water necessary to keep the guns in action.

Washington traveled back and forth along the line of Perrine Ridge during this part of the battle. He sent most of Lee's advanced guard to the road toward Englishtown to rest from their long, hot day. Though many had done little or no actual fighting, they had marched many miles back and forth that sweltering morning. At one time he stopped to observe the American artillery working and a stray British cannon ball hit nearby, sending dirt into the air and sprinkling the commander in chief with dirt and debris. Standing high in his stirrups for a better view, he was told by several officers to move but did so only when he saw something else that needed his attention. He then spurred

Molly Pitcher is one of the most famous names associated with the battle of Monmouth. Joseph Plumb Martin describes an unnamed woman's actions during the "Great Cannonade" that might have been the origin of the story. *National Archives, (Engraving by J. C. Armytage from painting by Alonzo Chappel, George Washington Bicentennial Commission. National Archives NAID: 532935 Local ID: 148-GW-923 Photographs and other Graphic Materials Covers: 1931–1932)*

his mount and briskly galloped off, leaving his aides and subordinates to try and keep up with him. Along with his military family, his personal slave and constant companion Billy Lee easily rode alongside the commander in chief. The Black man was just as accomplished a horseman as his master.

Oddly enough, except for the effects of heat and a few unlucky soldiers, the maelstrom of cannon fire inflicted only a small number of casualties on either side. Part of this was since many of the guns were firing at extreme range and most of the men of both sides were under cover; the British behind the hedgerow which had a solid dirt base, and the Americans up the slopes or even over the crest of Perrine Ridge out of the line of fire. Lord Stirling's adjutant, Lieutenant Colonel Francis Barber, was wounded during this action and a rising young officer, Major James Monroe of Virginia, took his place.

Several unlucky British soldiers died because of the cannon fire when they moved into shaded positions in a copse of trees closer to the American guns.

By avoiding the sweltering heat, they fell victim to the more lethal effects of the artillery. They were not the only ones who fell to cannon fire while seeking respite from the heat. Popular young Captain Henry Fauntleroy, commander of the 10th Company in the 5th Virginia, was celebrating his 32nd birthday on that blistering hot Sunday afternoon near Perrine Ridge when he lined up to get a drink of water at a well. It was Fauntleroy who had brought a pair of pistols as a gift to Washington back in April. Despite being exposed high on his horse, he patiently allowed several enlisted men to drink before him. A bouncing cannonball careened into his hip, knocking him from his mount. He never celebrated another birthday.

Tennent Meeting House

The first pastor of the new church built at the crossroads that led to Englishtown, South Amboy, and Monmouth Court House was the Reverend John Tennent in 1731. He died soon after and it was his brother, William Tennent, Jr., that built the church that the American army passed by that morning on their way to battle. The pastor had died recently and there were no services on that sultry Sunday morning. Yet several dozen local parishioners showed up to watch a battle not on a spiritual plane but on a more physical one. They were not the only ones. At the village of Freehold itself, community members hid among the buildings and in the nearby woods to watch Lee's soldiers' skirmish with Clinton's rear guard in the opening phase of the battle. Other locals watched throughout the battle, often in plain sight. British officers noted the locals skulking amidst bushes and trees and around buildings. They were not sure if they were militia or mere spectators.

With groups of locals watching the battle from different venues—Freehold, Perrine Ridge, Comb's Hill, and in the various woods—it's a wonder that not many civilians were hurt. At least one was killed near the Tennent Meeting House during the Great Cannonade. Sitting on a gravestone, a young man was hit by a careening cannonball that bounded into the graveyard, striking the marker he was sitting on, breaking off part of the stone, and fatally injuring him. He was one of many who would die in or near the building used as a hospital, though he was the only civilian.

Not far away, on the road to Elizabethtown, Charles Lee held court with any of the officers who would listen to him. Speaking contemptuously of those who lacked his experience, Lee calmly told of his battlefield exploits to the soldiers resting after the morning's action. One of the listeners was Washington's secretary, James McHenry. A former prisoner of war and veteran of many actions, McHenry noticed that Lee nervously told how he saved the army that day. The former English officer explained his frustration with the insubordination of others, the decisive superiority of the enemy cavalry, and gave the impression that the battle was finished. McHenry felt differently and returned to the commander in chief as Baron von Steuben brought up the last of the army.[21]

North of Spotswood Middle Brook

While Clinton led Cornwallis and his men in a direct attack down the main road, Sir Charles Grey's force moved across the John Craig and Sutfin Farms to outflank the American force along the main road behind the hedgerow. Moving into the open near Sutfin Farm, they were confronted by artillery fire from Carrington's guns on Perrine Ridge. Colonels Cilley and Richard Parker's picked men, stationed behind a rail fence at the base of the ridge facing the British, added musket fire to the fusillade. Grey retreated out of cannon range but left the Second Battalion, 42nd Foot, the Royal Highlanders, to shelter among the trees of the Sutfin Orchard in front of the ridge.

By late afternoon, the fire from the long cannonade began to slow down, and Washington decided to send out detachments to test the strength of the enemy. He rode over to Colonel Cilley on the lower slope of the ridge. "His excellency ordered me to take the battalion that I then commanded, consisting of 350 rank and file from Poor's, Glover's, Patterson's, Larnard's and Varnum's brigades, with Lieutenant Colonel Dearborn and Major Thair, (who were with me), and see what I could do with the enemy's right wing which was formed in an orchard in our front."[22] Colonel Richard Parker's 250 picked men would accompany him. Washington wanted Cilley to drive the British from the orchard near Sutfin Farm. Cilley gathered his own men, with Parker's, and a pair of 6-pounders, and moved to his left into the woods along the Spotswood North Brook. Cilley was an experienced officer from New Hampshire who had served in Roger's Rangers during the French and Indian War, fought in the abortive Canadian campaign, and earned lasting respect by capturing a British cannon single-handedly at Saratoga. Now he led the two detachments to the left, into the deep depression formed by the stream. Hundreds of men moved along the banks of the watercourse, screened by the trees, toward a position on the right flank of the Highlanders resting in the cover of the apple trees.

The Americans used the cover, and shade, to reach a position just to the north of the Highlanders' location, where they stopped. Filtering through the trees, the shaded darkness broken here and there by the probing fingers of the hot sun, Cilley and Parker moved through the ranks of the men and faced them toward the British position. Satisfied with his preparations, Cilley gave the signal, the cannon fired, and long lines of infantry in double ranks tumbled out of the trees, charging the orchard. In the glare of the bright sun, a Highlander captain spotted the Americans on the edge of the woods and alarmed the rest of the battalion.

The 42nd, seeking refuge from both the sun and the fire of the American cannons, had moved into the shade of the orchard. They were stunned out of their lethargy and quickly scrambled to form up behind one of the fences that enclosed the orchard. The Americans continued to fire with muskets and cannon, racing across a short space of open ground toward the enemy. The Highlanders gave a volley and then the Americans closed on the fence. Heavily outnumbered by the attacking Continentals, the Highlanders did not panic but skillfully withdrew through the orchard pursued by American fire, stopping occasionally to return that fire.

One of the men with Cilley was New Englander Joseph Plumb Martin, and for him the war became very personal: "When within about five rods of the rear of the retreating foe, I could distinguish everything about them, they were retreating in line, though in some disorder; I singled out a man and took my aim directly between his shoulders, (they were divested of their packs,) he was a good mark, being a broad shouldered fellow; what became of him I know not, the fire and smoke hid him from my sight; one thing I know, that is, I took deliberate aim at him as ever I did at any game in my life."[23]

The disciplined Highlanders fired volleys in reply to the American musketry but continued to retreat and eventually passed through the John Craig Farm to form up with Grey's main body and the artillery of the First Light Infantry. The British outnumbered the advancing Americans, who had moved into an open area out of range of their supporting artillery on the slopes of Perrine Ridge. Cilley and his lieutenant colonel, Henry Dearborn, wisely corralled their men and fell back to defensive positions in the orchard, a perfect spot to protect the guns along the lower slope of Perrine Ridge and the causeway over the West Ravine on their right.

North of Spotswood North Brook

Pushing north across the Spotswood North Brook near Forman's Mill were the British troops of Clinton's other flanking column under Brigadier General Sir William Erskine. The most successful tactic used by the British throughout the war had been flank marches around the end of American positions, facilitated by the professional marching ability and discipline of the British infantry. Long Island and Brandywine were excellent examples of significant British flanking maneuvers that resulted in major victories. In nearly every prior battle the British had tried to outmaneuver the Americans to get a crushing victory, but also to avoid needless casualties, as the king's soldiers and his mercenaries were expensive and their loss could not be taken lightly. Erskine was to march north with the Queen's Rangers, 1st Light Infantry, the 1st Battalion of the 42nd Foot, the 44th Foot, three Hessian Grenadier regiments, and a couple of 3-pound cannon nicknamed "grasshoppers," and then turn Washington's left flank near the Tennent Meeting House. If successful, they would outflank Stirling's men on Perrine Ridge, forcing Washington to retreat or face an enemy in both front and rear.

Erskine crossed the brook near Forman's Mill and moved west, seeking the rebel left flank. Militia had been active throughout the northern area above the Spotswood North Brook, watching the British right flank, and they reported Erskine's movement as soon as the British crossed the stream. Young Major James Monroe, a veteran officer who had been wounded at Trenton in 1776, reported the size of the British force to Washington after a short reconnaissance. The commander in chief ordered Lafayette, temporarily without a command, to take Poor's brigade, the 1st Maryland Brigade, the North Carolina Brigade, and Weedon's Virginia Brigade to the left and protect that flank, already protected by the militia under the indomitable Philemon Dickinson in the woods north of the Spotswood North Brook. The militia was used to fighting and running away. The situation was different now; they would stand firm when backed by hundreds of veteran Continentals under experienced officers led by the boyish Frenchman.

Erskine crossed the farm of Deacon John Craig and found boggy ground to his front and a creek to his left. As Erskine led his men to the west, there appeared to be large numbers of militia in the woods to his front and milling about all around him. Erskine made several tentative moves toward the Americans but couldn't gain any advantage. After only desultory firing, he fell back across Spotswood North Brook toward Clinton's main force. The militia, emboldened by their successful stand, pursued the British until they crossed the brook, nearly capturing a cannon bogged down in the mud.

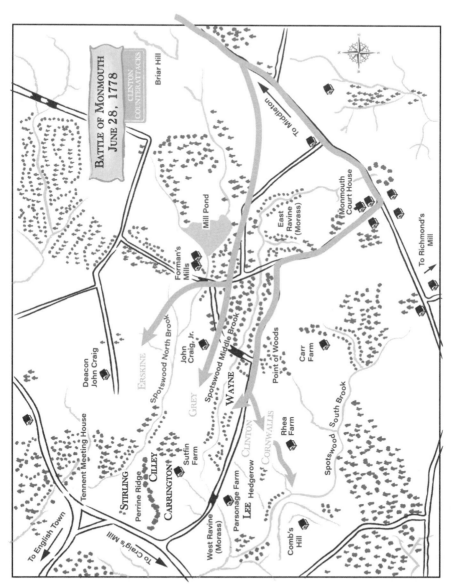

BATTLE OF MONMOUTH
JUNE 28, 1778

CLINTON
COUNTERATTACKS

While Lee maneuvered to obtain a more advantageous position, Henry Clinton skillfully turned his army about. Then he struck. *Megan Dacus*

Comb's Hill

Washington adroitly met each of the British moves. As the actions on the American left, at the Sutfin Farm, and near the causeway across the ravine were taking place, Nathanael Greene's column was moving southeast toward Craig's Mill on the British left. Greene moved his men quickly to the right, crossing Spotswood Middle Brook near the Huggins Farm and taking a position on the right of the army. David Rhea, the local officer detailed by Washington to guide Greene's march, led Greene toward Comb's Hill, a 160-foot height that clearly dominated the area.

Greene, a Rhode Islander often thought of as Washington's favorite general, had been chafing for action all winter. He had been "asked" to take over as quartermaster when the army moved into Valley Forge and experienced the first inadequacies of supply brought on by the poor performance of that department. Attacking the problem with customary energy, he quickly turned things around, started the flow of supplies back to the main camp, and in the process organized the department to work more efficiently. But he had only taken the post with the caveat that he would be given a field command in the next campaign. Washington gave him that command on the afternoon of June 28 when the Continentals under Greene followed Rhea to the crest of Comb's Hill.

Atop the hill, protected at its base by the swampy ground of the Spotswood South Brook and closely covered by Woodford's seasoned Virginia Brigade, four 6-pounders were positioned by the experienced eye of Brigadier General Thomas-Antoine de Mauduit Du Plessis. Du Plessis had attended the French school of artillery and now served as adjutant to the chief of artillery, Henry Knox. He thoroughly knew his business. By midafternoon he had the guns in position and firing on the British artillery battery and infantry along the hedge-row, essentially enfilading their line from their left. The fire abruptly surprised the red-coated infantry; it prevented them from crossing the West Ravine and made their position along the hedgerow and in the buildings of the Parsonage Farm untenable. The redcoats beat a hasty retreat. Without infantry support, the British artillery was forced to withdraw, and the Great Cannonade was over.

Clinton recognized the danger from the elevation on his left. Earlier, he detached Lord Cornwallis to take Comb's Hill with the 37th Foot, 44th Foot, and the two battalions of Guards. Unfortunately, they found the same reasons that had compelled Lee to forgo taking possession of the hill earlier in the day prevented them from making any headway toward the hill. The swampy ground that literally sucked the shoes from soldiers' feet was too wet to be traversed by artillery. The steep terrain made an ascent of the slope difficult.

Cornwallis found the heat had sapped the strength from many of his men and they moved as if in a stupor. Greene's cannon were firing and their ability to control much of the ground made an attack on the hill difficult. After trying a short movement toward the left of the hill, Cornwallis brought his troops back to the line behind the hedgerow and then continued further back to the Wikoff Farm. It was obvious that the British were outflanked; Clinton pulled back his infantry and cannon, ending the cannonading between the two lines of guns. The 1st Grenadiers stayed behind the rest of Cornwallis' detachment and took up an outpost position near the Wikoff Farm.

The Hedgerow, Part Two

Washington surveyed the battlefield after the cannons ended their exchange. Seeing the vacuum created by the British withdrawal from the hedgerow, he decided to take advantage. After sending Cilley across Sutfin Farm, he ordered Wayne to take a detachment, re-cross the causeway over the Middle Brook, and explore the British position. Wayne led part of his old Pennsylvania Brigade; the 3rd Pennsylvania under Colonel Thomas Craig; Spencer's Additional Regiment under Colonel Oliver Spencer; and Malcolm's Additional Regiment under Lieutenant Colonel Aaron Burr. All three were experienced officers. Craig was a veteran of the Canadian campaign and had served at Brandywine, Germantown, and Valley Forge. Spencer was a New Jersey militia officer who had seen more combat than many Continental officers, serving with such merit that he was chosen to form his own regiment in January of 1777 from men in Pennsylvania and New Jersey. Burr had been beside Brigadier General Richard Montgomery at the latter's death in the failed attempt to take Quebec in 1775. He had served in staff and field positions since, gaining a reputation as an excellent soldier and leader.

Wayne formed up his men, moved them across the brook as fast as possible and then reformed on the other side. With the three regiments on line, two ranks deep with flashing bayonets leading, the Americans stormed across Parsonage Farm and struck the isolated 1st Grenadiers near the small rise just east of the hedgerow near the Wikoff Farm.

The veteran grenadiers were surprised by the assault and gave way but did not panic. The action was close and hot, bayonets as well as muskets the dominant weapons. Men on both sides fell, including Lieutenant Colonel Rudolph Bunner of the 3rd Pennsylvania who was killed by a musket ball. During the fighting Burr's horse was killed, joining many other mounts that perished that hot day, some to enemy fire but many to the extreme temperature. The redcoats were pushed back toward the Carr House and the Americans followed but lacked the numbers to do much more than maintain contact, soon outdistancing their supporting artillery atop Comb's Hill. British artillery brought the charging Americans up short. The British and Americans traded shots for a few minutes across the fields of the farm until Clinton acted.

Clinton directed Lieutenant Colonel James Webster to advance his 33rd Foot into a position to support the retreating grenadiers. The red-coated infantry of the 33rd Foot counterattacked through their grenadier comrades, struck the pursuing Americans, and drove them back toward the Parsonage Farm. The British could not gain any advantage from their counterblow as American artillery fire from Comb's Hill made it too hot for Webster's men to remain near the hedgerow. American fire was heavy: one British platoon had a cannon ball travel down its front, injuring some and knocking muskets from the hands of some of the soldiers. Washington ordered Wayne to hold where he was and pushed across other troops, including more Pennsylvanians from Wayne's own brigade, to support him.

Aaron Burr's men had taken a position that exposed them to the direct fire of the British and were taking casualties when Washington's order to hold their position arrived. Burr thought it would be better to attack the British immediately but many of the men were exhausted, including Burr who was suffering some ill effect from the heat. Washington wanted them to hold until he could bring up fresh troops before advancing further. Burr's men took several casualties while waiting near the ravine and Burr felt Washington left his men exposed to enemy fire too long. As more troops arrived, Burr finally pulled his troops back across the ravine. He harbored ill will toward Washington from several earlier encounters, including an attempt by Washington to force him into a position on the commander in chief's staff. Burr felt the losses under close British fire were unnecessary and he blamed Washington for leaving his men in an exposed position.

Once they were safely under the guns of the battery atop Comb's Hill and protected by the grand battery of guns on Perrine Ridge, the Americans used the buildings of the Parsonage Farm, unoccupied as the pastor had died and not been replaced, to dispute the British advance. Clinton pulled the 33rd back after finding he couldn't take and hold the hedgerow with the dominating rebel artillery atop Comb's Hill. More American reinforcements built up a line and the fighting abruptly ended. Continental soldiers went through the bodies of those who had fallen earlier in the day searching for loot or wounded soldiers. Among the bodies of grenadiers killed earlier in the day was a well-dressed form, obviously an officer. The infantrymen of Captain William Wilson's company of Colonel James Chambers' 1st Pennsylvania finally took possession of the body of gallant Colonel Henry Monckton.

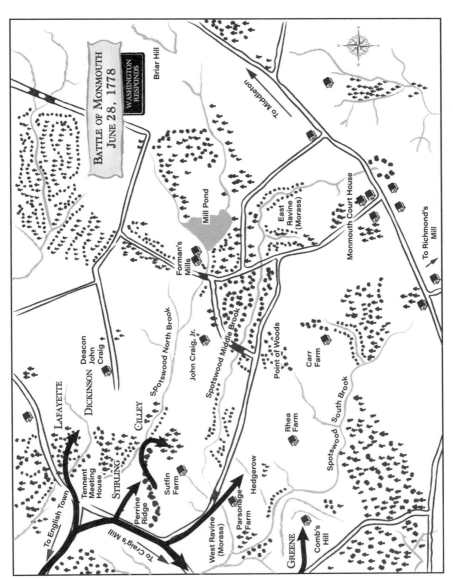

Washington parried each move by the British. Then he prepared to engage the British the following day. *Megan Dacus*

End of the Day

Clinton's men were at the end of a very long day, as it was nearly 6:00 pm, and the general realized if there was more fighting to be done, it would have to be done the next day. He ordered part of Knyphausen's division, the British 1st Brigade, to join him but Brigadier General James Grant,[24] commanding the forces in question, failed to move up. Cornwallis' division, especially his elite formations, had been moving and fighting since 4:00 am in great heat and humidity. They were exhausted. Clinton pulled Grey's men back across the Spotswood Middle Brook with Erskine's men to join the rest of the army near the original position the British had occupied that morning.

Weary soldiers from Lee's morning advanced guard were east of Englishtown, ordered to refresh themselves there by Washington after their busy day. Lee continued to converse with any officer who would listen, primarily his own aides, and told all within earshot of why the battle had been such a bad idea, frequently questioning those around him as to how they viewed his mental state during the action and espousing the superiority of the British cavalry.

Washington wasn't finished. He called for more troops to support an advance. Enoch Poor took his brigade and the North Carolina Brigade across the causeway to move in on the left of Wayne's detachment. Woodford's Virginians came down the slope east of Comb's Hill, to a position on Wayne's right. To support the movement, Baron von Steuben came forward with the reorganized remnants of Lee's division from Englishtown, and Brigadier General John Paterson followed with a force made up of his own Massachusetts brigade and the 2nd Maryland Brigade.

Poor's men failed to come to grips with the enemy, as the British fell back quicker than the Americans could close. The British moved back to a position east of the Carr Farm using the Middle Ravine as an obstacle to their front. It had been a long day and many soldiers, especially Lee's men, were exhausted; the heat had taken its toll on even the freshest troops who had hurried from Englishtown. Combat and the excitement of action had drained the fighting ability of many of the soldiers. Washington, usually a good judge of men, saw that an attack at the late hour might not achieve results that would be worth the effort. He ordered the regiments to halt in place. Washington sent Poor's relatively fresh brigade closer to maintain contact with the British outposts. Poor was one of the most respected and able of the army's brigade commanders but had been denied any role in the long day's fighting. A tough fighting man who had had made a name for himself in the heaviest fighting around Saratoga, Poor moved his men quickly into position near the British. They eagerly anticipated a renewal of action on the morrow.

In the waning hours of the long day, George Washington finished bringing up the main body of the army in preparation for the next day's action. Washington hoped to renew the battle the next morning and ordered the army to sleep on their arms in preparation for whatever the following day might bring. The American pickets were told to position themselves close enough to see their British counterparts. Washington wanted to prevent a surprise attack by the British but also wished to be close enough to fight in the morning.

Both armies were exhausted. Enemies slept fitfully, nerves on edge after the long battle, the exhaustion of a long day, and their closeness to their opponents. The voices of the pickets of each army carried through the darkness of the warm night. Washington found an oak tree and curled up in his cloak under it for a few hours' sleep. Lying next to him, sharing his cloak, was the Marquis de Lafayette.

CHAPTER 6

Order from Chaos

Clinton

Combat is a physically and mentally exhausting activity. In addition to the sheer physical exertion of lugging around a heavy weapon and many pounds of other gear, including canteens and cartridge boxes, there were long marches to new positions and quick rushes or advances. Short bursts of adrenaline from an enemy charge or in the anticipation of action took a toll just as heavy as that of the marching and running. The dry throat and heavy breathing of the fighting soldier is not always from the battle; it can come from the waiting and watching as opponents move toward you or assault positions near you. It affected everyone, the militiaman from Pennsylvania or the grenadier from Dublin, and by the time darkness engulfed the armies, most of the soldiers on the battlefield were worn out.

Gaunt and weary faces framed reddened eyes, lethargic arms cradled hot weapons, and wobbly legs slowly propelled tired soldiers, British and American, wherever their equally fatigued officers sent them. Parched and dry mouths, framed by grayish streaks caused by the opening of cartridges, longed for refreshment. As if mocking their condition, the late evening cooled only marginally, making sleep difficult. Joseph Plumb Martin summed up the exhaustion of the day's battle: "We then laid ourselves down under the fences and bushes to take a breath, for we had need of it. I presume everyone has heard of the heat of that day, but none can realize it that did not feel it. Fighting is hot work in cool weather, how much more so in such weather as it was on the twenty-eighth of June, 1778."[1] The darkness ended all activity.

Washington had a reputation as the "Fox" earned at Long Island, in New York, and after the second battle at Trenton, slipping away in situations in which his army appeared trapped in an unfavorable position. He was outdone on the night of June 28. As the darkness of the summer night slowly enveloped the battlefield, Henry Clinton was awake, weighing all his options. "It was not for me to give him [Washington] the advantage… by attacking him so posted; nor indeed could I have done it, as the troops were fairly spent."[2] Despite his personal wish to do battle, the long logistics train, the strong American position, and the fatigue of his own troops were factors that led Clinton to order his men to begin moving east at about 10:00 pm. Clinton gave up the possibility of renewing battle on the present ground and took advantage of the tired Americans to slip away in the night.

Officers prodded the exhausted troops and forced them onto the road in a well-orchestrated move that was so quiet nearby American outposts failed to notice any disturbance. Fortunately, the baggage train was already on the road and a good distance from the battlefield, leaving the army somewhat unencumbered. Taking advantage of a moonless night, the artillery and troops farthest away from the picket line moved first, then those closer to the Americans. The last to move were the light troops who had done so much fighting and marching during that long day. Cloaked in darkness, they moved out so silently that the rebel pickets didn't realize they were gone until three hours after the last British soldiers had left. The Queen's Rangers, who covered the retreat through Freehold, released 15 locals who had been detained for various reasons when they left the village to join the main body in retreat.

The British column, following its slow-moving baggage train, marched 13 miles the day after the battle before catching up with their comrades with the wagons. At first light they met Knyphausen and the rest of the army with the vast procession of wheeled vehicles at Nut Swamp. By mid-morning they reached Middleton and remained there the rest of the day. Clinton did not give up hope for a general action. Perhaps Washington would pursue him into the rugged country near the coast and he would use the terrain, as Washington had used Perrine Ridge and Comb's Hill, to defeat the Continental Army. "I waited two days in the hope that Mr. Washington might have been tempted to advance to the position near Middletown, which we had quited; in which case I might have attacked him to advantage."[3] Like many of the British generals, he was unable to give up on the idea that if given the right opportunity, he could end the war with a great victory over Washington. He also had the bad taste in his mouth so common to British generals that had the opportunity to destroy the American army in a major action but had failed to do so.

As the British retreat had put a great distance between the American army and themselves, and entered into territory unfavorable for pursuit, Washington was content to let the British attain New York City, harassed by American light troops and militia. The evening after the battle he and some of his staff

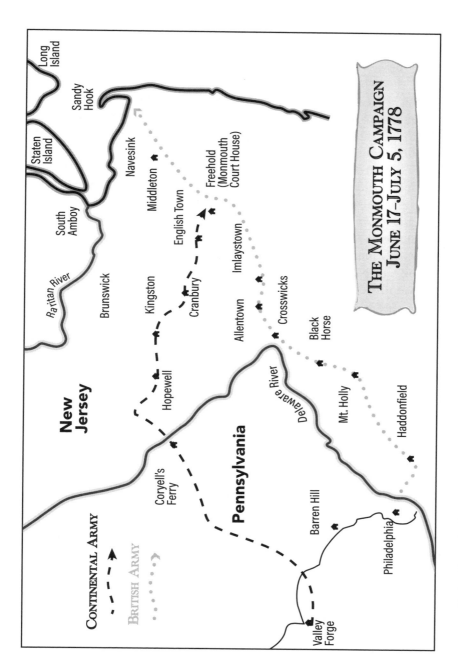

THE MONMOUTH CAMPAIGN
JUNE 17–JULY 5, 1778

CONTINENTAL ARMY

BRITISH ARMY

Long Island

Sandy Hook

Staten Island

Navesink

South Amboy

Middleton

Freehold (Monmouth Court House)

English Town

Raritan River

Brunswick

Imlaystown

Kingston

Cranbury

Allentown

Crosswicks

Hopewell

Black Horse

Delaware River

New Jersey

Mt. Holly

Haddonfield

Coryell's Ferry

Pennsylvania

Barren Hill

Philadelphia

Valley Forge

In the aftermath of Monmouth, the British retreat to New York City via rough country to Sandy Hook. *Megan Dacus* relaxed at the home of one Moses Laird, enjoying a filling meal with the man's engaging wife and daughters. The main Continental force remained in place around Freehold, parties scouring the battlefield for dead and wounded as well as looting British bodies, their Brown Bess muskets a particular trophy as many of the French muskets the rebels carried had proven unreliable. The day after the battle, Washington ordered the groups of "picked men" dissolved and the soldiers returned to their parent units. The militia and light troops under Maxwell and Morgan along with Moylan's dragoons followed the tired but wary British as Clinton made his way to Sandy Hook.

Deserters from the British force, especially Hessians, continued to be rounded up days after the battle. The American light troops captured "several prisoners, a number of horses, and some baggage"[4] during one of their annoying attacks on the long British column. Typical was an action described by Stephen Moylan: "within three miles of Midletown, we attackd a party of the enemy, this morning and took one Captain one Lieut. and one Ensign, with two privats, prisoners, & Killd a few more, the Brittish army is expected at that place this day or to morrow. quarters are taken for Gen. Clinton at Midletown, and for Lord Cornwallis at the place where we made the attack, which I suppose will be the rear of their army, the Baggage is still where it last night halted, badly guarded, I wish there was infantry in this Quarter a great stroke might Still be made upon it."[5]

The British commander continued to hope that Washington might attack him in the rugged hills near the coast, but he was continually disappointed. Clinton had to be satisfied with the completion of his assigned task, taking his army to the coast without major losses in wagons or baggage. Unfortunately for the British commander it appeared as if he was running from the American army, and leaving many of his wounded at Monmouth Court House added to the perception of defeat.

Arriving at the peninsula of Sandy Hook, the British found it to be an island separated from the mainland. The army paused long enough for the able Major John Montresor and his engineers to construct a floating bridge from the mainland to the island. From July 2 to July 5 the British army crossed over the bridge and embarked on ships to return to New York, harassed more by summer rains and mosquitoes than the irregular American troops.

Tensions were high one night when the British and their allies heard a great deal of musket and cannon fire coming from the nearest American encampment, but they soon realized that it was July 4 and the rebels were merely celebrating their declaration of independence. The rebels might have been celebrating even more if Clinton had not hurried across from Sandy Hook to New York City. On July 11, the French fleet appeared off Sandy Hook. The new American allies had barely missed Lord Howe's fleet in mid-June as it was leaving the Chesapeake with its load of refugees, and they missed interrupting Clinton's nautical retreat by only a few days. With his arrival in New York, Sir Henry had achieved his objective, the withdrawal of British forces from Philadelphia, without losing any major part of his army or stores. One account even compared his retreat across the countryside of New Jersey to the march of Greek general Xenophon's ten thousand from deep in Persia back to Greece in 401 BC.[6] Despite the accomplishment, and various accolades, it was the end of the inconclusive British occupation of Philadelphia and an indication of a new Imperial policy.

The Americans

Major Richard Howell had turned down a chance to visit his dying brother on June 28 and stayed with his regiment, taking part in the entire battle. Early the next morning, he left the army and journeyed to Black Horse Tavern to be with his twin, Lewis, who was the 2nd New Jersey regimental surgeon. He arrived in time to see his brother die.

General Lee received a note in the dawning hours of June 29, from Daniel Morgan, explaining what had kept the "Old Wagoner" out of the fight:

> Sir,
>
> General Lee wrote me yesterday at one o'clock in the evening, he intended to attack the enemy's rear this morning, and ordered me to attack them at the same time on their right flank.[7]

Morgan still thought it was on June 29 that Lee had intended to attack and Lee apparently made no attempt during the battle to contact Morgan, leaving his elite force out of the action. Misdating a letter seems a small thing but it may have had an impact on the outcome of the battle. It was not the last time that Lee would misdate a message.

Washington pushed out his light units, Maxwell, Morgan, McLane, and Moylan, to follow and harass the British, but the bulk of the Continental Army returned to reclaim their baggage and to rest around Englishtown. On July 1 the rested troops marched north to New Brunswick.

Also on July 1, Washington sent a letter to the president of Congress with his report on the action. In it, he paints a picture of positive action and lauds his troops' conduct while giving a brief description of their fatigue due to the weather. While he praises the officers of the army, "They seemed to vie with each other in manifesting their Zeal and Bravery," he praises only one individual officer: "Brigadier General Wayne whose good conduct and bravery thro' the whole action deserves particular commendation." Just before he ends the detailed letter, he inserts information about a controversy developing in the army: "The peculiar Situation of General Lee at this time, requires that I should say nothing of his Conduct. He is now in arrest. The Charges against him, with such Sentence as the Court Martial may decree in his Case, shall be transmitted for the approbation or disapprobation of Congress as soon as it shall have passed."[8] On the same date he issued a general order including a reference to the same controversy: "A General Court-Martial whereof Lord Stirling is appointed President will sit in Brunswick tomorrow (the hour and place to be appointed by the President) for the Trial of Major General Lee."[9]

A few days later the army celebrated the Fourth of July, a very special celebration with new meaning, as the average soldier did not view Monmouth as a draw but as a full-fledged victory. A chaplain with John Glover's brigade noted how the recent action added to the celebration: "The Consideration of the late defeat of the Enemy & divine providence having removed the gloom that seemed to shade our Independence invited the festivity."[10] George Washington was treated to an elaborate ceremony like that of the celebration at Valley Forge when the alliance with France was announced. From a second-story balcony at Ross Hall, across the Raritan River from the army, Washington watched the soldiers, decorated with boughs in their hats, fire a volley after a 13-gun salute by the artillery. The smoky celebration was repeated three times, a *feu de joie* comparable to the one the army had staged back at Valley Forge. It was followed by a celebration dinner attended by over 100 guests. One of the guests reported, "The running fire of musketry is grand of itself, but the cannon throwing out their columns of smoke, and adding their sounds at proper distances, made it magnificent beyond description."[11]

The rebel soldiers crossed the Hudson River at King's Ferry on July 17 and a week later settled in at White Plains, where they had been defeated two years prior. Events had brought great changes, with the defeat of Clinton and the entry of France into the war; Washington was free to focus on his dream since 1776, an attack on New York City.

Losses

Casualties for the battle were hard to determine. American soldiers and locals crisscrossed the battlefield in the days after the battle looking for wounded and dead. One was Dr. William Read of Georgia, who walked near the West

Ravine the morning after the battle and was shocked when he found large numbers of wounded and dead British soldiers, mostly grenadiers injured in the fight with Lee's men at the Hedgerow and subsequent pursuit of the retreating Americans. Most of the wounded were in a poor state; many had died of their wounds. Some of the casualties had been left in shade or buildings, but the dead were strewn about where the Continental artillery had done its work. The British left 44 privates and wounded officers at St. Peter's Episcopal Church in Freehold, which had been used as a hospital during the action.

Washington issued orders that the wounded, both British and American, be transported to hospitals in Princeton. In a note to Congress, Washington officially listed his losses as 69 killed, 161 wounded, and 132 missing.[12] New York Colonel Cornelius Van Dyke led a burial party, noting his men interred 217 British and 29 American soldiers.[13] It was difficult to count the exact cost because of the large numbers of militia involved, the use of "picked men" not fighting with their own regiments, and many independent detachments, like the commander in chief's guard, who were on detached duty with unfamiliar battalions or regiments. Most of the missing were those who were merely separated from their regiment and would return later. Unlike previous battles, the British captured only a few Americans. Washington does not differentiate between battle and heat casualties.

In a letter to William Livingston, the governor of New Jersey, Washington mentions how many of the enemy soldiers were lost: "They [burial parties] have returned 245 killed. Besides the enemy left behind them at Monmouth Court house, 4 wounded officers, and 40 privates exclusive of those we took on the field of battle. The prisoners taken since the enemy entered the Jersey amount to about 100. Our loss considering the severity and sharpness of the different contentions is very inconsiderable. We have 60 rank and file killed and 133 wounded."[14] He mentioned the same figure of 245 bodies buried in a letter to his brother.[15]

British sources also mentioned conflicting numbers. Clinton's adjutant, Stephen Kemble, recorded that the British forces lost a total of 65 killed, 170 wounded, and 64 missing.[16] As in the totals of American casualties, there were circumstances that make any count of the actual Crown losses on June 28 suspect. Hundreds of Germans and many British were deserting throughout this period. Clinton states that a further 59 died of "fatigue," which would indicate they perished because of the heat.[17] These are not included in the tally of dead. Captain Ewald of the Jaegers estimated that counting desertions and casualties, including those felled by the atrocious heat, "this march cost two thousand men."[18] The losses were especially heavy in the elite formations of the British. Lieutenant Hale reported that the 2nd Grenadiers lost 98, of whom 11 were officers, killed or wounded.[19] The elite battalions of light infantry and grenadiers were disbanded after the retreat from Monmouth. This may have made exact casualty counts problematic.

Overall casualties for the battle were surprisingly light, considering the fight lasted from early morning until the evening and large numbers of men were involved. The disjointed nature of the battle no doubt contributed to this, with detachments fighting in separate actions at different locations at different times and the full force of both armies never really involved in a single, heavy action. Much of the British army did not take part in the battle at all. Washington's army took part in relays; few of those in Lee's advanced corps that began the battle finished the day on the front line.

People searching the fields and woods of New Jersey found many victims. One of the wounded was Nathaniel Ramsey. The British had left him for dead when they scattered his detachment and that of Walter Stewart at the point of woods. Later in the day, British troops found him still alive and took him prisoner. While Ramsey's wounds were being treated, Henry Clinton learned of his one-man fight against overwhelming odds. Ramsey was treated with respect until he was released on parole on November 11, 1780.

The Americans also appreciated the heroic efforts of their transatlantic cousins. Henry Monckton was buried with full honors at the Tennent Meeting House. Washington mentioned the brave British officer in his report to the president of Congress. Clinton, ever the gentleman, sent a thank-you note to Washington, not only for the care of his wounded but also for the burial honors rendered to Henry Monckton.[20]

Aftermath: The British

It is difficult to know how much influence the battle around Monmouth had upon British policies, but Clinton made no attempt to test Washington's main army in the next two years and there were no major actions in the Middle States after Monmouth. The makers of Imperial policy in London changed the focus of operations to the Southern colonies where they expected large numbers of new American recruits. The setback at Monmouth may have encouraged the king's ministers to look elsewhere to an area where they didn't have to face Washington and his Continental Army. As if closing a book on the British efforts in the North, Congress informed the Carlisle Commission on August 11, 1778, that there would be no dealings with them.

For the British, victory would not come on the New Jersey battlefield or with diplomacy. Combining the events of the summer of 1778 can only lead to the conclusion that the campaign was a defeat for the British. The evacuation of Philadelphia, the harassed retreat across New Jersey, the defeat on the battlefield of Monmouth Court House, the retreat from the battlefield, the arrival of the French fleet off New York City, and the unsuccessful Carlisle Commission indicated the failure of the British campaign in 1778.

In August of 1778, the Americans and French attempted to force the British out of Newport, Rhode Island, which the redcoats had held since 1776. Unfortunate events forced the French fleet to withdraw and the American army, under Major General John Sullivan, conducted a fighting retreat in the presence of the superior British forces. Henry Jackson's troops proved especially valuable as light infantry under the command of Henry Beekman Livingston. The veteran Continental troops, trained by von Steuben, proved the backbone of Sullivan's force. The Continentals counterattacked the British, briefly pushing them back. Nathanael Greene compared it to June 28: "I had the pleasure to see them run in worse disorder than they did at the battle of Monmouth."[21] This action provided the breathing space needed for a successful amphibious withdrawal of the American forces.

When the new Imperial policy shifted the geographic focus of war in North America to the Southern States, Clinton was directed to move south and support the Loyalists there. In a skillful campaign, Clinton conquered the city of Charleston, delivering the worst American defeat of the entire war. The capture of the most prosperous city in the Southern Colonies appeared to be the key to the South and Clinton, satisfied with a job well done, returned to New York in triumph, leaving the mopping up to Lord Cornwallis. Unfortunately, Imperial policy makers were disappointed, as the capture of Charleston did no better in ending the war than the capture of Philadelphia in 1777.

While Clinton was in South Carolina conquering Charleston, his subordinate in New York City, Baron von Knyphausen, launched a raid into New Jersey on June 7, 1780, engaging a part of the Continental Army and local militia. The battle, sometimes referred to as the battle of Connecticut Farms, took place near Springfield, New Jersey and ended with Knyphausen retreating. When Clinton returned, the two generals led a multi-pronged raid into New Jersey on June 23 that resulted in another action near Springfield that ended with the British retreating again. Clinton never challenged Washington's army directly after Monmouth.

Aftermath: The Americans

The war was not over by any means for the main army after the British moved the scene of operations to the south. A difficult winter was spent in 1779–80 at Morristown, far worse than that at Valley Forge in 1777–78. There were several mutinies and attempted mutinies. Unable to strike the main British army entrenched in New York, Washington contented himself with an attack by Anthony Wayne against the British outpost at Stony Point on July 16, 1779, and an expedition against the Indians led by John Sullivan in the summer of 1779. Irregular warfare on Long Island, in the area north of New York City, and in the New Jersey countryside, kept the Continental Army and local militias occupied.

Washington wanted to attack New York City but was faced with various problems; weather, a lack of men and materiel, or British dispositions. It was an offer by his new French allies to go south to the Chesapeake that changed his mind and Washington finally gave up his fascination with New York. When he took his army to Yorktown in Virginia in 1781, he proved that he had learned many lessons during the war. The deception of his movement south and his ultimate success on the banks of the York River enabled him to eventually reenter New York without a fight on November 25, 1783. For George Washington, the satisfaction of the successful completion of the military phase of the American Revolution was the culmination of an educational experience for himself. He went from an inexperienced army commander with a natural military bearing to an accomplished and skillful military leader. One of the major turning points in his education was the battle of Monmouth.

CHAPTER 7

Aftermath of Battle

Charles Lee

While the Continental Army rested near the battlefield, petulant Charles Lee was not happy with his treatment during his meeting with Washington during the battle. His overall conduct in the battle at Monmouth Court House was a mixed bag. He failed to state his intentions to his subordinates or keep them informed. He missed an opportunity to attack the retreating British and gave up the tactical initiative to the more energetic Clinton. In the ensuing action, Lee lost control of his detachments, carried along by the retreat. Personally, he recovered to valiantly lead the defenders along the hedgerow until Washington could organize the army's defensive positions atop Perrine Ridge. Lee was not the only one who made errors that day. It was Charles Scott's precipitous withdrawal that had started the flood to the rear when he mistakenly believed a retreat was in progress and his men were being left behind. William Maxwell retreated with Scott despite the lack of clear orders. At the same time, Lee lost control of the various detachments and failed to keep everyone, his subordinates and Washington, informed of what was going on. Much of what had happened was just the fog of war caused by the lack of messengers and the actions of the British. There was no reason for him to feel dishonored, but he simmered over a perceived slight. He remained second in command of the army and performed his duties as required.

The angry words of Washington during their battlefield meeting had struck deep in the heart of the enigmatic Lee and he felt that the commander in chief owed him an apology or at least an explanation. Washington was too focused on directing the army to dwell on what had passed, especially a violent outburst in the heat of battle, and the commander in chief made no mention of the incident. Lee boiled all through the 29th, listening to the rumors and stories that swirled around him concerning his role in the retreat. One example of this gossip is a letter written by James McHenry, Washington's aide: "Whether it was owing to a defect in the original scheme of attack, or in its execution in the first instance under Gen. Lee, should be inquired into. For from one or other of these causes we lost the fairest opportunity this war has afforded to destroy the British army."[1] McHenry also expressed the opinion of many concerning the role of Washington in the battle: "However, by the exertions of our General, a small front was formed, that gave the first check to the enemy's progress till a more solid opposition was made."

Not only was much of the buzz around camp questioning Lee's decisions but it also was praising Washington for what Lee thought were his own actions. Typical was Major Joseph Bromfield: "[Washington's army] Drove the proud King's-Guards & haughty British-Grenadiers, & gained Immortal-honor, to the Shame & infamy of Genl. Lee who acted the part of the base in not engaging the Enemy when he had received positive orders to attack them. But History I expect will give a full account of this memorable action, justly censure Lee for his scandalous behavior & give due credit... to Genl. Washington's bravery & merit."[2] Instead of going to Washington and explaining what happened during the battle or writing his own account of the action, Lee bristled at the rumors.

The army rested the day after the battle. But the malicious talk about Lee's conduct continued to circulate. Oddly, Lee expected Washington somehow to come to him and apologize. Washington had moved on; his perception of what occurred on the battlefield was that he had only done and said what was necessary. Finally, that evening, as Lee received no communication on the subject, he made a grave mistake by penning a poorly worded note to Washington:

> Camp, English Town, July 1st [actually June 29] 1778
>
> Sir,
>
> From the knowledge I have of your Excy's character—I must conclude that the misinformation of some very stupid, or misrepresentation of some very wicked person, coud have occasioned your making use of so very singular expressions as you did on my coming to the ground where you had taken post—They implyed that I was guilty either of disobedience of orders, of want of conduct, or want of courage. Your Excellency will therefore infinitely oblige me by which of these three articles you ground your charge—that I may prepare for my justification which I have the happiness to be confident I can do the army, to the Congress, to America, and to the world in general. Your excellency must give me leave to observe that neither yourself, nor those about your person, could from your situation be in the least judges of the merits or demerits of our maneuvers—And to speak with a becoming pride, I can assert, that to these maneuvers the success of the day was entirely owing—I can boldly say, that had we remained on the first ground, or had we advanced, or had the retreat been conducted in a manner different from what it was, this whole army, and the interests of America, would have risked being sacrificed. I ever had (and

hope ever shall have the greatest respect and veneration for General Washington) I think him endowed with many great and good qualities, but in this instance I must pronounce that he has been guilty of an act of cruel injustice towards a man who certainly has some pretensions to the regard of every servant of this country—and, I think Sir, I have the right to demand some reparation for the injury committed—and unless I can obtain it, I must in justice to myself, when this campaign is closed, which I believe will close this war retire from a service at the head of which is placed a man capable of offering such injuries. But at the same time in justice to you I must repeat that I from my soul believe, that it was not a motion of your own breast, but instigated by some of those dirty earwigs who will for ever insinuate themselves near persons in high office—for I really am convinced that when General Washington acts from himself no man in his army will have reason to complain of injustice or indecorum. I am, Sir, and hope I ever shall have reason to continue your most sincerely devoted humble servt

Charles Lee[3]

This rambling letter was obviously a reaction to continued comments from others (the "earwigs" mentioned in the letter) in the camp about the incident. Officers in the Revolution were notoriously jealous of their honor and position, so much so that John Adams had likened them to animals: "They worry one another like mastiffs, scrambling for rank and pay like apes for nuts."[4] Previously some officers had gone as far as to challenge others in duels to protect their personal honor. Most of the offenses had been over rank or seniority but often it was merely a perceived slight that activated animosity between officers.

After Monmouth some officers, like McHenry, felt that an opportunity to inflict a defeat on the British had been lost, or at the very least that Lee had shown a lack of leadership. These men made sure everyone in earshot knew of their opinion of Lee. In response, Lee was stung by something more than the few comments by Washington on the battlefield. He indicates several times in his note that it may have been the remarks of others that put the angry words into Washington's mouth. But the spontaneity of Washington's outburst leaves no doubt as to whose thoughts they were. It is interesting to note how Lee perceived that his orders to retreat "saved" not just the army but the revolution as well. If he was requesting an apology from Washington with his meandering writing style, drifting back and forth from directly addressing the commander in chief and then using the third person, he failed miserably.

At this point Washington was content that the actions at Monmouth had been a success for the Continental Army. On June 29 he had issued the General Orders for the day with a proud proclamation: "The Commander in Chief Congratulates the Army on the Victory obtained over the Arms of his Britanick Majesty yesterday and thanks most sincerely the gallant officers and men who distinguished themselves upon the occasion and such others as by their good order & discipline gave the happiest presages of what might have been expected had they come to Action."[5] He also informed the president of Congress of the battle in a note with a positive twist: "I have the honor to inform you that about seven OClock yesterday Morning both Armies advanced on each other. About 12 they met on the Grounds near Monmouth Court House, when an action commenced. We forced the Enemy from the Field and encamped on the Ground."[6] Busy with the continuing campaign, Washington received Lee's surprising note sometime during the morning of July 30.

Washington must have expected some type of report about the battle from his subordinates and when he received Lee's note, he probably thought it was such a statement. Any feelings of friendship that may have remained after Lee's antics over the last two years evaporated immediately upon reading the missive. One of Washington's trademarks in writing was his brevity, a characteristic Lee should have cultivated, and the Virginian curtly answered Lee's rant the same day:

> Head Qr. English Town June 30th 1778
>
> Sir,
>
> I received your letter, (dated, thro' mistake, the 1st of July) expressed, as I conceive, in terms highly improper. I am not conscious of having made use of any very singular expressions at the time of my meeting you, as you intimate. What I recollect to have said was dictated by duty and warranted by the occasion. As soon as circumstances will permit, you shall have an opportunity either of justifying yourself to the army, to Congress, to America, and to the world in general; or of convincing them that you were guilty of a breach of orders and of misbehaviour before the enemy, on the 28th inst. in not attacking them as you had been directed and in making an unnecessary, disorderly, and shameful retreat. I am Sir, your most obt. servt,
>
> Go Washington[7]

Washington's perception of battle led him to mention the two specific areas of guilt. He had not seen any casualties or indications of a battle among the troops he encountered during the retreat. Indeed, many of the officers he met indicated there had been no attempt to attack the British. In addition, he had seen regiments and brigades moving without direction or orders and a mere captain tasked with organizing the troops at the West Ravine. Brief, dismissive, and to the point, Washington's response would have surprised those who thought him without humor. He pointedly, and sarcastically, included Lee's own phrase about "the army, to Congress, to America, and to the world in general." The commander in chief felt he had acted as required at the time and now wanted to move on to other things. At this point Washington had too much to do; the ruffled feathers of a subordinate were not the most important item to a focused general like Washington. He had an army to command.

That same day Washington received a note from Charles Scott and Anthony Wayne. The note was mildly critical of Lee's conduct on June 28 and probably was indicative of the talk going around camp. In the last paragraph they laid out their perception without mentioning Lee: "We have taken the liberty of stating these facts, in order to convince the world that our retreat from the Court-House was not occasioned by the want of numbers, position, or wishes of both officers and men to maintain that post."[8] The two generals were referring to the time after the initial repulse of the British cavalry. Of course, after Scott's retreat their wish to maintain that post was probably impossible.

Lee was not satisfied with his commander's brusque reply and the petulant general penned another note, keeping it brief this time but again misdating it:

> Camp June the 28th [actually the 30th] 1778
>
> Sir,
>
> I beg your Excellency's pardon for the inaccuracy in misdating my letter—you cannot afford me greater pleasure than in giving me the opportunity of shewing to America the sufficiency of her respective servants—I trust that the temporary power of office and the tinsel dignity attending it will not be able by all the mists they can raise to offuscate the bright rays of truth, in the mean time your Excellency can have no objection to my retiring from the army—I am Sir your most obt. hble srvt.
>
> Charles Lee[9]

But the querulous major general wasn't finished irritating and insulting the commander in chief. Without giving Washington time to reply or even digest his last missive, Lee sent him another nettlesome note, almost like an afterthought to his previous, brief, communiqué:

> Camp June 30th 1778
>
> Sir,
>
> Since I had the honor of addressing my letter by Col. Fitzgerald [Washington's aide] to your Excellency I have reflected on both your situation and mine, and beg leave to observe, that it will be for our mutual convenience, that a court of inquiry should be immediately ordered—but I could wish it might be a court martial—for if the affair is drawn into length it may be difficult to collect the necessary evidences, and perhaps might bring on a paper war betwixt the adherents to both parties which may occasion some disagreeable feuds on the Continent—for all are not my friends nor all your admirers—I must intreat therefore from your love of justice that you will immediately exhibit your charge—and that on the first halt, I may be brought to tryal—and am Sir your most obt. hble servt.
>
> Charles Lee[10]

There was no further note from Washington except to inform Lee of a court martial. Perhaps Lee really did not want just an apology from Washington, maybe it was also a few wagging mouths he wanted to silence publicly, but he found himself insulting the Virginian personally for the second time.

Court Martial[11]

An immediate inquiry or court martial was not possible, as the army was in motion, waiting to see if the British were really crossing over to New York. The movements of the army postponed any trial until July 4. Instead of following his own advice about avoiding "a paper war betwixt the adherents of both parties," Lee fired the first shots of such a war himself. He penned a note to Isaac Collins of the *New Jersey Gazette* on July 3 complaining of an inaccurate or, as he wrote, "invidious, dishonest, and false"[12] newspaper account of the Monmouth encounter that was published on July 1. He asked that his letter be published to refute the account and offered that he had asked for a court martial. He followed it with a second note that expounded upon the action itself. Charles Lee was not a patient man; he could not wait until the trial to remove the perceived personal affront and exonerate his name.

The court martial proceedings, chaired by Lord Stirling, began in a tavern at New Brunswick. The general officers present were Jedediah Huntington

William Alexander, Lord Stirling, proved to be a competent subordinate; he would command on Perrine Ridge. He presided over the court martial of Charles Lee. *The Miriam and Ira D. Wallach Division of Art, Prints and Photographs: Print Collection, The New York Public Library. "Lord Stirling"*

of Connecticut, Enoch Poor of New Hampshire, William Smallwood of Maryland, and William Woodford of Virginia. None of these officers had been in the thick of the fighting on June 28 and may have been chosen for that reason or possibly because they were readily available. Of the eight colonels appointed, only William Grayson had been closely engaged during the day of the battle. He was removed from the court the night before the trial began as he was to appear as a witness during the proceedings.

The formal charges were:

> First: For disobedience of orders, in not attacking the enemy on the 28th of June, agreeable to repeated instructions.
> Secondly: For misbehavior before the enemy on the same day, by making an unnecessary, disorderly, and shameful retreat.
> Thirdly: For disrespect to the Commander-in-Chief, in two letters dated the 1st of July and the 28th of June.[13]

Lee pleaded not guilty. The witnesses were called, some questioned by the court or by Lee, as he was defending himself. Lee provided an able defense and was articulate in addressing witnesses and making points occasionally in his defense. Unfortunately, he also degraded witnesses and dismissed their opinions. He referred to their testimonies on "the whole" as "one tissue of negatives, opinions and comments upon opinions of those who had seen nothing and knew nothing."[14] He wandered occasionally, taking time to lecture the court on tactics or military history. In particular, he pressed the witnesses about his demeanor during the action.

Against charge one, "not attacking the enemy on the 28th of June, agreeable to repeated instructions," Lee's defense was simple: he had discretionary orders that told him to attack unless there were circumstances against it. When the odds became too great, his discretion dictated that he retreat instead of waiting for Washington to come up. He stated his case during the trial: "I had set out in the morning, as has been already observ'd, with the idea that it was His Excellentcy's intention that I should strike some important but partial blow, and I had endeavoured, in the manner related, to execute these intentions."[15] Lee shows a clear understanding of Washington's intentions. His detractors observed that he failed to attempt an attack before the retreat began.

On June 28 Washington was initially under the impression that Lee was attacking. His perception after the battle, and many of the witnesses agreed, was that Lee failed to attack. Lee maneuvered his men into position to attack but never actually attacked. He failed to support Wayne in attacking the British, which would have fixed the British attention, and wasted too much time in moving Lafayette into position. The only action was the defensive rebuff of the British cavalry and the exchange of cannon fire. Then events took place that forced Lee to join the retreat.

Lee questioned witnesses about the discretionary wording of the attack orders. Most witnesses agreed with the wording. It was clear that the key word was "attack" and the court, as well as many witnesses, believed that the failure to initially attack outweighed the discretionary nature of the orders. Lafayette said it best when questioned if Lee had attacked: "I cannot say that I saw them make any attack on the enemy; I saw them setting out for that purpose."[16] Lee took too long to prepare his attack and Clinton took away the opportunity.

The second charge, "making an unnecessary, disorderly, and shameful retreat," was more complex. Was the retreat unnecessary? Before Scott pulled out, there was no reason for the rest of the advanced detachment to withdraw. After Scott withdrew, the rest of the advanced corps was forced to retreat. Lee was unable to exert control after that. He did not order a retreat except for a small part of his advanced guard. Paradoxically, Lee claimed credit for saving the Continental Army by ordering a retreat but during the trial he claimed the retreat was "in direct opposition to my then wish."[17] He also called Lafayette's movement falling back as a "fortunate mistake."[18] He left Wayne nearly cut off as he personally retreated.

Disorderly? Lee failed to go forward and view the situation from Wayne's position. He lost control of the advanced units and gave little direction to the troops or their commanders during the withdrawal, making the retreat in general terms "disorderly." Many of the officers termed parts of the retreat as disorderly; Stewart used the exact word in his statement in court.[19] Much of this was due to Lee's lack of orderlies to communicate his directions. He claimed he was unable to inform Washington of the retreat due to the lack of aides but neglected to use Laurens or Meade when they proffered their services.

On the large scale, it was obviously a disorderly retreat. The witnesses who claimed they didn't know who gave the order to retreat and where they were to go gave credence to the disorderly charge. However, on the smaller scale, most individual units, even the groups of "picked men," retreated in an orderly manner, although this was due more to von Steuben's training and their small unit leaders than to Lee's leadership. Tench Tilghman testified: "The two regiments we first met [Grayson's and Patton's], were in some disorder, the men exceedingly heated, and so distressed with fatigue they could scarcely stand; the others, so far as keeping their ranks in battalion or brigade, I think, were in tolerable good order; but as to columns respectively in great confusion, as

I am convinced a line could not have been formed of them in that situation. They neither kept proper intervals, nor were the heads of columns ranged."[20]

When witnesses disagreed with Lee's view of the retreat, he tried to either downgrade their experience or use semantics to show his view was correct. When General Forman, a very experienced officer of both militia and regular troops, was questioned as to whether he had ever seen a more orderly retreat, Forman replied that he had at White Plains.[21] Lee sarcastically questioned Charles Scott's ability to discern a disorderly retreat, "Did it appear to you that the men were running away, or were only hastening their steps to take a more advantageous post in their rear?"[22] Semantics failed to intimidate; Scott made it clear that the advanced guard was disorganized during their retreat. Scott did not mention that he was himself the cause of much of the overall appearance of disorderly withdrawal. Lee's demeanor during the trial indicated that he failed to realize that he was no longer the eminent military mind in the Continental Army who could overawe his juniors. In 1778 there were many veteran officers with a variety of experiences surrounding him, unlike the novices of 1775–76.

Was the retreat shameful? The Continental Army had experienced shameful retreats before, from the panic at Kip's Bay to the foggy withdrawal at Germantown, and this retreat was hardly shameful in comparison. In fact, the troops could look at their retreat at Monmouth with pride: there was no panic as at Kip's Bay, and no great loss of men as prisoners such as had occurred at Brandywine and Germantown.

During the trial Lee brought out that his demeanor or state of mind during the battle was calm and dignified. Lee emphasized during his own questioning of witnesses the fact that he was under control of himself and not flustered by events. Most of the witnesses agreed with that characterization. Even Alexander Hamilton, who could hardly be called an advocate for Lee, believed the general had been composed and under control throughout the action. His deportment was never really in question and had little to do with his guilt or innocence of the three charges. The difference in temperament between Lee and Washington showed that sometimes a general needed to be more than calm.

Of the three charges, it was the charge of Lee being disrespectful to the commander in chief in which his guilt appeared to be obvious. The letters were introduced during the trial with little comment. Lee attempted to get the trial officers to sympathize with him. He asked them if they would have reacted in the same manner if they had suffered Washington's chastisement. That was the shame of the whole incident; Lee's inability to deal with Washington's spur-of-the-moment censure gave the appearance that the case was one of personalities.

Nathanael Greene, who remained both a friend to Lee and an admirer of Washington, spoke for many when he wrote: "I am really Sorry for the Affair as I know it will create many Divisions in the Army."[23] Ultimately there could be no doubt of Lee's guilt on the charge of "disrespect," as his writings provided the evidence.

Now that a court martial was taking place, Alexander Hamilton could not contain his disgust with Lee. In a note to Elias Boudinot, Hamilton spoke in derogatory terms of the army's second in command: "This man is either a driveler in the business of soldiership or something much worse." He proceeded to tell his view of the entire battle, praising many of the officers but telling the story of Lee's part in a prejudiced, negative view. He concluded by postulating that Lee, in whom "America has placed a large share of the most ill judged confidence," would be saved by his admirers. At the end of his narrative, he states: "What think you now of General Lee? You will be ready to join me in condemning him: And yet, I fear a Court Martial will not do it. A certain preconceived and preposterous opinion of his being a very great man will operate much in his favour. Some people are very industrious in making interest for him. Whatever a court Martial may decide, I shall continue to believe and say—his conduct was monstrous and unpardonable."[24]

The trial took more than a day and due to the movement of the army took place in several locations. Thirty-nine people testified during the lengthy proceedings. The word "shameful" was removed from the second charge as the conduct of the soldiers themselves showed they had nothing to be ashamed of. Washington quietly allowed the case to go forward in the various locations where the court sat. He only mentioned it once, in a letter sent to his step-son on August 6: "I thank you for your cordial and affectionate congratulations on our late success at Monmouth, and the arrival of the French Fleet at the hook—the first might, I think, have been a glorious day, if matters had begun well in the Morning; but as the Court Martial which has been setting upwards of a Month for the tryal of Genl Lee, is not yet over, I do not choose to say any thing on the subject, further, than that there evidently appeared a capitol blunder, or something else, somewhere. The truth, it is to be hoped, will come out, after so long an investigation of it."[25]

On August 12 the court rendered its verdict after a couple of days of deliberations:

> Judgement of the Court. The Court having considered the first charge against Majr Genl Lee the evidence and his defence, are of opinion that he is guilty of disobedience of Orders, in not attacking the enemy on the 28th of June agreeable to repeated Instructions, being a breach of the latter part of Article 5th Section 2d of the Articles of War.

The Court having considered the second charge against Major Genl Lee the evidence and his defence are of opinion he is guilty of misbehaviour before the enemy on the 28th of June by making an unnecessary, and in some few instances a disorderly retreat being a breach of the 13th Article of the 13th Section of the Articles War.

The Court having considered the third charge against Majr Genl Lee are of opinion that he is guilty of disrespect to the Commander in chief in two Letters dated the 1st of July & 28th of June being a breach of the 2d Article Sectn 2d of the Articles of War.

The Court do sentence Majr Genl Lee to be suspended from any Command in the Armies of the united States of North America for the Term of Twelve Months.[26]

On August 16, 1778, the commander in chief, as he normally did, forwarded the results of the proceedings to president of Congress without comment. His perception of the battle was born out by the trial, and he had nothing to add. Lee had failed to attack before retreating. Lee had failed to conduct an orderly retreat as witnessed by Washington and the men he had questioned during the retreat. For the written insubordination by the second in command, there was no defense. The sentence was mild; after all, Lee was the next in line to Washington and many believed he still had value to the American cause. He could resume his service, properly chastised, later. An officer of lesser stature, like Adam Stephen after Germantown, would have been cashiered or forced to retire.

Many members of Congress had a high opinion of Lee, and this made it difficult for them to endorse the outcome and punishment. Congress agreed to the court's decision by a close vote, 13 to 7. Hamilton had been proved correct: Lee's reputation was very much in his favor. Yet there is no firm evidence that it was a vote on personal partisan lines, Lee advocates versus Washington's supporters. Some members of Congress felt that Lee was still needed in the army. From the beginning of the trial until Congress reached its decision, Washington stayed out of the controversy and contented himself with leading the army.

The trial pointed out a weakness of Charles Lee's leadership—that he didn't know his officers, didn't know his men, and had little faith in either group. Lee explained why he sent a junior officer to organize the advanced corps at the West Ravine: "As the regiments have no uniforms or distinguishing colours, and as I was unhappily almost an utter stranger to the names and faces of the Commanding Officers of the respective corps."[27] He failed to acquaint himself with the army upon his arrival at Valley Forge. He failed to assemble his officers as a group before the battle. The failure to try to rectify these shortcomings, either on the march or during the night at Elizabeth Town before the battle, was his responsibility.

Lee was second in command of the army, with years of experience in various armies around the world and over a year of experience in command of a wing of the Continental Army, and much had been expected of him. Yet he had done little on the battlefields of the Revolution to suggest the abilities he supposedly possessed. He had succeeded as the commander of small detachments, but a large command proved too much for him. During the battle on June 28, 1778, he played more of the role of a regimental or brigade commander, exercising command only over those near him. The wording in his guilty verdict to charge two had been changed by adding "in some few instances" to a disorderly retreat. This reflected Lee's control of those few troops around him during the withdrawal. Except at the hedgerow after Washington detailed him to hold that position, essentially acting as commander of a small brigade, Lee's personal leadership never exerted itself.

Washington made a mistake in allowing Lee to take Lafayette's command with battle looming. Washington had deferred to military protocol concerning seniority and because of this he made the error of changing commanders on the eve of battle, replacing an eager general who wanted to carry out the intent of his orders with a reluctant general who had no confidence in the army, its officers, or Washington.

After the trial Lee never seemed to understand that he had been marginalized and tried to exonerate himself through letters to Congress and in the newspapers, feeding the "paper war" he had wanted to avoid by asking for a court martial. The only results were the alienation of many of his supporters and of Congress. His personal attacks on Washington, and those close to the commander in chief, resulted in a duel with one of the men he had referred to as an "earwig" in a letter to Washington. John Laurens, the young son of the president of Congress, laid down the challenge. At the time appointed, Laurens, close friend to both Lafayette and Hamilton, wounded Lee in the side. Hamilton, Laurens' second, convinced the unwounded South Carolinian not to enter a second round of shots. Lee's wound was serious enough to persuade him to agree not to continue and to forgo fighting an additional duel with another of Washington's favorites, Anthony Wayne. After Wayne, six other officers were waiting for their turn to duel with the now wounded major general. Time would see that they would never get their chance. Prior to the fight with Laurens, Lee had narrowly avoided another duel with von Steuben through a placating letter.

Dueling wasn't confined to Lee and his detractors only. Samuel Smith and Eleazer Oswald almost came to blows when Smith took umbrage at Lee's editorial attacks on Washington. Lee learned little from these experiences and after his year of suspension ended, he sent Congress another, less than respectful, letter. On January 10, 1780, Congress, fed up with his attacks on them and seeing the continuing controversy as a detriment to the cause, finally cashiered Lee from the service.

Even before Lee was cashiered, some questioned the legality or propriety of the trial. Lee was provided with the opportunity to defend himself. He called witnesses and questioned witnesses. The trial was done correctly along the lines of other trials at the time. Few questioned the fairness of the proceedings. It was primarily the results of the trial that were debated at the time. Typical of the critics of the trial's outcome was Benjamin Rush. He lamented the outcome of the court martial as an example of the continued loss of the army's best leaders: "We destroy reputation, which is dearer to a military man than life itself. Conway, Mifflin, and Lee were sacrificed to the excessive influence and popularity of one man. They were the first characters in the army and are all honest men."[28]

It is too simple to say that the court martial was a face-off between Lee and the commander in chief. Many of the officers honestly believed that Lee somehow failed to do his duty by failing to attack. Others, like Charles Scott, were possibly covering for their own errors. Wayne believed they should have attacked the British rear guard and that Lee missed an opportunity. There were some that believed that Lee did his best under the circumstances, and he was innocent of any misconduct except lack of respect for the commander in chief.

Those officers close to Lee during the battle shared their leader's experiences and testified to a different picture. There is no indication that they were supporting Lee out of pure animosity for Washington. They honestly believed that Lee had done the best he could. Despite Washington's own errors, the court martial was not a reflection on the commander in chief's leadership but on Lee's. Unfortunately, to some the trial overshadowed the victory at Monmouth.

To Washington the results of the court martial agreed with everything he had seen or heard. Lee did not attack, discretionary orders or not. The retreat was disorderly, though some of this was beyond Lee's control, but he was ultimately responsible for the Advanced Corps' actions. Washington had seen the disorderly retreat with his own eyes. The lack of respect in the petulant letters removed any affection the commander in chief had for his second in command. Washington would have little to do with Lee for the rest of Lee's life.

A Court of Inquiry

Charles Lee was not the only man to suffer embarrassment due to his actions on June 28. Colonel Henry Jackson, who had brought three under-strength and recently recruited regiments to the army after it left Valley Forge, noticed that there were rumors circulating about his conduct on the battlefield. It was his detachment, made up of his own so-called "additional" regiment, Lee's Additional Regiment, and Henley's Additional Regiment, that had found itself in need of ammunition as it neared the village of Freehold and consequently held up the deployment of the advanced guard. It was also Jackson who was confronted by one of Washington's aides and Lee with orders to stand near the Parsonage Farm. Jackson had begged off, citing the seriously weakened condition of his overheated recruits, many of whom had fallen out, and in the end retreated to Englishtown with Charles Lee's permission. Jackson had readily admitted his lack of combat experience. Several of his officers accused him of "Misconduct, Confusion & Disobedience of Orders."[29] He demanded a court of inquiry to clear his name.

Jackson's court of inquiry was not assembled until April of 1779 and didn't finish until July of that year. The court heard testimony and decided: "The Court upon fully and maturely considering the Evidence & Col. Jackson's Defence and also the Confusion of the advanced Corps of Genl. Lee's Division on that Day are of the opinion that there appears not anything against Col. Jackson sufficiently reprehensible to call him before a Court Martial."[30] It is worth noting that this Court of Inquiry mentions the "confusing" conditions that were characterized as "disorderly" during Lee's court martial. Jackson suffered no ill consequences from the episode and commanded the first troops into New York City at the war's end.

Accolades

The men of the Continental Army received a great deal of praise for their performance. Washington gave credit to the individual soldier in a note to Henry Laurens: "The Behaviour of the troops in general, after they recovered from the first surprize occasioned by the Retreat of the advanced Corps, was such as could not be surpassed."[31] In doing so, he did not mention that the recovery was largely due to his personal intervention. The pivotal ambush at the point of woods and the subsequent action at the hedgerow occurred after Washington took over.

The individual American soldier proved himself the equal of his European enemies throughout the day at Monmouth. The Continental Army demonstrated a remarkable ability to stand toe to toe with the British and fight it out. One soldier clearly understood: "I think Genl. Clinton will get no Laurels by the expedition—they can't say we sculked in the bushes & fought like Indians—our Troops met them in the open field."[32] They had demonstrated, by their quick recovery after the initial retreat, the movement to Comb's Hill, and in the counterattacks across Sutfin Farm and the hedgerow, the skills necessary to make complex battlefield movements without losing their cohesion, thanks to experience, von Steuben, and the time at Valley Forge. Their behavior during the bayonet charges and in hand-to-hand combat in the woods, and along the hedgerow, showed the mettle of the individual Continental soldier. There was never any panic, never any frightened mass exodus from the field. For the first time in a major encounter, the British failed to capture large numbers of prisoners as few Americans gave up during battle.

Experience made a difference. In the first great battle of the war, Long Island in 1776, the American soldiers, except for the very few who had fought in the French and Indian War, counted their military experience in months with little combat experience compared to the British soldiers, especially officers, who counted their service in years with a leavening of combat across the ranks. By the time of the action at Monmouth, many of the American officers and men had three years of war behind them.

Things had changed, and no one knew it better than cynical Alexander Hamilton: "The behavior of the officers and men in general was such as could not easily be surpassed. Our troops, after the first impulse from mismanagement, behaved with more spirit & moved with greater order than the British troops. You know my way of thinking about our army, and that I am not apt to flatter it. I assure you I never was pleased with them before this day."[33] At Monmouth it was evident the Continental soldier had come of age.

It was not only the infantry that showed toughness, but the American artillery also demonstrated its expertise. Throughout the war American artillery had done reasonably well, but again and again at Monmouth the cannons of the Continental Army engaged the British and performed admirably. Oswald's guns and the guns of the individual regiments kept the British from closing during the opening stages of the action. During the retreat Oswald kept the British at bay, with as many as ten or as few as two guns. Seward and Cook, supported by various groups of infantrymen, held up the British long enough to allow the advanced corps to retreat across the West Ravine. The large battery at Perrine Ridge kept the British from crossing the West Ravine, stopped the Highlanders' advance through Sutfin Farm, and kept the British off-balance during the Great Cannonade. The battery atop Comb's Hill forced Clinton to retreat from the hedgerow twice. Washington praised the army, including the militia which he normally held in some contempt, in his general orders the day after the battle, but singled out the artillery: "It is with peculiar Pleasure... that the Commander in Chief can inform General Knox and the Officers of

Artillery that the Enemy have done them the Justice to acknowledge that no artillery could be better served than ours."[34] Lee also lauded the gunners: "I confess it is difficult to refrain from paying compliments to the artillery, from General Knox and Colonel Oswald down to the very driver."[35] It was high praise indeed for a group of amateurs led by a bookseller.

To point to one commander or group of men would be difficult for Washington in his report to Congress. John Laurens commented in a letter to his father on the commander in chief's reluctance to single out one or another: "I have seen the General much embarrassed this day on the subject of those who distinguished themselves in the battle of Monmouth. To name a few, and be silent with regard to many of equal merit wd be an injustice to the latter; to pass the whole over unnoticed wd be an unpardonable slight; indiscriminate praise of the whole wd be an unfair distribution of rewards; and yet, when men generally conducted themselves so well as our officers did, this matter is allowable and is eligible, because least liable to offence."[36] Washington avoided praising Virginians to forestall charges of favoritism toward his own state.

Yet there were many that deserved praise. Washington was well served by his "family"; his aides and secretaries appeared to be all over the battlefield during the action and ably assisted him, as well as Lafayette and Lee, in reconnaissance, as messengers, or as the eyes and ears of the commander in chief. Laurens, Harrison, Hamilton, Fitzgerald, McHenry, and Meade ranged far and wide during that long day, several suffering injuries and some losing their horses. In Laurens' post-battle letter to his father, he lauded his fellows: "My three brother aides gained themselves great applause by their activity and bravery, while the three secretaries acted as military men on this occasion and proved themselves as worthy to wield the sword as the pen."[37] Hamilton wrote to Elias Boudinot: "What part our family acted let others say. I hope you will not suspect me of vanity when I tell you that one of them, Fitzgerald, had a slight contusion from a Musket ball, another, Laurens, had a slight contusion also—and his horse killed—a third, Hamilton, had his horse wounded, in the first part of the action with a musket ball. If the rest escaped, it is to be only ascribed to better fortune, not more prudence in keeping out of the way."[38] These officers and others pressed into duty as messengers allowed Washington to communicate with his subordinates effectively throughout the battle, something Lee was unable to do.

One of the commanders singled out for his contribution was Philemon Dickinson. Washington was notorious for his disparaging view of the militia, telling the president of Congress back in 1776: "To place any dependance upon

Militia, is, assuredly, resting upon a broken staff. Men just dragged from the tender Scenes of domestick life—unaccustomed to the din of Arms—totally unacquainted with every kind of Military skill, which being followed by a want of Confidence in themselves when opposed to Troops regularly traind—disciplined, and appointed—superior in knowledge, & superior in Arms, makes them timid, and ready to fly from their own Shadows."[39]

On June 28, and in the days leading up to the battle as well as after, the militia performed well by shielding the Continental movements and threatening Clinton's baggage. Dickinson was mentioned in Washington's general orders for June 29: "General Dickinson and the Militia of this State are also thanked for the noble Spirit which they have shewn in opposing the Enemy on their march from Philadelphia and for the Aid which they have given by harrassing and impeding their Motions so as to allow the Continental Troops time to come up with them."[40] Lee also praised the militia general, despite their heated argument during the morning meeting: "[Dickinson] seems to inform himself of everything; it was his business to have informed himself of more fully than any other person for whom I was referred."[41] Other militia leaders like David Forman performed admirably in providing intelligence and serving as guides for the Continental troops.

The Continental Army was well served by the battalion and regimental commanders of the American army who proved as capable as their opponents. Early in the battle, Butler and Dickinson had given a glimpse of the day's possibilities. Men like Oswald, Stewart, Olney, Livingston, and Ramsey gave the British a rough time. They stood with their men and held the British long enough for the bulk of the Continental forces to enter the battle. Late in the afternoon, it was men like Cilley, Parker, and Burr who stepped up to counterattack the British. As a group, they had stood the test of battle well and paid in blood for it. Bunner, Wesson, Stewart, Ramsey, and Durkee all fell victim to enemy action. Hamilton mentioned them in his letter to Boudinot:

> A great number of our officers distinguished themselves this day. General Wayne was always foremost in danger. Col Stewart & Lt Col Ramsay were with him among the first to oppose the enemy. Lt Col Olney at the Head of Varnum's Brigade made the next stand. I was with him, got my horse wounded and myself much hurt by a fall in consequence. Col Livingston behaved very handsomely. Our friend Barber was remarkably active; towards the close of the day, he received a ball through his side—which the doctors think will not be fatal. Col: Silly, & Lt Col: Parker were particularly useful on the left—Col Craig, with General Wayne, on the right. The Artillery acquitted themselves most charmingly. I was spectator to Lt Col: Oswalds behaviour, who kept up a gallant fire from some pieces commanded by him, uncovered and unsupported. In short one can hardly name particulars without doing injustice to the rest.[42]

Washington lauded the officers' conduct as a group in his report to the president of Congress: "Were I to conclude my account of this days transactions without expressing my obligations to the Officers of the Army in general, I should do injustice to their merit, and violence to my own feelings. They seemed to vie with each other in manifesting their Zeal and Bravery."[43] When called upon to perform a duty, they responded as the professionals they had become. Even Scott and Maxwell's detachments conducted their retreats with efficiency, despite confusion from a lack of direction and orders.

Frenchman the Marquis de Lafayette was probably the most disappointed of all the officers with the battle. It was not the outcome of the battle that bothered him as much as his lack of opportunities to garner personal triumph. He eagerly accepted command of the advanced corps in anticipation of the glory he would attain, but things did not work out the way he expected. Relieved of command just before the battle, he thought when Lee assigned him to lead the flanking maneuver this would result in some glorious action. But his troops were pulled back and he lost his command again. Finally, in the afternoon he confronted the British move around the American left, but it proved to be another near miss. James McHenry sensed disillusionment: "The Marquis De La Fayette was sadly disappointed. He had flattered himself, from his advanced situation under General Lee, with the first laurels of the day. The honors of war you know have a distinguished place in the breast of a French nobleman. I could see that the Marquis on this occasion felt particularly unhappy."[44] Despite his lack of personal success, the young man had done all that was required of him and done it as well circumstances allowed. Henry Laurens thought enough of Lafayette's performance to send him a personal note, making reference to Lee's lack of success. "I congratulate with your Excellency on the partial victory over the enemy on the 28th Ulto. At Monmouth, to intimate why it had not been so brilliant might in this moment seem invidious, I regret, however, that Your Excellency had not continued on in the Command of the Van and everybody appears to be of my opinion."[45]

One general officer that rightly deserved high praise at Monmouth was Anthony Wayne. The talk of his failure at Paoli and inconclusive conduct at Germantown was now behind him. Of all the commanders on the field that hot June day, Wayne led an advance on the British, not once or twice but three times. He came the closest to carrying out Washington's order to attack the redcoat rear guard that morning with Grayson and Butler. Later he led Ramsey, Stewart, and Woods in the ambush of the pursuing British near the point of woods, a turning point in the battle. He led his own Pennsylvanians when he took the detachments across Spotswood Middle Brook in the late afternoon to counterattack through the farms east of the hedgerow. The former surveyor had much to be proud of and was mentioned glowingly in Washington's report to Congress: "The Catalouge of those who distinguished themselves is too long to admit of particularizing individuals: I cannot however forbear mentioning Brigadier General Wayne whose good conduct and bravery thro' the whole action deserves particular commendation."[46]

Washington's Accolades

Washington proved himself more than just an inspirational leader; he also showed signs that he was becoming a capable commander. However, his error when he replaced Lafayette with Lee just before the action caused a great deal of confusion. No one will ever know how things would have turned out with Lafayette in command but Washington's choice to replace him, based on his observance of military protocol rather than first thoughts, did have the consequence of disruption to the command structure of the advanced corps. Despite this decision, the rest of the day was an example of excellent generalship. Personal example, personal courage, and a deft hand in moving troops about the battlefield showed that Washington had evolved into a highly skilled combat commander.

Washington compared well with the more experienced professional soldier Henry Clinton. After Lee's advance, Clinton turned his column about and expertly developed the situation. He successfully pushed back the Continentals along the main road while sending out columns under Erskine, Cornwallis, and Grey to outflank the Americans. The British gained the initiative, but Washington parried each of those movements. He countered Clinton by making his own flanking movement in taking Comb's Hill and emplacing guns atop its height. The commander in chief organized the defense in the point of woods that delayed the British advance. He sent Lafayette with a detachment to meet Erskine's move around the Continental left. Most importantly, his personal presence brought spirit to the retreating troops, something Lee had failed to do. Even Lee had perked up after his encounter with the commander in chief and performed capably, courageously fighting and leading the stand along the hedgerow.

Washington received letters from many that lauded his part in the victory. William Drayton of South Carolina wrote directly to the commander in chief, effusively praising him: "I cannot resist the impulse I feel, to pay you my little tribute of thanks for the important Victory of Monmouth and to express, how much I feel myself tenderly & anxiously interested in every thing respecting your safety and glory. Your Excellency's invariable conduct, naturally exposes you to such intrusions; and I rely upon it, that your good nature will pardon this."[47] Gouverneur Morris of New York alluded to the previous criticism of Washington in his congratulations for the victory: "Let me however congratulate you on the affair at Monmouth. On the *whole* Affair. It might have been better it is said. I think not for you have even from Your Enemies the Honor of that Day."[48]

A great part of the victory at Monmouth was due to the physical intervention of George Washington. Hamilton, who was near Lee when the encounter between the two commanders occurred, noted Washington's personal and decisive actions: "I never saw the General in so much advantage. America owes a great deal to General Washington for this day's work. A general rout, dismay and disgrace, would have attended the whole army in any other hands but his... Other officers have great merit in performing their parts well, but he directed the whole with the skill of a master workman. He did not hug himself at a distance and leave an Arnold to win laurels for him, but by his own presence he brought order out of confusion, animated his troops, and led them to success."[49] Hamilton's opinion was based on personal observation in the thick of the action and included a bit of criticism of Horatio Gates with the mention of Benedict Arnold at Saratoga.

By comparison, British officers were not entirely happy with the personal performance of their own commander. At least one of Clinton's officers thought the British commander had been too close to the action, taking away control of Cornwallis' division and exposing himself to injury in the initial attack at the hedgerow. "Sir Henry Clinton showed himself the Soldier, but not the wise General, on this occasion, exposing himself and charging to the head of a few Dragoons."[50] Another officer noted a lack of respect for Clinton: "The General by his rashness in the last action has totally lost the confidence both of the Officers and soldiers, who were astonished to see the Commander of the army galloping like a New market jockey at the head of a wing of Grenadiers and expressly forbidding all form and order..."[51]

Whether this criticism is valid or not, Clinton moved his troops skillfully, trying to gain an advantage, but the Americans met each challenge at the hedgerow, at Sutfin Farm, in the employment of artillery, and with the attempts to flank Washington's positions. The British soldiers fought with the great courage and discipline that were expected of them, especially as the flower of the king's forces in America—the Guards, light infantry, grenadiers, and veteran foot regiments—took part in all phases of the battle. They fought well in extreme heat and difficult terrain. It was the experience and new military skills of the American soldiers, as well as the improved tactical abilities of the American leaders, that stopped the king's army, not Clinton's lack of direction or the incompetence of the British soldier.

The End for Charles Lee

Charles Lee's bitterness and subsequent trial cast a shadow on the victory at Monmouth Court House. A few officers and politicians continued to retain the opinion that Washington was merely lucky when successful and surrounded by sycophants who were inept but loyal. After the Lee court martial and controversy, some credited Lee with making the brave decision to retreat from the area around Monmouth Court House that saved the army. Even Henry Clinton, perhaps to deflect criticism for his inability to defeat the Americans, heaped praise on his former acquaintance. "Had Washington been blockhead enough to sustain Lee, I should have catched them between two defiles; and it is easy to see what must have happened."[52] Unfortunately, Lee's supporters failed to acknowledge that the general never really made the decision to withdraw and "save" the army—the feet of Scott and Maxwell's soldiers made the decision for him.

Lee went back to the cabin he shared with his dogs in Virginia. When his year of suspension was nearing an end, he made a poor choice and wrote an inflammatory letter to Congress. On January 10, 1780, Congress passed, by a narrow margin, a resolution: "That Major General Charles Lee be informed, that Congress have no farther occasion for his services in the army of the United States."[53]

Lee made peace with former enemies such as Anthony Wayne and the Baron von Steuben. After Wayne's successful attack on the British post at Stony Point on July 16, 1779, Lee wrote his former critic: "I gave it that you were a brave officer, and an honest man... if I was appointed to a command, and had my choice of brigadiers, you should be one of my first election... I do most sincerely declare, that your action in the assault of Stony Point is not only the most brilliant, in my opinion, through the whole course of this war, on either side, but that it is one of the most brilliant I am acquainted with in history."[54]

Lee spent much of his time writing encouraging notes to those still in action, and even entertaining ideas of going west on a filibuster into Spanish territory. He also continued to correspond with his former British colleagues. Writing "as a good Englishman, as a good American," to his Monmouth adversary John Graves Simcoe, he wanted his old enemy to "assure Sir Henry Clinton,

General Robinson, and General Leslie, of my personal respect and esteem, and I beg you will remember me kindly to General Phillip."[55]

Financially broken, he was forced to sell his home and move to Philadelphia. Lee died there a lonely, bitter man on October 2, 1782. He had once stated, "I desire most earnestly, that I may be not buried in any church, or church-yard, or within a mile of any Presbyterian or Anabaptist meeting-house; for since I have resided in this country, I have kept so much bad company while living, that I do not choose to continue it when dead."[56] Against his wishes, he was buried in Christ Church burial ground in Philadelphia.

After Lee's death, his sister Sidney needed a copy of Lee's will to settle his affairs. Unable to locate a copy of the document, she enlisted the help of George Washington. The general responded cordially to her request: "If upon receipt of it, it shall appear that any opinion of mine can be of Service to you, I will submit it to your consideration with great chearfulness. In the mean while, permit me to offer you compliments of condolence on the loss of so near a relation; who was possessed many great qualities—& to assure you of the respect and consideration with which I have the honor to be Madam, Yr Most Obedt & Most Hble Servant."[57] Eventually, he was able to grant her request.

In 1785 a friend of Lee, William Goddard, began collecting letters and notes to write a biography of the disgraced general. He wrote George Washington to gain information from the former commander in chief for the book. Washington replied in a simple letter:

> I never had a difference with that Gentleman but on public ground, & my conduct towards him upon this occasion, was such only, as I conceived myself indispensably bound to adopt in discharge of the public trust reposed in me. If this produced in him unfavourable sentiments of me, I yet can never consider the conduct I pursued, with respect to him, either wrong or improper; however I may regret that it may have been differently viewed by him, & that it excited his censure and animadversions. Should there appear in Genl Lee's writings anything injurious or unfriendly to me, the impartial & dispassionate world, must decide how far I deserved it from the general tenor of my conduct.[58]

The book was never completed.

CHAPTER 8

Perceptions of Battle

Americans' Contemporary Perceptions of the Battle

Combining their inability to hold Philadelphia, the retreat across New Jersey and abandonment of the Monmouth battlefield, the British appeared to have lost the campaign of 1778 to Americans all over the 13 states. John Bannister, a member of Congress from Virginia, saw the battle at Monmouth Court House as part of a string of auspicious incidents starting with the British evacuation of Philadelphia: "The next favourable Event was the Enemy's determination to evacuate this City. The good Effect of this Resolution expanded itself 'thro all Order of Men & Produced an amazing change in the Minds of the wavering & undetermined. To this succeeded our Victory at Monmouth & then the arrival of the Fleet under the command of the Count D'Estaing."[1] Samuel Adams also linked the evacuation with Washington's victory in a note to his cousin John: "I suppose you have been fully & officially informed of the State of our military Affairs since the Enemy evacuated this City and met with a Drubbing at Monmouth."[2] James Lovell, a Congressional critic of Washington, wrote from Philadelphia to Abigail Adams: "Disgrace pursues the Army of our Enemies in their Passage from this City. The particulars are not yet come to Hand of the Battle at Monmouth; but we know it has been very fatal to the best of the British troops."[3] Henry Laurens echoed the various events that spelled a victorious campaign and slammed the Carlisle Commission's attempts at bribery: "The evacuation of Pilada. and Rhode Island [where a French fleet and Allied troops threatened the British occupation], the Battle of Monmouth and the arrival of a French fleet will operate more powerfully to the ends of Peace upon the minds of our Enemies than Governor Johnstone's profer'd Gold wrought upon Congress."[4] Connecticut Congressman Andrew Adams saw a couple of reasons for optimism: "The Arival of the French fleet added to the Battle of Monmouth seems to put our affairs upon a respectable Footing and Difuses a general Joy among the friendly Inhabitants of this City."[5]

Victory or draw, whatever modern writers and historians believe, Americans at the time perceived Monmouth as a victory. Lafayette wrote Richard Henry Lee: "Congratulations for the advantage obtain'd by Gal. Washington and your troops over the flower of the english Army. I think theyr journey through the Jersays has been rather disagreable and bought very dear."[6] Anthony Wayne saw Monmouth as a victory, almost gloating in a letter to the secretary of war, mocking Howe's Mischianzia: "Tell the Philadelphia ladies that the heavenly, sweet, pretty red Coats—The accomplished Gent'n of the Guards & Grenadiers have humbled themselves on the plains of Monmouth. The Knights of the Blended Rose" & "Burning Mount"—have Resigned their Laurels to Rebel officers who will lay them at the feet of those Virtuos Daughters of America who cheerfully gave up ease and affluence in a city for Liberty and peace of mind in a Cottage."[7]

The enlisted soldiers shared the officers' feelings about the action. Private Elijah Fisher of the Commander in Chief's Guard wrote in his diary: "On Sunday our army had the Engagement with the British at Monmouth Court-house where Gen. Lee went Contrary to orders but our army Drove them and if he had managed according to his orders it is likely in all probability we should have taken the howl or the bigar Part of there army."[8] Fisher echoed the thoughts of many when he alluded to Lee's failure to act as robbing the Americans of total victory. It is unclear what a total victory would have been.

Members of Congress joined Fisher in wishing the victory more decisive. Henry Laurens wrote: "Every one whose opinion I have heard, say, if general Lee had done his part at the battle of Monmouth, Sir Henry Clinton would have been reduced to circumstances little, if any thing, better than those which Burgoyne experienced last year. The General's trial before a Court Martial is not yet ended."[9] Other members of Congress agreed. Thomas McKean wrote explicitly that: "The Army did well, but had some officers done their duty, it would have terminated in a compleat victory."[10] It is unclear as to what constituted complete victory for McKean and the others. Unfortunately, many who had not actually been at Monmouth questioned Lee's behaviors, not knowing the facts about the battle.

A definition of what constitutes victory is difficult. However, it important that it is understood the Americans believed, perceived, or thought they had achieved a battlefield success, just as they had supposed that the Monmouth campaign was a strategic success. Looking at four different, subjective criteria for victory provides the material that fueled the American perception of the battle as a success. Who controlled the battlefield after the battle? Who lost the most killed, wounded, and captured? Which side received a boost to their morale? Which general attained his battlefield objective? Previous to Monmouth, the American army of Washington had, but for a few occasions, lost possession of the battlefield, suffered the greater casualties, taken blows to their spirit that threatened their continuing the war, and failed to attain any type of objective other than survival. It was not the same at Monmouth.

Battlefield Losses

Americans believed that the British had suffered higher casualties than the Continental Army. John Hancock overstated the results of Monmouth when the former president of Congress wrote his wife that the battle had not only been a victory but possibly meant the end of the war: "I Congratulate you & all my Friends on the happy & glorious Issue of the Engagement on Sunday last. The Two Armies Engag'd in the Jersies, we forc'd them from the Field & Encamp'd on the Ground. The Loss on either Side not yet known, theirs much more than ours, they have lost some Field Officers, among their Slain is Col Monckton, brother to General Monckton; as soon as particulars come you shall know them… This will be a dear Remove to General Clinton's Army… Desertion has taken very deep root. This Battle has so discompos'd & Ruin'd Clinton's Army, that it is hardly possible they should be able to effect any Operations this year; in short the Game is over with them."[11]

Whatever the scope of victory or missed opportunities, the battlefield losses, including the many deserters, pointed to an American victory. Henry Knox wrote his wife and expressed the feelings of the American troops: "Indeed, upon the whole, it was splendid. The capital army of Britain defeated and obliged to retreat before the Americans, whom they despised so much! I cannot ascertain either ours or the enemy's loss, but I really think they have lost three times the number we have, I judge from the field of battle, which, to be sure, is a field of carnage and blood; three to one of British forces lie there."[12] Washington's reports to Congress and Clinton's figures do not show a large discrepancy in favor of the Americans but the perception was that the British suffered much more, probably fueled by the large number of deserters. Oddly enough, the British suffered from the same misconception of American losses, as illustrated by one of their newspapers: "It is certain the rebels have not suffered so heavy a loss as on this occasion, in any engagement since their defeat on Long Island."[13]

Possession of the Battlefield

Washington had been defeated many times before Monmouth. One of the reasons why his losses were victories for the British stemmed from his forced retreats. Throughout the New York campaign, at Brandywine and Germantown, Washington was compelled to take his army from the battlefield. At Monmouth Clinton had the opportunity to fight a decisive battle with a willing opponent and then declined to continue battle after the first day. By not giving battle the second day, it gave the appearance of a defeat. The British retreated in haste and under the cover of darkness, leaving many of their wounded behind. By all appearances, they were running away from the Continentals and their militia allies. The slow pace of the British march prior to the battle had been Clinton's intentional invitation for Washington to attack. He had hoped that Washington would give battle. Afterwards his withdrawal seemed to indicate a defeat.

James McHenry expressed this view of the victory: "Although the victory was not so extensive as we could wish, yet it has every substantial and unequivocal proof of it being one. We gained the field of battle before evening—We camped on the ground that night."[14] McHenry failed to note that the British camped on the same ground that evening and only gave up the battlefield after midnight. After fleeing from the Continental Army and finding themselves penned up in New York City, the campaign of 1778 for the British had ended.

Effect on Morale

After the difficult winter at Valley Forge there was naturally a question among the Americans on what the new campaign would bring. Monmouth provided optimism to the Revolutionary effort. Washington learned that Congress, on July 7, had declared:

> Resolved, unanimously, That the thanks of Congress be given to General Washington for the activity with which he marched from the camp at Valley Forge, in pursuit of the enemy; for his distinguished exertions in forming the order of battle; and for his great good conduct in leading on the attack and gaining the important victory of Monmouth over the British grand army, under the command of Lieutenant General Sir Henry Clinton, in their march from Philadelphia to New York.
>
> Resolved, That General Washington be directed to signify the thanks of Congress to the gallant officers and men under his command, who distinguished themselves by their conduct and valour at the battle of Monmouth.[15]

The president of Congress sent Washington a personal message alluding to the victory and its impact on the country: "Your Excellency will therefore be pleased to accept this as an address of an Individual intended to assure you Sir of my hearty congratulations with my Country Men on the success of the American Arms under your Excellency's immediate Command in the late Battle of Monmouth & more particularly of my own happiness at the additional Glory achieved by Your Excellency in retrieving the honor of these states in the Moment of an alarming dilemma."[16]

From the Southern States to the New England seaboard, Americans celebrated the action at Monmouth as a victory. Virginian Richard Henry Lee wrote his brother Francis Lightfoot Lee: "Upon the whole, the battle was fairly won by our Army, & the best troops of Britain beaten in an open field."[17] From Connecticut, Titus Hosmer included Washington in his praise: "I congratulate you now most cordially on this Auspicious Opening of the Campaign, may it close with equal Glory and success, one Circumstance should not be omitted, that the Victory is under God to be ascribed to the personal Address, Bravery & presence of Mind of our admired Genl. & Commander in Chief."[18]

The commander in chief was included in many of the expressions of victory. Congressman John Mathews sitting in Philadelphia described the battle and its results to Thomas Bee back home in South Carolina:

> I inclose you an account of the action of the 28th June, a day that I imagine will be remembered by Clinton all his life… Genl. Washington… had to contend with were the Grenadiers, light infantry, & Cavalry of the British Army, but both our Officers & Men were determined to Conquer, & nothing could stand aginst them, when led on, by their Great & illustrious Commander. Some of the Deserters who have come in since the actions, say, it is allowed by their Officers, they have never yet been so shamefully beaten, not that the loss of Men, have been so great, but that their choicest troops were defeated. It is said that the foreign troops peremptorily refused to fight. There was not one of the General's family, except himself, but what was either wounded, or had their horses shot.[19]

Other news from the British side of the lines also boosted American morale. Henry Laurens learned that Sir William Erskine, who had led the abortive attempt to flank the American left at Monmouth, was dismayed by the outcome of the action. When Erskine read that Charles Lee referred to the British defeat as a "handsome check," he said: "Lee may call it what he pleases but by ___ I call it a handsome flogging. We had not receiv'd such a one in America."[20] The numbers of deserters and their descriptions painted a picture of a defeated enemy. American morale surged, boosted by this perception.

Attainment of Tactical Objectives

George Washington had clearly stated his intention to engage the British in some action during the retreat across New Jersey. The battle of Monmouth gave Washington more action than he originally intended but it did fulfill his intention when he told Lafayette:

> You are immediately to proceed with the detachment commanded by Genl Poor and form a junction as expeditiously as possible with that under the commanded of Genl Scott. You are to use the most effectual means for gaining the enemys left flank and rear, and giving them every degree of annoyance—all continental parties that are already on the lines will be under your command and you will take such measures in concert with Genl Dickinson as will cause the enemy most impediment & loss in their march—for these purposes you will attack them as occasion may require by detachment, and if a proper opening shd be given by operating against them with the whole force of your command.[21]

Mission accomplished, Washington wrote: "The extreme heat of the Weather—the fatigue of the Men from their march thro' a deep sandy Country almost entirely destitute of Water, and the distance the Enemy had gained by marching in the Night, made a pursuit impracticable and fruitless. It would have answered no valuable purpose."[22] Washington wished to "annoy" the British with an attack on their rear but he got much more than that, fighting a major battle. In doing so he attained his objective.

In military terms, the perceptions at the time showed the American forces punished the enemy with heavy losses, held the field, forcing the enemy to retreat, obtained a boost in morale, and met their tactical objective of engaging the enemy during his march to New York. Washington was satisfied with the outcome of the campaign, mocking the British in New York and giving thanks:

> It is not a little pleasing, nor less wonderful to contemplate, that after two years Manœuvering and undergoing the strangest vicissitudes that perhaps ever attended any one contest since the creation both Armies are brought back to the very point they set out from and, that that, which was the offending party in the beginning is now reduced to the use of the spade and pick axe for defence. The hand of Providence has been so conspicuous in all this, that he must be worse than an infidel that lacks faith, and more than wicked, that has not gratitude enough to acknowledge his obligations—but—it will be time enough for me to turn preacher, when my present appointment ceases; and therefore, I shall add no more on the Doctrine of Providence.[23]

Conclusion

The battle of Monmouth Court House was an important event in the history of the small town of Freehold. Occasionally there are reminders of the battle, as men digging a basement found out when they uncovered the remains of soldiers killed in the battle. Today, the morning battlefield has largely disappeared beneath the urban sprawl of Freehold. For a tourist, it is possible to follow the morning battle with the assistance of an experienced guide. Except for Clinton's headquarters at the Covenhoven House, little is as it was in 1778. In contrast, a person interested in the afternoon battlefield of Monmouth finds that is well preserved and well maintained, remaining much the same as in 1778. Well placed interpretive signs make it easy to follow the flow of the action. The state of New Jersey, with help from the local Friends of Monmouth Battlefield, maintains the area with a visitor center atop Comb's Hill. Among the buildings still standing are the Rhea House, the Craig House, and the Sutfin Farm. The Tennent Church continues to hold services surrounded by the graves of many victims of the battle, including Colonel Monckton and Captain Fauntleroy. One of the pews is stained by what is purported to be the blood of the wounded from the battle on June 28, 1778. The only statue on the site of the battlefield park is a well-done portrayal of Baron von Steuben, near the visitor center.

On the one-hundred-year anniversary of the battle in 1878 former New Jersey Governor Joel Parker laid a cornerstone to a massive pillar. It was dedicated on November 13, 1884. Built along Court Street in an area where the first phase of the battle took place, it stands 94 feet in the air, capped by the figure of "Columbia Triumphant," celebrating the "victory" at Monmouth. In 1878, the people still had a perception of triumph. Enoch Cowart wrote a poem about the battle for the *Monmouth Democrat* newspaper at the event. Part of the poem celebrates:

> The treacherous Lee there made a retreat,
> Resulting almost in fatal defeat;
> But the troops were rallied and victory won
> By commander-in-chief, our Washington[1]

The people of Monmouth, one hundred years after the event, considered it a victory. Near the base of the monument are five bronze *bas-relief* panels depicting important scenes of the battle. Four of the panels show events that seem natural for depiction: Ramsey's bitter defense at the point of woods, Washington gathering the troops just east of the West Ravine, Anthony Wayne charging the British, and the ubiquitous Molly Pitcher. Most unusual is one panel depicting the council of war at Hopewell on June 24, with the figures of Washington, Lee, Greene, Stirling, Wayne, Knox, Poor, Woodford, Duportail, Scott, and Patterson. It is an odd choice, considering that Hamilton thought it was a council of midwives, but it indicates the respect the builders of the monument had for all the participants in that pre-battle meeting. It was those subordinate commanders who deserve credit for fighting the British to a standstill and then following Washington to take the battlefield.

Washington

The leader of the Constitutional convention, first president of the United States, and "Father of his Country" needed no monument at Monmouth to preserve his legacy. Yet his personal stamp is everywhere on the battlefield of Monmouth. Much of the success there can in some part be attributed to him. For him, Monmouth was just a step on the long path to the British evacuation of New York City five years later. There was no Mischianza to mark the end of his military career. His officers said goodbye at a solemn "turtle feast" at Fraunces Tavern in New York City in 1783.

While Washington makes no note in his voluminous writings of Monmouth being pivotal or important in his career, it is certain that he viewed Monmouth as a victory. Years later, when writing South Carolinian Charles Cotesworth Pinckney about the historic day on which South Carolina ratified the new United States' Constitution, he noted that it reminded him of another memorable June 28: "The day itself is memorable for more reasons than one. It was recollected that this day is the Anniversary of the battles of Sullivan's Island and Monmouth."[2]

The battle was significant as it showed the maturing of Washington's tactical and operational skills. The defeats of the Conway Cabal and attempts to limit his command by the Board of War during the winter and early spring of 1777–78 had solidified his political position as commander in chief. There were still doubts about his military skills and abilities; he lacked a significant victory. Monmouth provided a victory that removed many doubts about his ability to continue as commander in chief. There would still be critics, vocal critics, of his capabilities. Washington understood that, writing to Henry Laurens during the height of the Conway Cabal, "But why should I expect to be exempt from censure—the unfailing lot of an elevated station? Merits and talents, with which I can have no pretensions of rivalship, have ever been subject to it. My Heart tells me it has been my unremitted aim to do the best circumstances would permit; yet, I may have been very often mistaken in my judgment of the means, and may, in many instances deserve the imputation of error."[3]

One of those continuing critics was Dr. Rush, who wrote John Adams on October 27, 1778: "Charecters appear in One age, and are only to be known in Another. General CONWAY who was the nerves—MIFFLIN who was the Spirit—and LEE who was the Soul of our Army have all been banished from Head Quarters."[4] Fortunately, the critics were never strong enough to threaten his position again. Elias Boudinot expressed Washington's new standing as victorious in battle as well as against his critics in a letter to Alexander Hamilton: "The General I allways revered & loved ever since I knew him, but in this Instance he has rose superior to himself. Every Lip dwells on his Praise for even his pretended Friends (for none dare to acknowledge themselves his Enemies) are obliged to Croak it forth."[5] The sarcasm is unmistakable.

Monmouth would not be the end of Washington's military education as the Yorktown campaign in 1781 provided a completely different set of lessons. But the crucial action on June 28, 1778, between the main British and American forces in North America ended in American victory and his role in that victory was pivotal. The triumph at Monmouth, combined with the evacuation of Philadelphia and the arrival of the French fleet, signaled the campaign of 1778 as an American success. The British would attempt no major offensive move that year. The Revolutionary effort had another year of life. The optimism Washington felt back on that spring day at the parade ground at Valley Forge, celebrating the French alliance, had been rewarded. Not only had he defeated the British on the battlefield, but he defeated his military and political opponents as well.

Endnotes

Notes on Abbrevations

Papers of George Washington, Revolutionary Series unless otherwise noted—*PGW*
Writings of George Washington—*WGW*

Introduction

1 Edward G. Lengel, ed. *The Papers of George Washington, Revolutionary War Series, Vol. 15, May–June 1778* (Charlottesville, University of Virginia Press, 2006), 38.
2 "General Orders" May 6, 1778. Ibid, 57.

Chapter 1

1 Thomas Jefferson to Walter Jones, January 2, 1814. *Founders Online*, National Archives.
2 John Adams to Benjamin Rush, November 11, 1807. *Founders Online*, National Archives.
3 Thomas Jefferson to Walter Jones, January 2, 1814. *Founders Online*, National Archives.
4 John Adams to Abigail Adams, May 29, 1775. Edmund C. Burnett, ed. *Letters of Members of the Continental Congress, Volume 1, August 29, 1774 to July 4, 1776* (Washington, D.C., Carnegie Institute of Washington, 1921), 240.
5 Eliphalet Dyer to Joseph Trumbull, June 17, 1775. Paul H. Smith, ed. *Letters of Delegates to Congress, 1774–1789, Vol. 1* (Washington, Library of Congress, 1976), 499–500.
6 Worthington Chauncey Ford. *Journals of the Continental Congress, 1774–1789, Volume VI, 1776, October 9–December 31* (Washington, Government Printing Office, 1906), 1045–46.
7 Clarence Green. "DeKalb and His Hoosier Namesake," *Indiana History Bulletin*, (Indianapolis, Indiana Historical Commission, February 1924), 43.
8 Washington to John Hancock, September 11, 1777. Philander D. Chase and Edward G. Lengel, eds. *The Papers of George Washington, Revolutionary War Series, Vol. 11, 19 August 1777–25 October 1777* (Charlottesville, University Press of Virginia, 2001), 110–11.
9 Washington to John Hancock, October 5, 1777. Ibid, 394.
10 Henry Alonzo Cushing. *The Writings of Samuel Adams, Volume III* (New York, Putnam, 1906), 250.
11 Sergeant to Lovell, November 20, 1777. Burnett, 2:570.
12 Theodore Thayer. *Nathanael Greene: Strategist of the American Revolution* (New York, Twayne Publishers, 1960), 198.

13   Benjamin Rush to John Adams, October 21, 1777. L. H. Butterfield. *Letters of Benjamin Rush, Volume 1: 1761–1792* (Princeton, Princeton University Press, 1951), 159–60.

14   Major General Stirling to Washington, November 3, 1777. Frank E. Grizzard, Jr. and David R. Hoth, eds. *The Papers of George Washington, Revolutionary War Series, Vol. 12, 26 October 1777–25 December 1777* (Charlottesville: University Press of Virginia, 2002), 110–11.

15   Conway to John Sullivan, Jan. 3, 1778. Otis G. Hammond, ed. *Letters and Papers of Major-General John Sullivan, Continental Army* (Concord, N.H., New Hampshire Historical Society, 1931), 2.

16   William Duer to Philip Schuyler, June 19, 1777. *Letters of Delegates to Congress,* 7:229.

17   Alexander Graydon. *Memoirs of His Own Time with Reminnences of the Men and Events of the Revolution* (Philadelphia, Lindsey & Blakiston, 1846), 314.

18   Washington to Richard Henry Lee, October 16, 1777. *PGW,* 11:529.

19   Lafayette to Washington, December 30, 1777. *PGW,* 13:69.

20   James Craik to Washington, January 6, 1778. Edward G. Lengel, ed. *The Papers of George Washington, Revolutionary War Series, Vol. 13, 26 December 1777–28 February 1778* (Charlottesville: University of Virginia Press, 2003), 160.

21   Washington to a Continental Congress Camp Committee, January 29, 1778. Ibid, 376–409.

22   Lynn Montross. *The Reluctant Rebels: The Story of the Continental Congress 1774–1789* (New York, Harper & Brothers Publishers, 1950), 225.

23   Gouverneur Morris to John Jay, February 1, 1778. Smith. *Letters of Delegates,* 9:3–4.

24   Washington to Lieutenant Colonel John Fitzgerald, February 28, 1778. Ibid, 694.

25   Mercy Otis Warren to James Warren, March 10, 1778, James Warren and Samuel Adams, *Warren–Adams Letters: Being Chiefly a Correspondence Among John Adams, Samuel Adams, and James Warren; 1778–1814, Volume 2* (Boston, Massachusetts Historical Society, 1925), 2.

26   Ezra Sheldon, 1st Connecticut Regiment, to Doctor Samuel Mather, May 15, 1778, "Letters from Valley Forge," *Americanrevolution.org,* accessed December 5, 2020.

27   Benjamin Rush, October 10, 1777. Dr. S. Weir Mitchell, ed. "Historical Notes of Benjamin Rush," *The Pennsylvania Magazine of History and Biography,* Vol. XXVII, No. 2 (University of Pennsylvania Press, 1903), 147.

28   Nathanael Greene to Washington, April 24, 1779. Edward G. Lengel, ed. *The Papers of George Washington, Revolutionary War Series, Vol. 20, 8 April–31 May 1779* (Charlottesville: University of Virginia Press, 2010), 186–89.

29   Steuben to Washington, December 6, 1777. *PGW,* 12:567–68.

30   Washington to Francis Barber, March 24, 1778. *WGW,* 11:136.

31   Paul Lockhart. *The Drillmaster of Valley Forge* (New York, Harper Collins, 2008), 104.

32   General Orders, May 7, 1778. *PGW,* 15:69–70.

33   Washington to John Augustine Washington, June 10, 1778. Ibid, 373.

34   Clarence Green. "Baron DeKalb and his Indiana Namesake," *Indiana History Bulletin* (Indianapolis, Indiana Historical Commission, 1923), 43.

35   Washington to Thomas Nelson, Jr. May 15, 1778. *PGW,* 15:129.

36   Thomas Turner to George Washington, March 22, 1778. David R. Hoth, ed. *The Papers of George Washington, Revolutionary War Series, Vol. 14, 1 March 1778–30 April 1778,* (Charlottesville: University of Virginia Press, 2004), 277–78.

37   George Washington to Thomas Turner, April 25, 1778. *PGW,* 14:639–40.

38   See John W. Jackson. *With the British Army in Philadelphia 1777–1778* (San Rafael, California, Presidio Press 1979).

39   William B. Willcox. *Portrait of a General: Sir Henry Clinton in the War of Independence* (New York, Knopf, 1964), 44.

40 Wilken. *Some British Soldiers in America*, 250.

41 Mitchell Broadus. *The Price of Independence: A Realistic View of the American Revolution* (New York, Oxford University Press, 1974), 64.

42 Willcox, *Portrait of a General*, 85.

43 Ibid, 2262.

44 William B. Willcox, ed. *The American Rebellion; Sir Henry Clinton's narrative of his campaigns, 1775–1782, with an appendix of original documents* (North Haven, Conn., Archon Books, 1971), 96.

45 Matthew Spring. *With Zeal and Bayonets Only: The British Army on Campaign in North America, 1775–1783* (Norman, University of Oklahoma Press, 2008), 127–28.

46 Worthington Chauncey Ford, ed. *Journals of the Continental Congress, 1774–1789, Vol. X, 1778 January 1–May 1,* (Washington, Government Printing Office, 1908), 114–15.

47 *PGW*, 15:74.

48 Washington to Philemon Dickinson, June 5–7, 1778. Ibid, 323.

49 Ibid, 81.

50 Ibid, 84.

51 Washington to William Maxwell, May 7, 1778. Ibid, 74–75.

52 Moylan to Washington, May 13, 1778. Ibid, 119.

53 Ibid, 131–32.

54 Washington to Nathanael Greene, May 16, 1778. Ibid, 135.

55 Ibid, 137.

56 Washington to Lafayette, May 18, 1778. Ibid, 152–53.

57 Jackson, *With the British Army*, 226.

58 Washington to Philemon Dickinson, May 24, 1778. *PGW*, 15:208–9.

59 Washington to Maxwell, May 29, 1778. Ibid, 259.

60 Washington to Charles Lee, May 30, 1778. Ibid, 274.

Chapter 2

1 J. J. Boudinot. *The Life, Public Services, Addresses, and Letters of Elias Boudinot, LL.D., President of the Continental Congress, Volume I* (Boston, Houghton, Mifflin and Co., 1896).

2 Montross, *The Reluctant Rebels*, 206.

3 Joseph Galloway. "Reasons against Abandoning the City of Philadelphia," in Benjamin Franklin Stevens, ed. *B.F. Steven's Facsimiles of Manuscripts In European Archives Relating to America, 1773–1783: With Descriptions, Editorial Notes, Collations, References And Translations. London: Vol. 24, No. 2096* (London, Photographed and printed by Malby & Sons), 1895, 2085.

4 Captain Johann Ewald. *Diary of the American War: A Hessian Journal* (New Haven, Yale University Press, 1979), 132.

5 Ibid, 132.

6 Willcox, *The American Revolution: Sir Henry Clinton's Narrative of his Campaigns*, 89.

7 Mercy Otis Warren, *History of the Rise, Progress, and Termination of the American Revolution interspersed with Biographical, Political and Moral Observations, in Two Volumes, Volume I, Foreword by Lester H. Cohen* (Indianapolis: Liberty Fund 1994). Vol. 1. 8/20/2020.

8 "From John Adams to James Warren, 24 July 1775," *Founders Online*, National Archives.

9 "From John Adams to James Warren, 24 July 1775," *Founders Online*, National Archives.

10 David Lee Russell. *Victory on Sullivan's Island: The British Cape Fear/Charles Town Expedition of 1776* (Haverford, Pa., Infinity Publishing, 2002), 210.

11 Charles Lee to Benjamin Rush, November 20, 1776. *The Lee Papers, Volume II* (New York, New York Historical Society, 1873), 293–94.

12 Reed to Lee, November 21, 1776. *Lee Papers, II*:28.

13 Lee to Joseph Reed, November 24, 1776. *Lee Papers, II*:305–6.

14 Washington to Reed, November 30, 1776. *PGW* 7:237.

15 Dr. James Thacher. *The American Revolution, from the Commencement to the Disbanding of the American Army: Given in the Form of a Daily Journal, with the Exact Dates of All the Important Events; Also a Biographical Sketch of All the Most Prominent Generals* (Hartford, Conn., Hurlbut, Kellog and Company, 1860), 565–66.

16 William S. Baker. "Exchange of Major General Charles Lee," *The Pennsylvania Magazine of History and Biography, Vol. 15, No. 1, 1891*, 32.

17 Charles Lee to Horatio Gates, October 14, 1776. *Lee Papers, II*:261–62.

18 Theodore George Thayer. *The Making of a Scapegoat: Washington and Lee at Monmouth* (Port Washington, N.Y: Kennikat Press, 1976), 20.

19 Lee to the President of Congress, April 17, 1778. *Lee Papers, II*:290.

20 *PGW*, 15:403–8.

21 Ibid, 416.

22 Benjamin Rush. *A Memorial containing Travels Through Life of Sundry Incidents in the Life of Dr. Benjamin Rush* (Philadelphia, Louis Alexander Biddle, 1903), 120.

23 Diary of Dr. Albigence Waldo, January 4, 1778, "Valley Forge, 1777–1778. Diary of Surgeon Albigence Waldo, of the Connecticut Line," *The Pennsylvania Magazine of History and Biography, Volume 21.* (The Historical Society of Pennsylvania, University of Pennsylvania Press, 1897), 320.

24 *PGW*, 13:288–89.

25 Harlow Giles Unger. *Lafayette* (Hoboken, N.J., John Wiley & Sons, Inc. 2002), 23.

26 *PGW*, 12:81.

27 Thacher, *The American Revolution*, 537.

28 Marquis De Chastellux. *Travels in North America in the Years 1780–81–82* (New York, 1828), 71.

29 Washington to John Hancock, May 31, 1777. *PGW,* 9:569.

30 Albert Cook Myers. *Sally Wister's Journal, A True Narrative: Being a Quaker Maiden's Account of Her Experiences with Officers of the Continental Army, 1777–1778* (Philadelphia, Ferris & Leach Publishers, 1902), 81–82.

31 Samuel Holden Parsons to John Adams, August 15, 1776. *Founders Online*, National Archives, founders.archives.gov/documents/Adams/06-04-02-0212, accessed December 22, 2017.

32 Horatio Gates to the President of Congress, September 30, 1776. Thomas Egleston, LLD. *The Life of John Paterson, Major General in the Revolutionary Army* (New York, G. P. Putnam's Sons), 90.

33 Wayne to Horatio Gates, December 1, 1776. Paul David Nelson. *Anthony Wayne: Soldier of the Republic* (Bloomington, Indiana University Press, 1985), 34.

34 Robert Howe to the Virginia Convention, January 2, 1776. Henry Steele Commager and Richard B. Morris, eds. *The Spirit of 'Seventy-Six, The Story of the American Revolution as told by Participants* (New York, Harper & Row, 1975), 114.

35 Edward W. Hocker. *The Fighting Parson of the American Revolution, A Biography of General Peter Muhlenberg, Lutheran Clergyman, Military Chieftain, and Political Leader* (Philadelphia, Edward W. Hocker, 1936), 70.

36 Barnardus Swartwout, Jr., of the 2nd New York Regiment. Jerome Greene, *The Guns of Independence: The Siege of Yorktown, 1781* (New York: Savas Beatie, 2005), 95.

37 Jedediah Huntington to Thomas Pickering, December 22, 1777. *WGW*, 10:183–84.

38   Washington to Henry Laurens, November 16, 1778. Edward G. Lengel, ed. *Papers of George Washington, Revolutionary War Series, Vol. 18, 1 November 1778–14 January, 1779* (Charlottesville, University of Virginia Press, 2008), 168.

39   Jedediah Huntington to Washington, June 18, 1778. *PGW*, 15:445.

Chapter 3

1   Several sources were used for both British and American Orders of Battle: Mark Edward Lender and Garry Wheeler Stone. *Fatal Sunday: George Washington, the Monmouth, and the Politics of Battle* (Norman, University of Oklahoma Press, 2016); Brendan Morrissey. *Monmouth Courthouse 1778, the Last Great Battle in the North* (Oxford, Osprey Publishing, 2004); *The Battle of Monmouth*, New York (Simulations Publications Inc.), 1982; Samuel Stelle Smith. *The Battle of Monmouth* (Philip Freneau Press, Monmouth Beach, N.J., 1964); and *Worcester Polytechnic Institute Battle of Monmouth Staff Ride*, www/wpi.edu/Academics/Depts/MilSci/BTSI/Monmouth, 1999.

2   Dickinson to Washington, June 20, 1778. *PGW*, 15:480.

3   Benedict Arnold to Washington, June 21, 1778. Ibid, 485.

4   Dickinson to Washington, June 21, 1778, Ibid, 487.

5   Washington to Henry Laurens, June 22, 1778. Ibid, 506.

6   Dickinson to Washington, June 21, 1778, Ibid, 488.

7   William Livingston to Washington, June 22, 1778, Ibid, 507.

8   William B. Willcox, ed. *The American Rebellion; Sir Henry Clinton's narrative of his campaigns, 1775–1782, with an appendix of original documents* (North Haven, Conn., Yale University Press, 1971), 91.

9   Dickinson to Washington, June 23, 1778, Ibid, 513.

10   Mark Urban. *Fusiliers: The Saga of a British Redcoat Regiment in the American Revolution* (New York, Walker & Company, 2007), 150.

11   Washington to Morgan, June 24, 1778. *PGW*, 15:532.

12   Dickinson to Washington, June 23, 1778. Ibid, 511.

13   An excellent look at the British infantryman is found in Matthew Spring's *With Zeal and Bayonets Only: The British Army in North America* (Norman, University of Oklahoma Press, 2008).

14   Dickinson to Washington, June 23, 1778. *PGW*, 15:513.

15   *WGW*, 12:116–17.

16   Unger, *Lafayette*, 76.

17   *PGW*, 15:521.

18   Harold C. Syrett. *The Papers of Alexander Hamilton, Vol. I, 1768–1778* (New York, Columbia University Press, 1961), 510.

19   Washington to Wayne, June 24, 1778. *PGW*, 15: 535.

20   Washington to John Rutledge, May 7, 1779. *PGW*, 20:371.

21   Washington to Scott, June 24, 1778. *PGW*, 15:534.

22   Greene to Washington, June 24, 1778. Ibid, 526.

23   Lafayette to Washington, June 24, 1778. Ibid, 528–29.

24   Jackson to Washington, June 24, 1778. Ibid, 527–238.

25   Mark E. Lender and James Kirby Martin, eds. *Citizen Soldier—The Revolutionary War Journal of Joseph Bloomfield* (Newark, New Jersey Historical Society, 1982), 135–36.

26 Henry B. Carrington. *Washington the Soldier* (Boston, Lamson, Wolffe, and Company, 1898), 227.

27 Washington to Lafayette, June 25, 1778. *PGW*, 15:539.

28 Ewald, *Diary*, 135.

29 Joseph Plumb Martin. *A Narrative of a Revolutionary Soldier: Some of the Adventures, Dangers, and Sufferings of Joseph Plumb Martin* (New York, Penguin Books, 2001), 107–8.

30 General Orders, *PGW*, 15:492.

31 Washington to Lee, May 30, 1778. Ibid, 274.

32 Martin, *Narrative*, 107.

33 Ibid, 109.

34 Moylan to Washington, June 25, 1778. *PGW*, 15:544–45.

35 Lee to Washington, June 25, 1778. Ibid, 541.

36 Ibid, 539.

37 Lafayette to Washington, June 26, 1778. Ibid, 551.

38 To Lafayette from Washington, June 26, 1778. Ibid, 552–53.

39 Washington to Lafayette, June 26, 1778. Ibid, 555.

40 Washington to Lee, June 26, 1778. Ibid, 556.

41 Washington to Gates, June 27, 1778. Ibid, 563.

42 William Maxwell's recollection at Lee's court martial. Charles Lee, *The Lee Papers, Vol. III* (New York, New York Historical Society, 1873), 89.

43 Stryker's *The Battle of Monmouth* and Maxwell's statement at the trial indicate Washington made a special effort to address Maxwell.

44 Lee to Washington, June 27, 1778. *PGW*, 15:564.

45 From Moylan to Washington, June 27, 1778. Ibid, 565.

46 Ibid, 565.

47 Martin, *Narrative*, 109.

48 *PGW*, 15:573.

Chapter 4

1 *Lee Papers*, *III*:6.

2 Ibid, 8.

3 Ibid, 7.

4 Ibid, 124.

5 Doctor Thomas Henderson in the *New Jersey Gazette*, August 5, 1778, quoted in William S. Stryker. *The Battle of Monmouth* (Princeton, Princeton University Press, 1927), 97.

6 Catherine R. Williams. *Biography of Revolutionary Heroes: Containing the Life of Brigadier Gen. William Barton, and Also, of Captain Stephen Olney* (New York, Wiley & Putnam, 1839), 243–45.

7 *Lee Papers*, *III*:38.

8 Ibid, 180.

9 Ibid, 78.

10 *PGW*, 15:580.

11 *Lee Papers*, *II*:6.

12 Ibid, 120.

13 Ibid, 231.

14 Martin, *Narrative*, 110.

15 *Lee Papers, III*:56.

16 Ibid, 183–84.

17 Ibid, 28–29.

Chapter 5

1 *Lee Papers, III*:172–73.

2 Ibid, 194.

3 Ibid, 157, 159.

4 Ibid, 72.

5 Ibid, 73.

6 Ibid, 73.

7 Patrick K. O'Donnell. *Washington's Immortals: The Untold Story of an elite Regiment Who Changed the Course of the Revolution* (New York, Grove Press, 2016), 361.

8 *Lee Papers, III*:191–92.

9 Ibid, 147. Lee also gives a detailed account in his statement for the court.

10 Unger, *Lafayette*, 79.

11 *Lee Papers, III*:194.

12 *PGW*, 15:580.

13 Mark M. Boatner III. *Encyclopedia of the American Revolution* (Stackpole Books, Mechanicsburg, Pa., 1994), 1059.

14 W. H. Wilkin. *Some British Soldiers in America* (London, H. Rees, Ltd., 1914), 258.

15 William Hale. Letter of 14 July, 1778. Ibid, 118.

16 Wilkin, *Some British Soldiers in America*, 259.

17 Urban, *Fusiliers*, 151.

18 Williams, Otho. "Calendar of the General Otho Holland Williams," *The Maryland Historical Records Survey Project*, Baltimore, Maryland Historical Society, November 1940, 5.

19 Lloyd A. Brown and Howard H. Peckham, eds. *Revolutionary War Journals of Henry Dearborn* (Chicago, The Caxton Company, 1939), 127.

20 Martin, *Narrative*, 115.

21 *Lee Papers, III*:79.

22 Dennis R. Ryan, ed. *A Salute to Courage* (New York, Columbia University Press, 1979), 132–34.

23 Martin, *Narrative*, 113.

24 Willcox, *The American Revolution: Sir Henry Clinton's Narrative of his Campaigns*, 236.

Chapter 6

1 Martin, *Narrative*, 131.

2 Clinton to Lord Germain, Willcox. *Portrait of a General*, 235.

3 Stryker, *The Battle of Monmouth*, 271.

4 Joseph Clark. "Diary of Joseph Clark, Attached to the Continental Army," May 1777 to November 1778, *Proceedings of the New Jersey Historical Society, Vol. 7*, (Edison, N.J., New Jersey Historical Society, 1854), 93–110.

5 Moylan to Washington, June 29, 1778. *PGW*, 15:588.

6 Ewald, *Diary*, 138.

7 *Lee Papers, III*:120.

8   David R. Hoth, ed. *The Papers of George Washington, Revolutionary War series, Vol. 16, July–September 1778* (Charlottesville, University of Virginia Press, 2006), 5–6.

9   Ibid, 1.

10   William Van Horne, letter to Joseph Hart, July 13, 1778, "Revolutionary War Letters of the Reverend William Van Horne," Spruance Library, Bucks County Historical Society, Doylestown, Pennsylvania. Quoted in John U. Rees, "What is this you have been about to day? The New Jersey Brigade at the Battle of Monmouth," 35.

11   Francis B. Lee, ed. *Documents Related to the Revolutionary History of the State of New Jersey, Volume II, Extracts from American Newspapers, Vol. II, 1778* (Trenton, John L. Murphy Publishing Company, 1903), 281.

12   Washington to William Livingston, July 4, 1778. *WGW,* 12:158–59.

13   Cornelius Van Dyck. "A Report of the British & American Troops, Fallen in the Action near Monmouth & buried under the care of Col. Van Dyke," *Lee Papers. Vol. II. 1776–1778* (New York, New York Historical Society, 1872), 447.

14   Washington to William Livingston, July 4, 1778. *PGW,* 16:23.

15   Washington to John Augustine Washington, July 4, 1778. Ibid, 26.

16   S. Kemble, D. Jones, H. Clinton and W. Howe. *Journals of Lieut. Col. Stephen Kemble, 1773–1789: and British Army orders: Gen. Sir William Howe, 1775–1778; Gen. Sir Henry Clinton, 1778; and Gen. Daniel Jones, 1778* (Boston: Gregg Press, 1972), 30.

17   *Lee Papers*, II:466–67.

18   Ewald, *Diary*, 139.

19   Wilkin, *Some British Soldiers in America*, 119.

20   Stryker, *The Battle of Monmouth*, 230.

21   *Greene Papers*, II:501–2.

Chapter 7

1   Thomas S. Montgomery. "The Battle of Monmouth, as described by Dr. James McHenry, Secretary to General Washington," *The Magazine of American History with notes and queries, Vol. III, Part 1* (New York, A. S. Barnes & Company, 1879), 357–58.

2   Lender and Martin, *Citizen Soldier*, 137.

3   *PGW*, 15:594–95.

4   David McCullough. *John Adams* (Simon & Shuster, New York, 2001), 168.

5   *PGW*, 15:583.

6   Washington to Laurens, June 29, 1778. Ibid, 587.

7   Washington to Lee, June 30, 1778. Ibid, 595–96.

8   Jared Sparks, ed. *Correspondence of the American Revolution; being the Letters of Eminent Men to George Washington, From the Time of His Taking Command of the Army to the End of His Presidency, Volume II* (Boston, Little and Brown, 1853), 152.

9   Lee to Washington, June 30, 1778. *PGW,* 15:596.

10   Lee to Washington, June 30, 1778. Ibid, 596–97.

11   The best single account of the trial is found in Christian McBurney's *George Washington's Nemesis: The Outrageous Treason and Court-Martial of Major General Charles Lee during the Revolutionary War* (El Dorado Hills, Ca., Savas Beatie, 2020). In addition, the transcripts of the trial provide an accurate first-hand account of the events surrounding battle.

12   *The Lee Papers*, II:452–53.

13   *The Lee Papers*, III:2.

14 Ibid, 201.

15 Ibid, 192.

16 Ibid, 13.

17 Ibid, 194.

18 Ibid, 194.

19 Ibid, 88.

20 Ibid, 79–82.

21 Ibid, 26.

22 Ibid, 29.

23 *Papers of Nathanael Greene, Vol. II*:451.

24 Harold C. Syrett, ed. *The Papers of Alexander Hamilton, Vol. 1, 1768–1778* (New York, Columbia University Press, 1961), 510–14.

25 *PGW*, 16:242.

26 Ibid, 319.

27 *Lee Papers, III*:186.

28 Benjamin Rush to David Ramsey, November 5, 1778. L. H. Butterfield, ed. *Letters of Benjamin Rush, Volume I: 1761–1792* (Princeton, Princeton University Press, 1951), 220.

29 *Lee Papers, III*:211.

30 Ibid, 228.

31 Washington to Laurens, July 1, 1778. *PGW*, 16:5.

32 Letter from J. Huntington to his father, June 30, 1778. Copy in Monmouth County Historical Association, Box 72.

33 Syrett, *The Papers of Alexander Hamilton*, 513.

34 *PGW*, 15:584.

35 *The Lee Papers, II*:452–53.

36 John Laurens to Henry Laurens, July 2, 1778. *WGW*, 7:85–86.

37 William Gilmore Simms. *The Army Correspondence of Colonel John Laurens in the years 1777–1778* (New York, Bradford Club, 1867), 204.

38 Syrett, *The Papers of Alexander Hamilton*, 510–14.

39 Washington to John Hancock, September 25, 1776. Philander D. Chase and Frank E. Grizzard, Jr., eds. *The Papers of George Washington, Revolutionary War Series, Vol. 6, 13 August 1776–20 October 1776* (Charlottesville: University Press of Virginia, 1994), 396.

40 *PGW*, 15:583.

41 *Lee Papers, III*:186.

42 Syrett, *The Papers of Alexander Hamilton*, 510–14.

43 Washington to Henry Laurens, July 1, 1778. *PGW*, 16:5.

44 John Austin Stevens, et al., *Magazine of American History with Notes and Queries, Vol. III* (New York, A. S. Barnes & Co., 1879), 360.

45 Henry Laurens to the Marquis de Lafayette, July 10, 1778. Paul H. Smith, et.al. *Letters of Delegates to Congress, 1774–1789, Volume 16, June 1–September 30, 1778* (Washington, Library of Congress, 1985), 254.

46 Washington to Laurens, July 1, 1778. *PGW*, 16:5.

47 William Henry Drayton to Washington, July 12, 1778. Ibid, 59.

48 Morris to Washington, August 2, 1778. Ibid, 223.

49 Syrett, *The Papers of Alexander Hamilton*, 510–14.

50 Wilkin, *Some British Soldiers in America*, 257.

51 Ibid, 120.

52 *The Greene Papers, II*:501–2.

53 Worthington Chauncey Ford, ed. *The Journals of the Continental Congress, Volume16* (Washington, Government Printing Office, 1910), 33.

54 *Lee Papers, II*:357.

55 Ibid, 453.

56 *Lee Papers, IV*:31.

57 *WGW*, 26:342.

58 George Washington to William Goddard, June 11, 1785. W. W. Abbot, ed. *The Papers of George Washington, Confederation Series, Vol. 3, 19 May 1785–31 March 1786* (Charlottesville: University Press of Virginia, 1994), 50.

Chapter 8

1 John Banister to St. George Tucker, August 11, 1778. *Letters of Delegates to Congress*, 10:423.

2 Samuel Adams to John Adams, October 25, 1778. *Letters of Delegates to Congress*, 11:116.

3 James Lovell to Abigail Adams, July 3, 1778. *Letters of Delegates to Congress*, 10:219–20.

4 Henry Laurens to William Smith, July 28, 1778. Ibid, 367.

5 Andrew Adams to Oliver Wolcott, July 22, 1778. Ibid, 336.

6 Stanley Idzerda. *Lafayette in the Age of the American Revolution: Selected Letters and Papers, 1776–1780, Vol. II, April 10, 1778–March 20, 1780*, (Ithaca, N.Y., Cornell University, 1983), 96.

7 Charles Stille *Major General Anthony Wayne and the Pennsylvania Line in the Continental Army* (Cranbury N.J., The Scholar's Bookshelf, 1968), 153–54.

8 Carlos E. Godfey. *The Commander in Chief's Guard* (Genealogical Publishing Company, Baltimore, 1972), 280.

9 Henry Laurens to John Burnet, July 24, 1778. Paul H. Smith, et al. *Letters of Delegates to Congress, 1774–1789, Volume 10, June 1–September 30, 1778* (Washington, Library of Congress, 1983), 345.

10 Thomas McKean to William Atlee, July 7, 1778. *Letters of Delegates to Congress*, 10:236.

11 John Hancock to Dorothy Hancock, July 1, 1778. Ibid, 217.

12 Samuel Smith. *The Battle of Monmouth* (Morristown, New Jersey Historical Commission, 1975), 25.

13 *New-York Gazette and Weekly Mercury*, July 6, 1778, in John U Rees, "What is this you have been about to day? The New Jersey Brigade at the Battle of Monmouth," Appendix L, 7.

14 Thayer, *The Making of a Scapegoat*, 64.

15 Washington to Congress, July 12, 1778. *WGW*, Vol. 12:173–74.

16 Laurens to Washington, July 7, 1778. Burnett, *Letters, Volume 10*, 237.

17 Richard Henry Lee to Francis Lightfoot Lee, July 5, 1778. *Letters of Delegates to Congress*, 10:223.

18 Titus Hosmer to Thomas Mumford, July 6, 1778. Ibid, 227.

19 John Mathews to Thomas Bee, July 7, 1778. Ibid, 234.

20 Henry Laurens to Lachlan McIntosh, August 23, 1778. Ibid, 494.

21 Washington to Lafayette, June 25, 1778. *PGW*, 15:539.

22 Washington to Laurens, July 1, 1778. *PGW*, 16:5.

23 Washington to Brigadier General Thomas Nelson, Jr., August 20, 1778. *PGW*, 16:340.

Conclusion

1   William Griffith. "Monmouth Monday: Centennial of the Battle of Monmouth, June 28, 1878," *Emerging Revolutionary War Era.*

2   Washington to Charles Cotesworth Pinckney, June 28, 1788. Abbot, W. W. et. al. *The Papers of George Washington; Confederation Series, Vol. 6., 1 January 1788–23 September 1788* (Charlottesville, University of Virginia Press, 1997), 361.

3   *PGW*, 13:420.

4   Benjamin Rush to John Adams, October 27, 1778. *Founders Online*, National Archives, last modified June 13, 2018.

5   Elias Boudinot to Alexander Hamilton, July 8, 1778. Paul H. Smith, et.al. *Letters of Delegates to Congress, 1774–1789, Volume 10, June 1–September 30, 1778* (Washington, Library of Congress, 1985), 238.

Bibliography

A special note of acknowledgement to the late Jim Raleigh and to Dr. David Martin, president and vice president respectively of the Friends of Monmouth Battlefield during one of my visits to the battlefield. They each gave a personal, guided tour of each part of action. Thanks also to the staffs of the Monmouth County Historical Association and the David Library of the American Revolution for their assistance. In addition, I would like to thank Eric Olsen of the National Park Service for his resources and help at the start of this project.

Abbot, W. W. ed. *The Papers of George Washington, Confederation Series, Vol. 3, 19 May 1785–31 March 1786*, Charlottesville: University Press of Virginia, 1994

——. *The Papers of George Washington, Confederation Series, 6.* Charlottesville, University of Virginia Press, 1997

Alden, John Richard. *General Charles Lee: Traitor or Patriot*, Louisiana State University Press, Baton Rouge, 1951

Andre, John. *Major Andre's Journal: Operations of the British Army under Lieutenant Generals Sir William Howe and Sir Henry Clinton,* New York Times and Arno Press, 1968

Bilby, Joseph G. and Katherine Bilby Jenkins. *Monmouth Court House: The Battle that Made the American Army*, Westholme Publishing Company, Yardley, Pennsylvania, 2010

Boatner III, Mark M. *Encyclopedia of the American Revolution*, Stackpole Books, Mechanicsburg, Pa., 1994

Boudinot, J. J., ed. *The Life, Public Services, Addresses and Letters of Elias Boudinot, LL. D.: President of the Continental Congress*, Boston, Houghton, Mifflin, and Company, 1896

Brant, Irving. *James Madison*, Bobbs-Merrill, New York, 1941

Broadwater, Robert P. *American Generals of the Revolutionary War: A Biographical Dictionary*, Jefferson, North Carolina, McFarland & Company, Inc., Publishers, 2007

Brown, Lloyd A. and Howard H. Peckham. *Revolutionary War Journals of Henry Dearborn, 1775–1783*, The Claxton Club, Chicago, 1939

Butterfield, L. H. *Letters of Benjamin Rush, Volume 1: 1761–1792*, (Princeton, Princeton University Press, 1951), 159–60

Burnett, Edmund C., ed. *Letters of Members of the Continental Congress*, 26 volumes, Washington, D.C., Carnegie Institute of Washington, 1921

Busch, Noel E. *Winter Quarters: George Washington and the Continental Army at Valley Forge*, Mentor Books, New York, 1974

Carrington, Henry B. *Battles of the American Revolution 1775–1781 including Battle Maps and Charts of the American Revolution*, A. B. Brand & Co, New York, 1881

——. *Washington the Soldier*, Boston, Lamson, Wolffe, and Company, 1898

Chadwick, Bruce. *The First American Army: The Untold Story of George Washington and the Men behind America's First Fight for Freedom*, Sourcebooks, Inc., Naperville, Illinois, 2005

Chase, Philander P. and Frank E. Grizzard, Jr., eds. *The Papers of George Washington, Revolutionary War Series, Vol. 6, 13 August 1776–20 October 1776*, Charlottesville, University of Virginia Press, 1994

Chase, Philander P. *The Papers of George Washington, Revolutionary War Series, Vol. 7, 21 October 1776–5 January 1777*, Charlottesville, University of Virginia Press, 1997

——. *The Papers of George Washington, Revolutionary War Series, Vol. 9, 28 March 1777–10 June 1777*, Charlottesville, University of Virginia Press, 1999

Chastellux, Marquis de. *Travels in North America, in the years 1780–81–82*, New York, 1828

Clark, Joseph. "Diary of Joseph Clark, Attached to the Continental Army," May 1777 to November 1778, *Proceedings of the New Jersey Historical Society, Vol. 7*, Edison, N.J., New Jersey Historical Society, 1854

Clary, David A. *Adopted Son, Washington, Lafayette, and the Friendship that Saved the Revolution*, New York, Bantam Books, 2007

Cook, Fred J. "Allan McLane: Unknown Hero of the Revolution," *American Heritage*, Oct. 1956, Vol. 7, Issue 6

Cushing, Henry Alonzo, ed. *The Writings of Samuel Adams, Volume III*, New York, Putnam, 1906

Dann, John C., ed. *The Revolution Remembered: Eyewitness Accounts of the War for Independence*, University of Chicago Press, Chicago, 1980

Davis, Matthew. *Memoirs of Aaron Burr, Vol. I*, Freeport, N.Y., Books for Libraries Press, 1836/1970

DePeyster, John Watts. *The Battle of Monmouth, Monmouth Court House or Freehold, 28th June 1778*, New York, A. S. Barnes & Co., 1878

Downey, Fairfax. "The Girl Behind the Guns," *American Heritage*, Dec. 1956, Vol. 8, No. 1, 46–48

Editors. "Washington at Monmouth," *American Heritage*, June 1965, Vol. 16, No. 4, 14–17

Ethier, Eric. "Clash at Monmouth," *American History*, Vol. 34, issue 4, Oct. 1999, 48–57

Ewald, Captain Johann. *Diary of the American War: A Hessian Journal*, New Haven, Yale University Press, 1979

Fitzpatrick, John C. *The Writings of George Washington from the Original manuscript sources, 39 volumes*, Washington, U.S. Government Printing Office, 1931–1944

Ford, Worthington Chauncey. *The Journals of the Continental Congress, 34 volumes*, Washington, Government Printing Office, 1904–1937

——. *The Writings of George Washington, 14 Volumes*, New York, G. P. Putnam's Sons, 1889—1893

Godfrey, Carlos E. *The Commander in Chief's Guard*, Genealogical Publishing Company, Baltimore, 1972

Greenman, Jeremiah. *Diary of a Common Soldier in the American Revolution, 1775–1780*, Northern Illinois University Press, DeKalb, Ill, 1978

Griffith, William. "Monmouth Monday: Centennial of the Battle of Monmouth, June 28, 1878," *Emerging Revolutionary War Era*, https://emergingrevolutionarywar.org/2022/09/19/monmouth-monday-centennial-of-the-battle-of-monmouth-june-28-1878/

Gruber, Ira, ed. *John Peebles American War*, Mechanicsburg, Pa., Stackpole Books, 1998

Hagist, Don. *British Soldiers, American War: Voices of the American Revolution*, Yardley, Pa, Westholme Publishing, 2012

Hammond, Otis G., ed. *Letters and Papers of Major-General John Sullivan, Continental Army*, Concord, N.H., New Hampshire Historical Society, 1931

Headley, J. T. *Washington and His Generals*, New York, A. L. Burt Company, 1847

Heitman, Francis B. *Historical Register of Officers of the Continental Army During the War of the Revolution, April 1775, to December, 1783*, Washington, D.C., The Rare Book Shop Publishing Company, 1914

Horner, William. "Eve of the Battle of Monmouth," *This Old Monmouth of Ours*, Moreau Brothers, Freehold, N.J., 1932

Hoth, David R., ed. *The Papers of George Washington: Revolutionary War Series, 15*, Charlottesville, University of Virginia Press, 2004

——. *The Papers of George Washington, Revolutionary War Series, Volume 16, July–September 1778*, Charlottesville, University of Virginia Press, 2006

Huntington, J. Letter to father, June 30, 1778. Copy in Monmouth County Historical Association, Box 72

Idzerda, Stanley. *Lafayette in the Age of the American Revolution: Selected Letters and Papers, 1776–1780, Vol. II, April 10, 1778–March 20, 1780*, Ithaca, Cornell University, 1983

Jackson, John W. *With the British Army in Philadelphia 1777–1778*, Presidio Press, San Rafael, California, 1979

Kaminski, John P. *George Clinton: Yeoman Politician of the New Republic*, Madison, Madison House, 1993

Katcher, Philip R. N. *King George's Army 1775–1783: A handbook of British, American and German regiments*, Stackpole Company, Harrisburg, 1973

Kemble, S., Jones, D., Clinton, H., Howe, W. *Journals of Lieut. Col. Stephen Kemble, 1773–1789: and British Army orders: Gen. Sir William Howe, 1775–1778; Gen. Sir Henry Clinton, 1778; and Gen. Daniel Jones, 1778*, Boston, Gregg Press. 1972

Lancaster, Bruce. *From Lexington to Liberty: The Story of the American Revolution*, Doubleday & Company, Inc., New York, 1955

Laurens, John. *The Army Correspondence of Colonel John Laurens in the years 1777–1778*, Bradford Club, New York, 1867

Lee, Charles. *The Lee Papers. Vol. II, 1776–1778*, New York Historical Society, 1872

——. *The Lee Papers, Vol. III, 1778–1782*, New York Historical Society, 1873

——. *The Lee Papers, Vol. IV, 1782–1811*, New York Historical Society, 1874

Lee, Francis B., ed. *Documents Related to the Revolutionary History of the State of New Jersey, Volume II, Extracts from American Newspapers, Vol. II, 1778*, Trenton, John L. Murphy Publishing Company, 1903

Leiter, Mary Theresa. *Biographical Sketches of the Generals of the Continental Army of the Revolution*, Cambridge, University Press, 1889

Lender, Mark. *Cabal: The Plot Against George Washington*, Yardley, Penn., Westholme, 2019

——. "The Politics of Battle: Washington, Lee, and the Battle of Monmouth," *New Jersey Heritage*, Spring 2003, 10–21

—— and Garry Wheeler Stone. *Fatal Sunday: George Washington, the Monmouth, and the Politics of Battle*, Norman, University of Oklahoma Press, 2016

Lender, Mark E. and James Kirby Martin, eds. *Citizen Soldier—The Revolutionary War Journal of Joseph Blomfield*, Newark, New Jersey Historical Society, 1982

Lengel, Edward, ed. *The Papers of George Washington: Revolutionary War Series, Vol. 13, December 1777–February 1778*, Charlottesville; University of Virginia Press, 2003

——. *The Papers of George Washington: Revolutionary War Series, Vol. 15, May–June 1778*, Charlottesville; University of Virginia Press, 2006

Lockhardt, Paul. *The Drillmaster of Valley Forge*, Harper Collins, New York, 2008

Lomask, Milton. *Aaron Burr: The Years from Princeton to Vice President, 1756–1805*, New York, Farrar-Straus-Giroux, 1979

Lossing, Benson. *Pictorial Field Book of the Revolution, Vol. II*, New York, Harper & Brothers Publishing, 1859

Mappan, Marc, and David Martin. "Good Golly, Miss Molly: In Search of the Real Molly Pitcher," *New Jersey Heritage*, Spring 2003, 22–29

Martin, David G. *The Philadelphia Campaign, June 1777– July 1778*, Conshohocken, Pennsylvania, Combined Books, 1993

——. *A Molly Pitcher Sourcebook*, Hightstown, N.J., Longstreet House, 2003

Martin, Joseph Plumb. *A Narrative of a Revolutionary Soldier: Some of the Adventures, Dangers, and Sufferings of Joseph Plumb Martin*, New York, Signet Classics, Penguin books, 2001

Mazzagetti, Dominick. *Charles Lee: Self Before Country*, New Brunswick, Rutgers University Press, 2013

McBurney, Christian M. *George Washington's Nemesis: The Outrageous Treason and Court-Martial of Major General Charles Lee during the Revolutionary War*, El Dorado Hills, Ca., Savas Beatie, 2020

McCullough, David. *John Adams*, New York, Simon & Shuster, 2001

McHenry, James. *Journal of a March, a Battle, and a Waterfall, Being the Version Elaborated by James McHenry from his Diary of the Year 1778, Begun at Valley Forge, & containing accounts of the British, the Indians, and the Battle of Monmouth*, Greenwich, Connecticut, Helen & Henry Flynt, 1945

Mitchell, Boadus. "The Battle of Monmouth through Alexander Hamilton's Eyes," *Proceedings of the New Jersey Historical Society, Volume LXXIII, Number 4, October 1955*, New York, New Jersey Historical Society, 1955

——. *The Price of Independence: A Realistic View of the American Revolution*, New York, Oxford University Press, 1974

Mitchell, Dr. S. Weir, ed. "Historical Notes of Benjamin Rush," *The Pennsylvania Magazine of History and Biography, Vol. XXVII, No. 2*, 1903

Montgomery, Thomas S. "The Battle of Monmouth, as described by Dr. James McHenry, Secretary to General Washington," *The Magazine of American History with notes and queries, Vol. III, Part 1*, New York, A. S. Barnes &Company, 1879

Montross, Lynn. *The Reluctant Rebels: The Story of the Continental Congress 1774–1789*, New York, Harper & Brothers Publishers, 1950

Morgan, John D. F. *Old Tennent Church and the Battle of Monmouth Court House and Washington Crossing and the McKonkey Ferry House*, Haddonfield, N.J., 1952

Morrissey, Brendan. *Monmouth Courthouse 1778*, New York, Osprey Publishing, 2004

Moultrie, William. *Memoirs of the American Revolution, as far as it related to the States of North and South Carolina, and Georgia, Volume 1*, New York, David Longworth, 1802

Myers, Albert Cook. *Sally Wister's Journal, A True Narrative: Being a Quaker Maiden's Account of Her Experiences with Officers of the Continental Army, 1777–1778*, Philadelphia, Ferris & Leach Publishers, 1902

Nelson, Paul David. *William Alexander: Lord Stirling*, Tuscaloosa, The University of Alabama Press, 1987

O'Donnell, Patrick K. *Washington's Immortals: The Untold Story of an elite Regiment Who Changed the Course of the Revolution*, New York, Grove Press, 2016

Ogden, Aaron. *Autobiography: An original document written by Col. Aaron Ogden for his children*, Paterson, N.J. Press Printing and Publishing Co., 269 Main Street, 1893.

——. *Our Country: A Household History for all Readers from the Discovery of America to the Present Time, Vol. II*, Henry J. Johnson Publishers, New York, 1877

Pappas, Phillip. *Renegade Revolutionary: The Life of General Charles Lee*, New York, NYU Press, 2014

Patterson, Samuel White. *Knight Errant of Liberty: The Triumph and Tragedy of General Charles Lee*, New York, Lantern Press, 1958

Peckham, Howard H. *The Toll of Independence: Engagements & Battle Casualties of the American Revolution*, Chicago, University of Chicago Press, 1974

Procknow, Gene. "Personal Honor and Promotion Among Revolutionary Generals and Congress," *Journal of the American Revolution*, January 23, 2018, allthingsliberty.com/2018/01/personal-honor-promotion-among-revolutionary-generals-congress/#_edn13

Rees, John U. "What is this you have been about to day? The New Jersey Brigade at the Battle of Monmouth,"https://revwar75.com/library/rees/monmouth/MonmouthToc.htm

——. "'The great Consumption of Cannon ammunition…' Continental Artillery at Monmouth, 28 June 1778," *Military Collector and Historian*, Washington, D.C., Vol. 60, No. 1 Spring 2008

——. "'One of the best in the army.' An Overview of the 2nd New Jersey Regiment and General William Maxwell's Jersey Brigade," *Continental Line Newsletter*, Spring, 1998, Volume XI, Number 2

Rush, Benjamin. *A Memorial containing Travels through Life or Sundry Incidents in the Life of Benjamin Rush*, Lanorie, Louis Alexander Biddle, 1905

Russell, David Lee. *Victory on Sullivan's Island: The British Cape/Fear/Charles Town Expedition of 1776*, Haverford, Pa., Infinity Publishing, 2002

Ryan, Dennis R. ed., *A Salute to Courage*, New York, Columbia University Press, 1979

Showman, Richard K., ed. *The Papers of Nathanael Greene, Vol. II*, Chapel Hill, University of North Carolina Press, 1980

Simms, William Gilmore. *The Army Correspondence of Colonel John Laurens in the years 1777–1778*, New York, Bradford Club, 1867

Siry, Steven. *Liberty's Fallen Generals: Leadership and Sacrifice in the American War of Independence*, Washington, D.C., Potomac Books, 2002

Sivilich, Daniel M., and Garry Wheeler Stone. "The Battle of Monmouth: The Archaeology of Molly Pitcher, the Royal Highlanders, and Cilley's Light Infantry," self-published pamphlet available at Monmouth Battlefield State Park

Smith, Paul, ed. *Letters of Delegates to Congress, 1774–1789, 26 Volumes*, Washington, Library of Congress, 1976

Smith, Samuel. *The Battle of Monmouth*, New Jersey Historical Commission, 1975

——. *The Battle of Monmouth*, Monmouth Beach, N.J., Philip Freneau Press, 1964

Sparks, Jared, ed. *Correspondence of the American Revolution; being the Letters of Eminent Men to George Washington, From the Time of His Taking Command of the Army to the End of His Presidency, Volume II*, Boston, Little and Brown, 1853

Spofford, Ainsworth R. *Eminent and Representative Men of Virginia and the District of Columbia*, Madison, Wisconsin, Brant and Fuller, 1893

Spring, Matthew. *With Zeal and Bayonets Only: The British Army on Campaign in North America, 1775–1783*, Norman, University of Oklahoma Press, 2008

Stevens, Benjamin Franklin, ed. *B. F. Steven's Facsimiles of Manuscripts in European Archives Relating to America, 1773–1783: With Descriptions, Editorial Notes, Collations, References And Translations. London: 25 volumes*, London, Photographed and printed by Malby & Sons, 1889–95

Stevens, John Austin, et al., *Magazine of American History with Notes and Queries, Vol. III*, New York, A. S. Barnes & Co., 1879, pp. 355–60

Stewart, Mrs. Catesby Wills. *The Life of Brigadier General William Woodford of the American Revolution*, Richmond, Virginia, Whittel & Shepperson, 1973

Stille, Charles. *Major General Anthony Wayne and the Pennsylvania Line in the Continental Army*, Cranbury, N.J., The Scholar's Bookshelf, 2005, reprint of 1893 edition

Stone, Garry Wheeler. "A Deadly Minuet. The advance of the New England 'Picked Men' against the Royal Highlanders at the Battle of Monmouth, 28 June 1778," *The Brigade Dispatch*, Vol. XXVI, No. 2, Summer, 1996

Stryker, William S. *The Battle of Monmouth*, Princeton, Princeton University Press, 1927

Syrett, Harold, ed. *Papers of Alexander Hamilton, Vol. I, 1768–1778*, New York, Columbia University Press, 1960

Taaffe, Stephen R. *The Philadelphia Campaign, 1777–1778*, Lawrence, University Press of Kansas, 2003

Taylor, David. *Farewell to Valley Forge*, Philadelphia and New York, J. B. Lippincott, 1955

Thacher, James. *Military Journal of the American Revolution*, New York, New York Times/Arno Press, 1969

Thayer, Theodore George. *Nathanael Greene: Strategist of the American Revolution*, New York, Twayne Publishers, 1960

——. *The Making of a Scapegoat: Washington and Lee at Monmouth*, Port Washington, N.Y., Kennikat Press, 1976

Trudeau, Noah Andre. "Charles Lee's Disgrace at Monmouth," *Military History Quarterly*, Autumn, 2006

——. *Nathanael Greene: Strategist of the American Revolution*, New York, Twayne Publishers, 1960

Trussell, John B. B. *The Pennsylvania Line: Regimental Organization and Operations, 1775–1783*, Harrisburg, Pennsylvania Historical and Museum Commission, 1993

Unger, Harold Giles. *Lafayette*, Hoboken, New Jersey, John Wiley & Sons, Inc., 2002

Urban, Mark. *Fusiliers: The Saga of a British Redcoat Regiment in the American Revolution*, New York, Walker & Company, 2007.

Wade, David. "Washington Saves the Day at Monmouth," *Great Battles: Turning Points in the American Revolution*, Special edition from the editors of *Military History Magazine*, Leesburg, Virginia, PRIMEDIA Publications, 2005

Waldo, Dr. Albigence. "Valley Forge, 1777–1778. Diary of Surgeon Albigence Waldo, of the Connecticut Line," *The Pennsylvania Magazine of History and Biography, Volume 21*. The Historical Society of Pennsylvania, University of Pennsylvania Press, 1897

Ward, Christopher. *The War of the Revolution, Vol. II*, New York, The Macmillan Company, 1952

Ward, Harry M. *General William Maxwell and the New Jersey Continentals*, Westport, Connecticut, Greenwood Press, 1997

Warren, James and Samuel Adams, *Warren–Adams Letters: Being Chiefly a Correspondence Among John Adams, Samuel Adams, and James Warren; 1778–1814, Volume 2*, Boston, Massachusetts Historical Society, 1925

Warren, Mercy Otis. *History of the Rise, Progress, and Termination of the American Revolution interspersed with Biographical, Political and Moral Observations, in Two Volumes, Volume I, Foreword by Lester H. Cohen, Vol. I*, Indianapolis: Liberty Fund 1994. 8/20/2020. https://oll.libertyfund.org/titles/815

Welsch, William. "Washington's Indispensible, Yet Unknown Lieutenants," *American Revolution*, Volume 1, Camden, S. C., American Revolution Association, May 2009, 7–12

Wilkin, W. H. *Some British Soldiers in America*, London, H. Rees, Ltd., 1914

Willcox, William. *The American Rebellion; Sir Henry Clinton's narrative of his campaigns, 1775–1782, with an appendix of original documents* (North Haven, Conn., Archon Books, 1971)

——. *Portrait of a General: Sir Henry Clinton in the War of Independence*, New York, Knopf, 1964

Williams, Catherine R. *Biography of Revolutionary Heroes: Containing the Life of Brigadier Gen. William Barton, and Also, of Captain Stephen Olney.* New York, Wiley & Putnam, 1839

Williams, Otho. *Calendar of the General Otho Holland Williams Papers in the Maryland Historical Society*, Baltimore, The Maryland Historical Society Project, 1940

Index